Schooner Port

Schooner Port
-Two Centuries of Upper Mersey Sail

First published in 1983.
This edition 1998.

© H. F. Starkey 1998

Design © W. D. Roberts - Avid Publications. 1998

ISBN 09521020 5 6

Other publications from Avid are detailed at the rear of this book

Garth Boulevard,
Bebington, Wirral,
Merseyside. U.K.
L63 5LS
Tel/Fax (44) 0151 645 2047
email: avid@publications.freeserve.co.uk
website http:\\merseyworld.com\avid

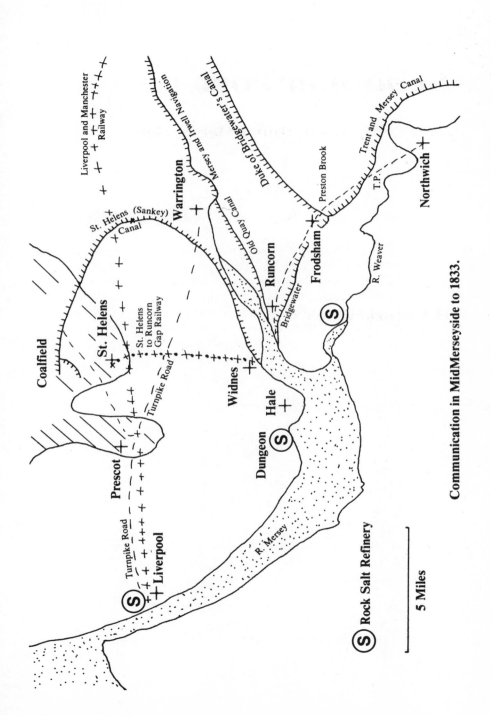

Communication in MidMerseyside to 1833.

Liverpool and Manchester Railway

Mersey and Irwell Navigation

Duke of Bridgewater's Canal

Trent and Mersey Canal

St. Helens (Sankey) Canal

Old Quay Canal

Warrington

Preston Brook

T.P.

Northwich

Runcorn

Coalfield

St. Helens to Runcorn Gap Railway

St. Helens

Frodsham

R. Weaver

Bridgewater

Turnpike Road

Widnes

Hale

Dungeon

Prescot

Turnpike Road

Liverpool

R. Mersey

Rock Salt Refinery

5 Miles

Schooner Port

Two Centuries of Upper Mersey Sail

H. F. Starkey

To Irene and Catherine

Contents

List of Illustrations

The schooner *Volant* under repairs at Stubbs' yard in the 1930s 185
The Runcorn District Council badge 210
Runcorn's Bridgewater docks crowded with schooners about 1886 rear cover

Illustrations

© H.F. Starkey, with the exception of:
p.70b,©Mrs. F. Stubbs
p.185a,©Mr. J. Collins
p.185b,©Mrs. F. Stubbs

List of Tables *page*

List of Graphs

Acknowledgements

A work of this kind must draw heavily upon the good will and experience of others and I have been most fortunate in the help I have received from many generous friends. For their assistance in indicating the essential documentary source material I owe a special debt to Mr. A. Hayman, formerly manager of the Bridgewater Docks of the Manchester Ship Canal Company; the late Mr. H. Hobley, former manager of the Weaver docks at Weston Point; Mr. W. Snelson, formerly Clerk to the Upper Mersey Navigation Commissioners; Mr. David Burrell of Lloyds of London; Miss P.A. Pemberton, formerly group archivist of Pilkington Brothers, St. Helens; Mr. M. Stammers, curator, the Merseyside Maritime Museum; Mr. N.E. Upham of the National Maritime Museum, Greenwich; Mr. J.P. Greene, Archaeology and Museums Officer, Norton Priory Runcorn; Mrs. J. Spruce, curator, the Museum, Stanley, Falkland Islands; Mr. Maurice Schofield, Widnes; Mr. Peter Norton, Warrington; and to the staff at the Cheshire County Record Office and at H.M. Customs and Excise Houses at Runcorn and Liverpool.

I believe that oral history is a valuable source of information and for their accounts of the last days of sail on the upper Mersey I am most grateful for the patient consideration afforded me by Mr. A. Cooke and Mr. W. Dutton of the M.S.C. Company, Eastham; the late Mr. F. Stubbs, ship-builder, Mr. H. Darbyshire, Mr. G. Evans; Mr. T. Williams, the late Mr. G. Weedall, the late Mr. H. Sandbach; Mr. P. Collins; Mr. A. Walker and Mr. A. Coleshill, all of Runcorn; Mr. E. Dorrian of Great Sankey, Warrington and Dr. W.N. Howell of Hale.

I am indebted to Dr. Dennis Brundrit of Kelowna, British Columbia, and to Mr. J.S. Brundrit of Wirral for the details of their family's commercial activities.

To Bill Leathwood, J.P. of Weston, I owe a great deal for, in addition to providing me with information from his collection of documents, he read the script, made useful suggestions and saved me from many mistakes. I am also grateful to Mrs. Rosalind Denton for typing the manuscript.

Finally I hasten to acknowledge that none of my friends and helpers can be held responsible for any errors or serious omissions which may occur. The design and execution of the work has been my responsibility and I accept the blame for its shortcomings.

H. F. Starkey

Introduction

Although it was overshadowed by the enormous volume of trade and commerce a dozen miles down river at the Port of Liverpool, Runcorn, for a brief period in the last century, showed promise of developing into a successful minor port. Unfortunately the expectations of the local manufacturers and shippers were never fully realised because geographical forces intervened to make serious and lasting problems for navigation in the upper Mersey estuary and as a consequence the town remained a canal port for shallow draught vessels.

Unaccountably the story of the canal port of Runcorn has never been fully explored and historians have paid scant attention to Runcorn's role in promoting the economic development of Liverpool, Manchester, Stoke-on-Trent and the mid Merseyside industrial region. Of course frequent references to Runcorn do appear in the many publications which are specifically concerned with the inland waterways but invariably these accounts give little indication of Runcorn as a port in its own right. The town is regarded simply as a place through which trade passed en route to major centres of industry and commerce.

Besides the navigable Mersey and Weaver rivers there were, within the boundaries of the Customs Port of Runcorn, the termini of the Sankey Canal, the Bridgewater Canal, and also that of the Runcorn to Latchford Canal of the Mersey and Irwell Navigation Company and yet no research appears to have been undertaken in order to explore the immense up river traffic in small craft which flourished for more than a hundred and fifty years. Even after the advent of good roads and railways the bulk of the raw materials required by the textile, pottery, chemical, glass and salt refining industries were conveyed by water. Until well into the twentieth century the upper reaches of the Mersey constituted a major highway which was essential for the prosperity of the areas in which these industries were situated.

In addition to the through traffic in cotton, grain and timber to Manchester and the trade in potters' materials to the Five Towns, four other commodities ensured that the Port of Runcorn should survive the difficulties caused by silting and by intense railway competition. It was through Runcorn that Welsh roofing slates were distributed to centres of population over a wide area of the North West and the Midlands. The demand for Cheshire salt from industry, agriculture and from the fishing ports of the United Kingdom and northern Europe never slackened in the second half of the last century and Lancashire coal was always available for ships which had discharged cargo at Runcorn. Lastly, from mid century, the development of the chemical industry in the Runcorn Gap district brought new trade to the port in the carriage of materials to the alkali works which were established on canal or on riverside sites.

The Port of Runcorn saw much enterprise and innovation. For instance the Sankey Canal was the first industrial canal in England and the Runcorn Gap railway dock is believed to have been the world's first purpose-built railway dock. The earliest paddle steamers to operate on the Mersey were financed and built by Runcorn men and for a brief period in the 1850s the Warrington ship builders pioneered the construction of great iron sailing vessels which were amongst the largest of their time.

Even though it would be impossible to write about maritime Runcorn without making some reference to the impact of the Bridgewater Canal, the Weaver Navigation and the Manchester Ship Canal, I have avoided these famous waterways except where they have influenced the immediate local scene, because there is much authoritative literature concerning these undertakings readily available in our public libraries. Also because of the limitations imposed by the size of this book I have not made adequate consideration of Weston Point which was within the nineteenth century port of Runcorn but which was not incorporated in the Urban District Council of Runcorn until 1936 by which time the days of the sailing ship were almost over.

History can be unappetizing fare and I make no apology for flavouring the work with a seasoning of trivial occurences which have no bearing upon the course of events. The accounts of the day to day happenings, the actions of local personalities, the practices of the times and the stories of shipwrecks over a century ago might have detracted from the academic ethos of the work but then it has been truly said that "In its amplest meaning history includes every trace and every vestige of everything that man has done".

1

The Inland Waterways and the Development of the Region in the Eighteenth Century

Daniel Defoe that most inquisitive and perceptive chronicler of early eighteenth century England, visited Liverpool three times between 1690 and 1724. He was astounded by the rapid expansion of the town's industrial and commercial activity which had more than doubled Liverpool's population within a decade. In 1725 he wrote:

> The town has now an opulent, flourishing and increasing trade not rivalling Bristol in the trade to Virginia and the English Island Colonies in America only, but is in a fair way to exceed and eclipse it, by increasing every way in wealth and shipping. They trade around the whole Island, send ships to Norway, to Hamburg and to the Baltic, as also to Holland and Flanders, so that in a word, they are almost become like Londoners, universal merchants.[1]

When Thomas Steers was called upon to build the first wet dock in Liverpool in 1708 the population was an estimated eight thousand inhabitants and there were eighty-four ships belonging to the port none of which had a capacity of more than seventy tons.[2] The town had suffered the chagrin of being an outpost of Chester during the seventeenth century but by Defoe's time the silting up of the Dee had brought about a decline at Chester and Liverpool's spectacular ascendancy was well under way. By 1773 Liverpool's population was an estimated 34,407 inhabitants and this had grown to 77,655 by the first census of 1801.[3]

A number of factors can be identified as being responsible for the town's rapid growth. Liverpool had become an independent port and the relaxation of statutes prohibiting its trade with Ireland and with the West Indies resulted in the establishment of sugar refineries and the development of salt works and metal industries which traded with the town's hinterland. Before long the Port of Liverpool could accommodate larger ships of up to 300 tons and by 1710 it ranked third among the country's ports contributing £50,000 in customs revenue.[4]

Cheshire salt played a significant part in the rise of Liverpool to prominence. The importance of the salt trade was recognised by John Holt who observed in 1790:

> The salt trade is generally acknowledged to have been the nursing mother and to have contributed more to the first rise, gradual increase and present flourishing state of the town of Liverpool than any other article of commerce.[5]

Salt was an essential basic raw material for Liverpool's glass and metal industries. In the Irish trade it was exported to be used as a fertilizer and for use on dairy farms. It was also an ideal ballast material and ships carried it to the Baltic, the West Indies and to North America. The Newfoundland trade was largely based on the export of salt which was exchanged for cod which

5

was taken to the West Indies. Dried salt-fish was also carried from Labrador to the Mediterranean in the same ships which had brought the salt from England. In Italy, Spain and Greece the salt-fish was then exchanged for cargoes of fruit and wine to be sold in England.

The first large scale salt works in Liverpool was established by two Warrington brothers called Blackburne. In 1697 they built a refinery at Dungeon Point at Hale with a quay to accommodate the sailing barges which brought the salt from Cheshire. Refineries were also established later at Liverpool's docks and from 1723 to 1753 the annual tonnage of salt shipped down the river Weaver increased from 7,954 tons to 14,359 tons.[6]

The salt trade expanded and prospered because the waterways of the region were made navigable for small craft. The improvements made to the rivers Mersey and Weaver in the 1730s also enabled Liverpool to become the chief port for the export of goods from the Midlands and from Manchester and south east Lancashire.

Even more important for the successful growth of Liverpool was the need to improve transport facilities for the carriage of coal. The town's manufacturers were totally dependent upon a regular supply of coal and in spite of the improvements which had been made to the roads between Liverpool and the Prescot and St. Helens coal pits in the first forty years of the eighteenth century the demands for coal could not be met. The cost of moving large quantities of coal by road became almost prohibitive because of the heavy tolls which were demanded to keep the turnpike in good condition after the passage of heavy carts and wagons.

But coal was only one of a number of heavy bulk materials whose transport costs were becoming exhorbitant, for, dead weight shipments of building stone, roofing slates, timber, pig iron and metal ores could not be transported economically in quantity along the soft surfaces of the roads of early eighteenth century Lancashire.

It was the need to transport these heavy commodities which inspired improved methods of carriage by water in north west England from the third decade of the century. Of these heavy goods coal was the most important. Professor T.S. Willan has observed: "The more we study in detail the history of communication by water, in England, the more do we realise how closely it was interwoven with the history of coal".[7]

Manchester's rate of population increase was as spectacular as that of Liverpool. Estimates made in 1717 gave the figures of 10,000 inhabitants in Manchester and another 2,500 in Salford. By 1728 the township of Manchester, according to local census, was 17,000 and in 1758 the estimated figure was nearly 43,000.[8] This expansion in population occurred at a time when there was a national demand for Manchester's major manufactured product-textiles. The mechanisation of the cotton spinning industry caused

British cotton goods to rise in value from £46,000 in 1751 to £200,000 by 1764 and to nearly £5½ million by the end of the century.[9]

Manchester, situated on the Irwell, a major tributary of the Mersey, was already a natural road centre but from about 1760 the wealthier Manchester merchants were beginning to concentrate their selling of cloth to overseas markets and their success in business depended upon the improvement in communications to the sea. Like their Liverpool counterparts they looked to the inland waterways to solve the problem of high transport charges.

Professor Willan believes that communications have generally been improved in order to meet the requirements of established industry and not to call a new one into being. He presents the view that improvements to navigable rivers and the canal expansion of the eighteenth century were intended to meet the demands of an existing trade which was growing rapidly. The remarkable development of water transport after 1750 was not due to any great technical advance but rather due to the pressures created by established business. This was certainly the case in both Liverpool and Manchester where the business communities of the two towns sought ways to ensure the efficient supply and delivery of their raw materials and finished manufactured goods.

Capitalism played the principal role in improving communications. The increasing wealth of the merchant classes in Liverpool and Manchester and their districts made possible the financing of extensive engineering schemes which were designed to deepen and widen the rivers. The prosperous merchant entrepreneurs became the "undertakers" who financed and carried through major waterway projects. They provided the means by which capital was raised in order to exploit the trade potential between the two regions by first improving the Mersey and Weaver rivers and, from 1757, by financing the construction of the canal system of the area.

While it may not be possible to discern how far the expansion of the market for agricultural produce influenced canal and river works, the waterways of the region did carry potatoes, corn, butter and cheese in increasing quantities but this traffic may have been the result and not a cause of improved communications by water. Certainly, the phenomenal growth of Liverpool and Manchester did create markets for agricultural produce and the merchants, farmers and consumers in the towns supported any means of establishing and maintaining the efficient transport of food. This included the improvement of transport facilities by water as well as by road.

Nowhere in the eighteenth century was the expansion in improved rivers and canals more apparent then in the mid Merseyside region. Strategically positioned between Liverpool and Manchester and between Liverpool and the Midlands, the Mersey's upper estuary was to become a vital waterway throughout the eighteenth and nineteenth centuries. In addition to the traffic to and from Manchester by way of the improved Mersey and Irwell route, no less than five major canal undertakings were constructed in the vicinity of

Runcorn. All were devised to supply the Port of Liverpool with the products of the Industrial Revolution from factories and mines in inland centres of population. The Duke of Bridgewater's Canal, the Mersey and Irwell Company's Runcorn to Latchford Canal, and the Sankey Canal with its later extension to Woodend (Widnes) - all had their termini near Runcorn.

The contribution of the canal port of Runcorn in furthering the growth of Liverpool, Manchester, the Potteries and the industrial areas of mid Merseyside has never been fully investigated. Yet the Runcorn area became the axis of a network of important waterways. Geographically it was an epicentre of trade routes through which passed vast tonnages of cargo to major manufacturing and commercial regions. Before the days of good roads and railways Manchester's raw cotton and finished products were shipped via Runcorn. The bulk of the potters' materials required in the Five Towns came through the town docks and the crated pottery came into the Bridgewater docks to be transhipped to Liverpool for distribution to a world market. Later the establishment of the chemical industry in the region brought about an immense barge traffic on the upper Mersey and much of the raw materials needed in alkali manufacture came to the Runcorn docks or to West Bank Dock at Widnes and to the St. Helens (Sankey) Canal.

Navigable rivers in the seventeenth century gave England what commercial unity she possessed. The improved waterways and the canals of the eighteenth century made possible the Industrial Revolution which was to make Britain the workshop of the world. Situated at a focal position among the inland waterways of the fastest growing industrial and commercial region of Britain, Runcorn had a significant role to play in the economic advancement of the nation.

Notes

I . Defoe, Daniel, *A Tour Through the Whole Island of Great Britain,* 1726, (ed.), Pat Rogers, Penguin, Harmondsworth, 1971, p.541.

2. Tracey, W., *Port of Manchester,* Hind, Hoyle and Light Ltd., Manchester, 1901, p.4.

3. Lawton, R., "Genesis of Population," in Smith, W., (ed.), *A Scientific Survey of Merseyside,* British Association, Liverpool University Press, 1953, p.120.

4. Bagley, J.J., *A History of Lancashire,* Darwen Finlayson Ltd., Henley on Thames, 1970, p.49.

5. Ibid, p.56.

6. Willan, T.S., *The Navigation of the River Weaver in the Eighteenth Century,* Chetham Society (3rd Series), 1951, pp.39-40.

7. Willan, T.S., *River Navigation in England,* Frank Cass and Co., London, 1964, p. 135.

8. Carter, C.J., *Manchester and Its Region,* British Association for the Advancement of Science, Manchester University Press, 1962, p.132.

9. Ibid., p. 133.

2
Early Traffic on the Upper River

We know little about the early navigation on the Mersey but it has been estimated that the average size of ships passing up the uncharted river in 1540 was about 14 tons burthen and in view of the uncertain conditions prevailing in the river for vessels proceeding as far as Warrington this estimate would appear to be a reasonable one. By the end of the seventeenth century Thomas Patten had sailing barges transporting copper ore to his works at Bank Quay and until the third decade of the eighteenth century this was the navigation limit.[1] Beyond this point the shallows, bends and mud banks made further passage up river impossible but, as a consequence of the Mersey and Irwell Navigation Act of 1721 new cuts and locks were introduced into this difficult stretch of river, a towing path was constructed and the waters of the Mersey and the Irwell were made passable to allow vessels of fifty tons to reach Manchester. The Mersey and Irwell Navigation Company had a warehouse at the Old Quay adjoining George's Dock in Liverpool and as a result the Company became known as the Old Quay Company.

Gore's Liverpool Directory for 1766 gives some indication of the extent of river traffic between Liverpool and Manchester by the improved waterway. The directory lists the names of thirteen sailing flats engaged in carrying to "Old Key", Manchester, with another six vessels trading to "Salford Key" and three craft are given as being on regular passage between Liverpool and 'Bankey' at Warrington.

The volume of traffic on the upper Mersey increased considerably with the construction of the Sankey Canal from St. Helens to the Mersey. The canal was built in response to Liverpool's insatiable demand for fuel. Coal was required in large quantities for the town's salt refineries, sugar boilers and soap makers. There was also a growing domestic requirement. As the turnpike road from St. Helens to Liverpool had proved to be inadequate for the transportation of large consignments of coal the Liverpool Corporation employed two surveyors, Henry Berry and William Taylor, to explore the possibility of making the Sankey Brook navigable from the St. Helens coalfield to the Mersey.

The surveyors rejected the notion of making the Brook navigable but they submitted new proposals which showed that a canal was feasible. The Corporation accepted the report and petitioned Parliament for permission to introduce the necessary bill. In March 1755 the Royal Assent was obtained and the Sankey Canal was complete by the end of 1757 to become the first industrial canal in England. The venture provided the means of transporting large quantities of coal cheaply not only to Liverpool but to many small ports and landing places in north west England, Ireland and Wales.

From about the middle of the eighteenth century the Mersey and Weaver sailing barge or "flat" evolved into a recognised type of vessel particular to the canals and rivers of the region and especially suited for the carriage of such heavy bulk cargoes as coal, building stone, salt and metal ores. The flats were so called because of their flat construction. There is a brief reference to the little craft in the customs letter books of the Port of Liverpool:

> They are chiefly employed in the coal trade (and they are) from 40 to 60 tons and their construction (is) very flatt and (they) are decked and carry coals free of duty to the salt refineries in Cheshire.[2]

During the early years of the century these sturdy vessels often made journeys to North Wales and up as far as the north Lancashire coast. But they were specifically designed as Mersey river craft to operate between Liverpool and Warrington and up the river Weaver as far as the tidal limit. The improvements to the two rivers in the 1720s and 1730s extended the range of the sailing flats to enable them to proceed as far as Winsford by the Weaver and to Manchester on the waters of the Mersey and Irwell. The sailing flat *George* of Warrington, Master, David Jones, was a typical early example. She displaced 30 tons and had a crew of three. Between June 1729 and May 1730 *George* was employed in carrying roofing slates between Beaumaris and Warrington.[3]

A vast fleet of sloop rigged flats came into being in the second half of the century and the busy little craft were always fully employed. They were so numerous that although Gore's Liverpool Directory of 1766 names twenty-three which were plying the Mersey to Warrington and to Manchester, the author declined to list the names of those engaged on the Weaver because "The Northwich flats are so numerous, it would take too much room to insert them". Henry Holland writing in 1808 asserted that there were more than two hundred and fifty on the Weaver. He noted that they carried between sixty and eighty tons but that some of the larger flats could transport a hundred tons of coal or salt.[4]

The single mast sailing flats made no small contribution towards Liverpool's economic success. As early as 1770 the port was able to export 48,000 tons of white and rock salt most of it going to Ireland and to the American colonies. The sailing barges helped to bring an end to Liverpool's fuel crisis of the 1750s. It has been estimated that by 1791 Liverpool was exporting 80,000 tons of coal of which 57,000 tons went to foreign countries and the remainder as cargoes in coast-wise shipping.[5] Much of the coal and every ton of salt to be exported from Liverpool in this period reached the port in the first instance by means of river flats.

When the scale of copper mining increased in Anglesey in the 1770's there was also an intensification in shipping between the island and the Mersey as cargoes of ore were shipped from Amlwch to be smelted in Lancashire at the coalfield. Some of the ore was destined for the Warrington

Copper and Brass Company and in the years 1769 to 1772 vessels belonging to Beaumaris, Caernarvon, Aberystwyth, Cemaes, Liverpool and Amlwch itself were engaged in the trade.[6] In 1771 twenty-three different vessels carried 2236 tons of copper ore to Warrington, some of them making several voyages. Among these small craft were *Speedwell* of Pwllheli, *Morning Star* of Conway, *Molly* of Cemlyn, *Blessing* of Aberdovey and *Providence* of Caernarvon. Cargo tonnages were small because the navigation of the Mersey required the use of small, shallow draught vessels. The *Sea Horse* carried just 16 tons of ore and the largest cargoes appear to have been the seventy tons carried on each of the ten voyages made by the *William and James*.[7]

St. Helens coal was shipped to the Anglesey copper mines as back cargo. In 1780 the Ravenhead and Thatto Heath mines supplied the Parys Company with an average of 700 tons of coal per week and in that same year Thomas Williams, who had become the exclusive proprietor of the island's copper mining industry was shipping his ore to two smelting works in St. Helens; the Stanley works in which he held a financial interest and to the Ravenhead works.[8] Williams employed a fleet of sloops to carry the copper ore from Anglesey to the Sankey Canal where the cargoes were reloaded into barges to be conveyed to the St. Helens refineries. The sloops then returned to Anglesey with coal which was used to part smelt the ore so as to reduce its weight and thus lessen the freight costs to the Mersey.[9]

The volume of traffic in the upper estuary grew substantially when the Bridgewater Canal was completed. The Canal was opened locally at Runcorn in 1773 and throughout its length from Manchester in 1776. It was constructed to accommodate the river flat but vessels using the canal had to be designed so that they could lower their masts or unship them because of the low fixed bridges.

At Runcorn by 1785 the line of canal locks ended in a tidal basin. Here there was a warehouse and, two locks up from the tideway, a small dry dock. The Duke had built himself a temporary home near the terminus of his canal in order that he could supervise the construction of the Runcorn end of his waterway. To the south of Bridgewater House there was another warehouse on the east side of a dock which led to another tidal basin. This dock allowed the Duke's small sea going craft to enter the canal and also those of the independent carriers who paid a charge on tonnage carried.

Before 1780 Runcorn could not have been described as even a minor port. River traffic to the township consisted almost entirely of the shallow draught river flats employed by the Duke to operate between Liverpool and his Runcorn Docks. In 1783 the Duke had completed a handsome eight storey warehouse at his dock adjoining the Salthouse Dock at Liverpool and this became known as Duke's Dock. The dock, which was extended in 1790, was specifically intended for the flats which carried cargoes up to Runcorn. At first no provision was made either at Liverpool or Runcorn for the berthing of the larger sea going vessel because previous attempts at sailing up river with large heavily laden craft had proved frustrating. Some appreciation of the difficulties entailed in navigating the upper estuary with sailing ships can be gleaned from the Customs Letter Book of the Port of Liverpool which contains an observation on Runcorn and Warrington trade. The reference of August 1785 noted:

> Vessels from foreign parts have some years ago delivered iron at Warrington but the expense of officers and the delay occasioned were greater than the convenience of landing it there and all goods are now landed here (Liverpool) except a few instances of Limestone from Ireland which by special sufferance are allowed to be landed there.

> Vessels of burthen 120 tons have recently discharged clay from Poole and Exeter and flint stones from London at Runcorn, but as it frequently occasioned much delay by missing the channel and grounding on the banks for a whole neap, the masters in general prefer delivering their cargoes here which are afterwards carried up by flat bottomed vessels.[10]

However in spite of its hazards to navigation the upper Mersey by the last decade of the century had become a waterway of considerable importance. The coastal trade in roofing slates from North Wales to the Mersey had its origin in medieval times and during the 1770s and 1780s Runcorn and Liverpool were the chief distributing ports for Penrhyn slates. The Penrhyn quarries dealt only with customers who bought whole cargoes of slates and such importers were to be found in Runcorn and Frodsham.[11]

The slate trade to Runcorn received a boost in February 1793 with the outbreak of war with France when the cost of sending slates from North Wales to London by sea rose from twelve shillings and nine pence a ton to thirty-six shillings a ton in 1794. The insurance rates for cargoes on the London route where the risks from French privateers were greatest rose steeply within a few weeks of the start of the war. The agent at the Dinorwic quarry wrote:

> There is not a vessel that will take cargo now for London. The insurance runs now at £10 per cent which is more than the freight. I think it lucky to have the Runcorn trade at present.[12]

Frodsham too, had ancient links with the North Wales slate ports and in 1805 Lord Penrhyn supplied slates at a preferential rate to William Hayes, shipbuilder and slate merchant of Frodsham Bridge, the reason being that "he was an old customer".[13] Even before the upper reaches of the Weaver were made navigable Ormerod described the scene below Frodsham Bridge as being "crowded with vessels which unloaded there and assumed the appearance of a petty port".[14]

In the late eighteenth century the river traffic at Warrington was considerable. It had become "incessant, and the brick dust coloured sails of the barges are seen every hour of the day on their passage flickering in the wind". Warrington in 1795 was described as being:

> . . in some measure a port town, the Mersey admitting by the help of the tide, vessels of 70 or 80 tons burthen to Bank Quay, a little below the town where warehouses, cranes and other conveniences for landing goods are erected.[15]

The old river was well used. The hemp and flax needed by the Warrington sail making establishments were discharged at Liverpool then carried by barge up the Mersey. Joseph Crosfield in 1815 established a soap works in Warrington and he imported tallow, palm oil and kelp by river from Liverpool. Transport by the river was cheap and Crosfield and other Warrington merchants were able to obtain Lancashire coal and Cheshire salt by this route. The manufactured soap, copper and wire were carried by canal and river to centres of population and, by way of the Port of Liverpool to overseas markets.[16]

However, there was one maritime venture which appears to have been of short duration. An attempt had been made to ship coal from staithes which were built into the river at Halebank. In 1791 a Mr. Willis was shipping Whiston coal down the Mersey. Undoubtedly the absence of good roads from the pit head to the river helped to make his enterprise unprofitable for apart from a brief reference in a littoral survey no further evidence of the activity appears to have survived.[17] It is more likely however that his staithes were unwelcome to the shippers who were using the busy channel and that Willis ceased business because of their protestations.

From the first decade of the nineteenth century Runcorn and Weston Point began to eclipse the other petty ports of Frodsham and Warrington. In 1804 the Mersey and Irwell Company completed their Runcorn to Latchford 'Old Quay Canal' and this enabled vessels to by pass the difficult stretches of the Mersey near to Fiddlers Ferry. The new waterway quickened traffic on the Mersey and Irwell undertaking and it placed the company in a more favourable position to compete with the Bridgewater system. The docks and the terminus of the Old Quay's Runcorn to Latchford Canal were little more than a mile from those of their rival.

When the Sankey or St. Helens Canal was extended to Woodend at Runcorn Gap in 1833, Widnes became an important outlet for the St. Helens collieries and from 1847 the alkali manufacturers began to ship their ores, limestone, salt and finished products via the old river.

Throughout the Industrial Revolution the upper Mersey was an essential highway. As early as 1796 the *Liverpool Guide* acknowledged the contribution made by the efficient system of inland waterways to the rapid development and prosperity of Liverpool. The town's position as the second commercial centre of the kingdom was in large measure due to

the advantage the town possesses in its near connexion and ready communication by internal rivers and canals with the extensive manufacturing town and neighbourhoods of Manchester, the coal country of Wigan, the unrivalled Potteries of Staffordshire, the exclusive export of salt and its central position on the western coast of the kingdom.[18]

Pre-Industrial Runcorn

John Leland, England's first antiquary, travelled extensively throughout the country in the reign of Henry VIII. He has left a detailed account of his travels and it is in his *Itinerary* that there appears the first description of Runcorn village. Leland dismisses the hamlet of Runcorn in 1540 as being a place of no importance. He described it as "now a poore hamlet by a salt creke"[19]. This is a brief comment, sufficient to describe the tiny isolated community of little consequence, but can one read any significance into Leland's use of the work "now"? Is it possible that the Runcorn he described in the first half of the sixteenth century had been a place of some importance in earlier times? It must be admitted that there is no documentary or archaeological evidence available to suggest that before the end of the eighteenth century Runcorn was ever anything other than a lonely cul-de-sac. And yet the tithe map of the district of 1844 shows a web of ancient field tracks and lanes in what is now an area of Victorian streets.

Of course this 'evidence' is far too slight to enable any serious conclusions to be made but is it possible that a larger settlement existed prior to Leland's day? Could medieval Runcorn have been a minor port or landing place which had decayed into insignificance by Tudor times? A possibility perhaps but in the light of existing evidence we know that only Frodsham is mentioned in medieval documents as being a port on the Mersey's Cheshire shore.

From the earliest times there had been craft on the upper Mersey. During the construction of the Manchester Ship Canal prehistoric dug-out canoes were unearthed but the earliest evidence of ships on the Mersey's upper reaches appears when William Camden, the great Elizabethan antiquary, recorded the finding of twenty pigs of lead on the river's edge at Norton marsh.[20] The position of the find together with Camden's precise description of the inscribed ingots leaves no doubt that the lead was part of the cargo of a Roman vessel which was trading on the Mersey during the first century of the Roman occupation of Britain. But in medieval times the waters of the Mersey carried little traffic. Irish merchants were bringing cargoes of grain into Frodsham and here the ship tolls in 1280 amounted to ten pounds.[21] There is also some record of trade between Runcorn and Ireland. An entry in the Patent Rolls for November 1289 states, "There is a safe conduct for the men of the Prior of Norton going with a ship to Ireland for victuals and other things". Richard Starkey in 1354, claimed to have boats on the Mersey "to fish and to carry to all manner of lands being in the place of the Lord the King"[22].

Throughout the Middle Ages the river was regarded more for its fish than for its trade potential. Staked nets anchored in the river bed were a hindrance to barge traffic and in 1388 the Abbot of Norton was charged with making two fish garths called *Charity* and *Gracedieu* which impeded the passage of the lord's boat of eight oars which was on its way from Freshpool to Thelwall. Five years later the abbot was again in trouble for a similar offence and for the next three centuries staked nets in the sailing channels continued to hamper traffic on the river.[23]

Towards the end of the fifteenth century it appears that Runcorn had begun to assume sufficient importance as a landing place to cause concern to the merchants of Chester. The burgesses of the city persuaded Edward IV, as Earl of Chester, to instruct the Mayor of Dublin that no goods from Ireland should be landed in the county Palatine except at the Port of Chester and in 1481 the Sheriff was ordered to arrest all vessels attempting to discharge cargoes at Runcorn.[24]

The first attempt to improve the river for navigation in the vicinity of Runcorn was made towards the end of the seventeenth century. In 1696 Thomas Patten of Warrington wrote to Richard Norris, the Member of Parliament for Liverpool, pointing out the benefits to the trade of south Lancashire if the Mersey could be made navigable to Manchester.[25] Patten stated that he had already made some improvements as far as Warrington and in his letter he claimed that two thousand tons of cargo were being shipped annually between Liverpool and Warrington. How Patten had improved the upper river has not been recorded. He probably removed the salmon nets and marked the sailing channel with buoys and perches and perhaps even provided beacons in order to aid navigation at night.

It was to be another twenty-five years before Patten's ambitious project became a reality. In 1712, Thomas Steers, the engineer who was engaged on the building of the first of Liverpool's docks was consulted by a number of prominent merchants from Manchester. They sought to avoid the expensive cost of land carriage between Manchester and Liverpool. They declared

The inland parts of Lancashire and Yorkshire being favoured with great variety of valuable manufactures in woollen, linen, cotton etc and that in very great quantities, has made that neighbourhood as populous, if not more so (London and Middlesex excepted), as the same extent of any part of Great Britain. The trades of these counties extend considerably through the whole Island, as well as abroad, and the consumption of Groceries, Irish Wool, Dyeing Stuff and other imported goods, consequently very great but as yet not favoured with the conveniency of water carriage.[26]

The Manchester men wanted a navigable waterway from "Bank-Key (wither from Leverpool the navigation is at present used) so that Trade (be) made more easy by an expensive Land Carriage being turned into an easy and cheap water carriage, and Cheshire served with Coals, Flaggs and slate far cheaper than at present"[27].

As a consequence of Steers' favourable report the Parliamentary Act for the Mersey and Irwell Navigation was given Royal Assent in 1720 and this resulted in the canalizing of both rivers between Warrington and Manchester.

The improvements carried out under the Act soon proved to be "beneficial to trade, advantageous to the poor, and convenient for the carriage of coals, stone, timber, wood, wares and merchandises"[28]. The enterprise cut the cost of transporting goods from forty shillings a ton when carried by packhorses, to twelve shillings a ton when shipped by barge between Liverpool and Hunt's Bank in Manchester.[29]

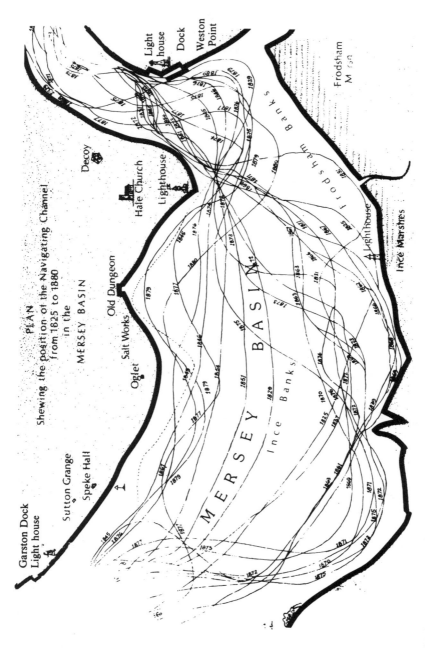

PLAN
Shewing the position of the Navigating Channel
from 1825 to 1880
in the
MERSEY BASIN

Garston Dock
Light house

Sutton Grange

Speke Hall

Decoy

Hale Church

Lighthouse

Old Dungeon

Salt Works

Oglet

MERSEY BASIN

Ince Banks

Frodsham Marsh

Frodsham Banks

Lighthouse

Ince Marshes

Light house

Dock

Weston Point

(Adapted from charts submitted in evidence for the Manchester Ship Canal Bill of 1884. Mersey Conservancy
Reports; *drawn by G. Starkey*)

16

But navigating on the Mersey's upper reaches was never plain sailing. Some of the difficulties encountered by sailing vessels might be illustrated by the following comment from the Admiralty's "West Coast of England Pilot" which notes: "No sailing directions for the upper Mersey would be of any service as they could not be depended upon as correct for any length of time"[30]. The constant mobility of the navigable channels in the river is so unpredictable that the situation might best be summarized in a comment made by Sir Benjamin Baker who was the consulting engineer for Manchester Corporation when the Ship Canal was being built. Baker's opinion was frank. Of the Mersey channels he said:

> No engineer would attempt to predict where the channel would go under unstable conditions. It depends on complicated physical conditions exactly the same as those which regulate the weather. If I endeavoured to predict where a channel would be six months hence, I should be acting on the same basis as the man who used to write Old Moore's Almanack and say what the weather would be on a particular day.[31]

The inner estuary of the Mersey is 2,400 yards across at Dingle Point, 3,200 yards at Otterspool, two and a quarter miles between Garston and Eastham and three miles at its greatest width between Speke and Ellesmere Port. At Hale Head the river narrows to one and a half miles and between Widnes and Runcorn it is reduced to a quarter of a mile. Above the narrows of Runcorn Gap, between Cuerdley and Norton, the Mersey once again widens out into a basin. A few more miles upstream it has become a narrow meandering water course to Warrington where the first bridge up river from the estuary was sited in medieval times.

At low water the inner estuary is a wide expanse of sand with stretches of mud. Some of this material has been deposited in the estuary as a result of the constant erosion of the shore line and through the sand banks at low tide the Mersey winds in a number of shallow channels, some of them less than three feet in depth. It was once possible to cross the river at low tide by following recognised fordable routes. Hale Ford was the best known and this often hazardous crossing was frequently used particularly after skirmishes in Lancashire and Cheshire during the Civil War in the 1640s.

Navigating the upper Mersey was always a difficult and risky operation and in the eighteenth and early nineteenth centuries merchants with shipping interests were anxious that landowners whose estates bordered the river should do nothing which interfered with the tidal scour. In a report in 1818 a Mr. Whidby observed that if the marshes near to Ince and Runcorn were embanked the natural reservoirs of backwater would be greatly diminished so that the reduced scour of the ebb tide would be "insufficient to prevent the total ruin of Liverpool."[32] Four years later a report produced by Messrs. Whidby, Chapman and John Rennie drew attention to jetties which had been built into the river so as to slow the velocity of the tide in order to protect the shore line. The authors of the survey declared that the jetties had caused alluvial deposits to form banks and shoals which were "highly injurious to navigation". They were particularly anxious about sand banks which were growing near Halton and near the entrance to the Mersey and Irwell Navigation Company's Old Quay Canal.[33]

Developments in the upper river were kept under close observation and in 1826 concern about the silting up of the navigable channels was once again expressed when Messrs. Whidby, Giles and George Rennie drew attention to the serious situation caused by newly built "piers, jetties and chevrons which are built into the river from Fiddlers Ferry to Halton Point". They recommended that these obstructions to the tidal flow should be removed as well as an embankment which Sir Richard Brooke had constructed on Norton marsh.[34]

The Mersey's sailing channel up to Runcorn was ever unpredictable. In some years the natural deep would lie along the Lancashire shore but a few months later it had migrated to mid-stream. Another couple of years and it could be miles away from its original route now following the Cheshire shore. Sometimes the navigable channel was reasonably straight and deep but as often as not it followed a winding shallow course. Always difficult and frequently nearly impassable the upper Mersey's rapid changes presented a formidable challenge to even the most experienced masters of small craft.

In 1800 the channel lay along the northern shore and vessels destined for the Duke of Bridgewater's dock at Runcorn were obliged to pass through the narrows and then turn downstream to approach the Cheshire bank near to Runcorn Island. This route was a hazardous one for there were rocks all along the Lancashire shore as well as a barrier of rock in mid river at the Gap. Vessels were forced to reach Runcorn at high tide precisely in order to avoid these obstacles.[35] River navigation by night was feasible by 1820 and contemporary paintings executed by the Reverend J. Allen of Runcorn, show white beehive-type structures on the shore line at the Gap and at Weston Point. These were almost certainly aids to navigation and the probable sites of beacons which were used to guide shipping at night.

By 1831 the safe journey from Liverpool to Runcorn necessitated a passage in mid stream to the mouth of the little River Gowy then directly north across the Mersey to Hale Head followed by another crossing of the river to Weston Point where the deep water once more lay along the Cheshire bank.[36] Although this was a tortuous approach at a time when traffic on the river had vastly increased, it did make the passage safer and easier. But for vessels which were passing further up river beyond Runcorn, the new danger was the promontory of Runcorn Island. In 1773 the Duke of Bridgewater had cut a narrow channel across the promontory. This construction, known as the Duke's Gut, was made so as to funnel the ebb tide towards his dock in order that it might scour away the mud and sand which tended to accumulate across the entrance to the canal.

The Duke's Gut was not entirely satisfactory but when it did function efficiently its tidal race could imperil small craft by pulling them towards the Cheshire bank.

Runcorn, "the Montpelier of Manchester"

Towards the middle of the reign of George III the township of Runcorn became to be known as a watering place. The *Universal British Directory* for 1792 states that many visitors came to bathe in the river during the summer months. Such was the appeal of the place that in 1822 public salt water swimming baths were built on the river's strand below the ancient parish church[37] and boarding houses were built specifically to accommodate summer visitors. The new baths appear to have had every requisite for enjoyment. There was a large central bath open to the river and the side wings of the building had private baths, one for ladies and the other for gentlemen. The baths afforded "the greatest comfort, cleanliness and privacy" and a warm bath or a shower bath could be obtained at short notice. From a central reservoir the public could "be accommodated with clean salt water at their own convenience or, if they preferred, they may bathe with the greatest privacy in the open river when the tide is in."[38]

In an article in the *Gentleman's Magazine* of March 1824 Runcorn was described as "the Montpelier of Manchester and where the invalids of that town resort for their health". The Reverend G. Fowler had no doubts about the beneficial nature of Runcorn spa. He declared that :

> To persons of nervous, relaxed habits the air generally proves very friendly and favourable. Those who are healthy will have their health preserved by it.

In 1834 Mr. Fowler observed:

> A medical gentleman who had been acquainted with this neighbourhood for many years thus expresses his opinion. 'The air of Runcorn is well suited to invalids of strumous habit, convalescents from various types of fever, chronic affection of the viscera, which are accompanied by every modification of dyspepsia. In fact the purity of the air and the equable state of the atmosphere render the place inferior to none for the invalid and valetudinarian.[39]

Certainly pre-industrial Runcorn and its neighbourhood were known for the attractive scenery and rural aspect of the countryside. John Aikin a traveller in 1795 found the river's edge to be particularly alluring:

> The shore all round to Weston Point is protected by a low ridge of rock rising almost perpendicular from the beach. The lovers of botany may find a pleasing variety of plants both maritime and inland varieties in the vicinity of this place.[40]

Old etchings of Runcorn of this period present an idyllic aspect of parkland with a wooded area of mature trees to the west of the medieval church and with only a scatter of houses in the landscape.

The river frontage at Runcorn in 1800 was much the same as it had been for centuries. The ruins of Halton Castle, the windmill at Delph Bridge and the little pre-Reformation church with its square tower were the main features of the Cheshire bank of the river. Runcorn township with a population of 1470 inhabitants was situated in the present High Street and Bridge Street area of the modern town. There was then a natural inlet from the river which formed a creek which was known as the "Old Gut" or the Boat House Pool. This was the public landing place and the site of the ferry crossing to Woodend (Widnes).[41] Around the pool was clustered the few dozen small houses which comprised the township. The main sources for employment were the Duke of Bridgewater's undertaking, some ship and boat building, agriculture and the Runcorn and Weston sandstone quarries.

Across the narrows of Runcorn Gap the Lancashire side of the river was completely rural. Apart from the distant view of Farnworth church tower and Bold windmill the only buildings to be seen were a few isolated farm houses and the inn at the ferry landing place. The population of Widnes cum Appleton, comprising the hamlets of Appleton, Ditton and Woodend was a mere 1065 inhabitants.[42] This pleasant prospect of quiet, empty countryside was to be obliterated by the phenomenol growth of the unsightly chemical industry from the middle of the century onwards.

Throughout the years Runcorn had remained a hamlet of little consequence. Its growth had been retarded because of its cul-de-sac position and by poor communications by road with the rest of the region. It has been said that the Runcorn of 1750 "had become, at least in commercial terms more remote than it had been in medieval times."[43] Other settlements notably Frodsham and Warrington had grown in importance but Runcorn had remained solitary and unfrequented. The town was by passed by the road from Chester to Warrington and by the bulk of shipping activity on the river so that it did not enjoy any sizeable share in the trade and commerce of the district. If communications to the rest of Cheshire were bad those into Lancashire were wretched in the extreme. The only outlet to the north was by way of the often unreliable ferry. The ferry had been a recognised service since the twelfth century and by 1800 it was leased by the Marquis of Cholmondeley for £10 per annum.[44] The ferrymen provided an intermittent service which was available according to demand. As there were few travellers crossing the river the ferryman had a second occupation in order to make a living. Indeed, before the coming of the Bridgewater Canal Runcorn was an obscure village: "The peculiar geographical position of the township placed it far out of the reach of the great highways, and outside its own limits, the hamlet was little known."[45]

Gradually things began to change. By 1803 there was a regular passenger service by sailing packet to Liverpool and in that year the Liverpool Directory advertised:

The Runcorn Packet sails every day for Runcorn about four hours before high water. Fare; First cabin two shillings, second cabin one shilling and six pence. William Woods, Master of the packet.

Commercial expansion became obvious in the first years of the century and the Salford Directory for 1802 described Runcorn as "having become an astonishing place of business". Growth occurred because of increased demand for stone from the local quarries and also as a result of the establishment of ship building yards but the principal agent responsible for the surge in trading activity was the competition between the Duke of Bridgewater's Canal undertaking and that of the Mersey and Irwell Company.

Although the Bridgewater Canal with its terminus at Runcorn, had for a quarter of a century been a vital link between Manchester and the Midlands and the port of Liverpool, the town's growth had been slow because traffic had passed *through* the town. Between the first census of 1801 and that of 1811 the population had risen by only 590 inhabitants to a total of 2060 and much of this increase was the result of employment created by the Mersey and Irwell Company at their Old Quay docks.

In 1804 the Runcorn to Latchford canal was cut under powers embodied in the Mersey and Irwell Navigation Act which gave powers to make "new cuts" without the necessity of further recourse to Parliament. This Old Quay Canal enabled vessels to proceed to the canalized Mersey beyond Warrington without vessels being inconvenienced by being neaped by the ebb tide near Fiddler's Ferry. The new canal ended in the centre of Runcorn township at the Boat House Pool and from the beginning it provided a serious new challenge to the Bridgewater undertaking. The Old Quay Company made extravagent claims declaring that the journey from Liverpool to Manchester would be cut to twelve hours by this route but in fact it was seldom accomplished in less than eighteen hours.[46]

For most of its length the new canal was crossed by turn bridges and the absence of locks enabled the river flats to use a small sail to assist the horses if the wind allowed. The canal could be used by craft carrying a cargo of up to a hundred tons as far as Warrington.

The rivalry between the two canal companies was to become keenest in the passenger carrying service. The Duke of Bridgewater had passenger boats on his canal from 1781.[47] The journey from Runcorn to Manchester took eight hours with passengers alighting and boarding at Preston Brook, Stockton Heath, Lymm and Altrincham and the canal packet boats could each accommodate a hundred passengers. The sedate but efficient service was popular and the leisurely sail through the fields of Cheshire must have been appreciated by the passengers who could avail themselves of light meals and tea which was served by the boat's stewardess. Many passengers made the canal journey for pleasure or for the purpose of shopping in a market town. In 1806 the Mersey and Irwell Company entered the passenger carrying business[48] and their packets from Old Quay Docks soon began to provide serious competition to those of the Bridgewater Trustees. Fares were about the same on both waterways. On the Bridgewater boats the charge from

Runcorn to Knott Mill Wharf in Manchester was three shillings in the first saloon and two shillings in the rear saloon.

The inland waterways helped to lessen the complete isolation of Runcorn but travel by road remained a difficulty and the unsatisfactory crossing of the Mersey was not fully resolved until the construction of the famous transporter bridge in the early years of the twentieth century.

Runcorn Gap Bridge Schemes

There had been a number of proposals for bridging the Gap at Runcorn but ironically the plans for improving north to south communications were frustrated by merchants with shipping interests who wished to preserve the east-west link on the river. They did not wish to see piers in the river which would limit the sailing vessel's room for manoeuvre nor did they want to see the already powerful current increased in the narrows. They believed that bridge works built into the river would cause sand banks to form in the sailing channel and also that the arches of a bridge would narrow the passage through which ships could pass without endangering their top masts.

The first of the schemes was James Brindley's proposal to build an aqueduct to carry the Duke of Bridgewater's Canal over the river to Liverpool. In July 1768 Brindley met several influential Liverpool men "to ascertain the expense that may attend the building of a bridge over the Mersey."[49] This most ambitious scheme was never taken up and without doubt had the plan been implemented it would have severely restricted or even ended the movement of the larger sea going vessel up beyond the Gap but as a monument to eighteenth century engineering expertise it would have been matchless. It is also interesting to reflect how the barrier created by the presence of such a great aqueduct would have effected the plans for the ship canal to Manchester which were being advocated a century later.

A similar scheme for a cast iron aqueduct of three or five arches with a road on each side of the bridge channel was proposed by Ralph Dodd in 1800.[50] The estimated costs were £57,000 and like Brindley's proposals, the aqueduct would carry Bridgewater traffic into Liverpool docks. Once again the Mersey shippers found the idea unacceptable and they succeeded in suppressing the plans.

A suspension bridge was the obvious answer and in 1813 James Dumbell of Mersey Mills, Warrington put forward a design to the Mayor of Liverpool in which he stressed the advantages his bridge would bring by reducing by eight hours the carriage of mail between Liverpool and London.[51] At the end of the Napoleonic war bridge schemes proliferated. William Nicholson of London deposited plans in 1813 and a committee "for carrying the Undertaking into effect" was formed at a public meeting held at the White Hart Inn (later Royal Hotel) in Runcorn on 22nd October 1816. There was an impressive attendance. The Marquis of Stafford, the Marquis of Cholmondeley, the Earl of Derby, the Earl of Sefton, Earl Grosvenor and the Mayors of Chester and Liverpool were invited to serve on the committee.[52] When the committee members met on 29th November 1816 they were overwhelmed by a mass of new plans and estimates. It appears that there were no less than six separate schemes placed before them. A stone bridge of seven arches, an iron bridge of five, a framed timber bridge of five, a timber bridge with two arches, a 1600 feet chain bridge to carry the roadway 110 feet above high water and an iron bridge of similar dimensions. The Committee also considered correspondence from three other engineers who were preparing plans including a letter from Thomas Telford.[53]

The Committee resolved to meet again early in 1817 to receive further plans and estimates and a resolution was passed requesting Liverpool Council to "give their countenance and support to the Undertaking". However, the bridge Committee did not succeed in achieving the essential support of the Council and the movement to provide a Mersey crossing lost its impetus. Nearly two years later in December 1818, the Liverpool Council revived interest when they presented a Parliamentary Bill relative to a bridge at Runcorn. The plans for this suspension bridge were prepared by Telford and he claimed that as a result of his experiments he could provide "a roadway independent of timber, which is impervious to water, has perfect elasticity and appears indestructable". The design was similar to the one he later used for his bridge at Menai. The first estimates for Telford's Runcorn bridge at £84,890 were considered to be too high and his revised costing came to £62,500 but even this was too great for his proposals were not adopted and the suspension bridge scheme was abandoned.[54]

The untoward consequences in not providing a permanent road bridge were still being experienced on both sides of the river a hundred and forty-three years later. Until the arrival of the railway in 1868 communications and the carriage of freight to and from Runcorn depended upon the inland canals and the tides and the unpredictable navigable channel of the upper river. The absence of a road bridge retarded the growth of the town and the quarter of a mile of water effectively severed the mid Merseyside chemical region until 1961 when the Mersey road bridge was completed. The effects of years of procrastination became obvious when the new bridge began to make an immediate and striking impact on the social, economic and industrial structure of society over a wide area of north Cheshire.

Notes

1. Paget-Tomlinson, E., *Mersey and Weaver Flats,* Wilson, Kettering, 1974, p.6.

2. Jarvis, R.C., *Customs Letter Books of the Port of Liverpool 1711-1813,* Vol. VI (3rd Series), Chetham Society, 1954, p.126.

3. Eames, A., *Ships and Seamen of Anglesey,* 1558-1918, Anglesey Antiquarian Society, 1973, p.540.

4. Holland, Henry, *A General View of the Agriculture of Chester,* Phillips, London, 1808, p.307.

5. Hyde, F.E., *Liverpool and the Mersey,* David and Charles, Newton Abbot, 1971, p.30.

6. Eames, A., op.cit. p.187.

7. Eames, A., op.cit. p.188.

8. Harris, J.R., "Michael Hughes of Sutton. The Influence of Welsh Copper on Lancashire Business 1780-1815", *Transactions of the Lancashire and Cheshire Historical Society,* Vol. 101, 1950, p.186.

9. Ibid., p. 187.

10. Jarvis, R.C., op.cit., p.126.

11. Lindsay, Jean, *A History of the North Wales Slate Industry,* David and Charles, Newton Abbot, 1974, p.47.

12. Ibid., p. 191.

13. Ibid., p.82.

14. Ormerod, G., *History of the County Palatine and City of Chester,* (ed. T. Helsby), Vol. 2, 1882, p.46.

15. Aikin, J., *A Description of the Country from Thirty to Forty Miles Around Manchester,* Stockdale, London, 1795, p.300.

16. Musson, A.E., *Enterprise in Soap and Chemicals, Joseph Crosfield and Sons Ltd.,* Manchester University Press, 1965, p.14.

17. Boult, J.; "A Littoral Survey of the Port of Liverpool," *Transactions of the Lancashire and Cheshire Historical Society,* Vol . 22, 1869, p.220.

18. Moss, W., *The Liverpool Guide,* Crane and Jones, London, 1795, p.1.

19. Smith, Lucy, *Leland's Itinerary in England and Wales,* Vol. 5, Centaur Press, London, 1964, p.24.

20. Watkin, W.T., *Roman Cheshire,* 1886, E.P. Publications (Reprint), Wakefield, p.294.

21. Calendar of Patent Rolls, Vol. 1281-1292, November 20th 1289, p.334.

22. Hewitt, H., *Medieval Cheshire,* Manchester University Press, 1929, p.76.

23. Dunlop, G.A., "Early Warrington Fisheries", *Proceedings of the Warrington Literary and Philosophical Society,* 1929, p.7.

24. Parkinson, C.N, *The Rise of the Port of Liverpool,* Liverpool University Press, 1950, p. 17.

25. Carlson, R., *The Liverpool and Manchester Railway Project 1821-1831,* David and Charles, Newton Abbot, 1969, p.25.

26. Tracey, W.B., *Port of Manchester,* Hind, Hoyle, Light Ltd., Manchester, 1901, p.4.

27. Ibid., p.5.

28. Ibid., p.5.

29. *Bridgewater Department Handbook,* Manchester Ship Canal Company, 1968, p.23.

30. Allison, J.E., (as quoted in) *The Mersey Estuary*, Liverpool University Press, 1949, p. l0.

31. Unidentified newspaper cutting. Evidence arbitration between Fairclough and Sons and the MSC regarding Widnes Dock 1895.

32. British Association for tbe Advancement of Science, Report from the Mersey Inquiry Committee. Taylor and Francis, London 1856. Report 17.7. 1818, p.8.

33. Ibid., Report 25.5. 1822, p.9.

34. Ibid., Report 26.6. 1826, p.l0.

35. Mather, F.C., *After the Canal Duke,* Clarendon Press, Oxford, 1979, p.20.

36. Mersey Conservancy Reports, Upper Mersey Sailing Channels, evidence produced at MSC Parliamentary Bill, 1884.

37. Architects plans 1822. Amenities Officer Runcorn.

38. Fowler, G., *A Visitor's Guide to Runcorn,* Walker, Runcorn, 1834, p.34.

39. Ibid., p.34.

40. Aikin, J., op.cit., p.418.

41. Boult, J., op.cit., p.220.

42. Abstract of the Answers and Returns, Census 1801.

43. Porteous, J.D., *Canal Port. The Urban Achievement of the Canal Age,* Academic Press Ltd., London 1977, p.58.

44. Cholmondeley Papers, Cheshire CRO DCH/E/92 VI.

45. Nickson, C., *A History of Runcorn,* Mackie, London, 1887, p.26.

46. Hadfield, C. and Biddle G., *The Canals of North West England,* David and Charles, Newton Abbot, 1970. Vol. I, pp.87-88.

47. Ibid., p.89.

48. "Diary of Richard Lea", *A Brief History of Holy Trinity Church,* Centenary Publication, Runcorn, 1938.

49. *Williamson's Liverpool Advertiser,* 19th July 1768.

50. *Runcorn River Crossings,* Cheshire Education Committee Publication 1976.

51. James Dumbell, Letter Relative to a Bridge at Runcorn (1813), Local Collection, Warrington Library.

52. *Liverpool Mercury,* 1st November 1816.

53. *Liverpool Mercury,* 29th November 1816.

54. Telford's Report, Liverpool 13th March 1817, Local Collection, Runcorn.

3

The Growth of Runcorn as a Port 1786-1830

In spite of the difficulties of up-river navigation the Duke of Bridgewater began to use the larger, sea going vessel to Runcorn dock and from 1790 a number of sizeable ships were built for him at Runcorn. Three brigantines each of 140 tons and a 'snow' of 120 tons were constructed in local yards between 1792 and 1800.

Unlike Frodsham, a few miles down river, Runcorn before 1790 had no tradition for shipbuilding. Undoubtedly small craft were repaired on primitive slipways but the first reference to Runcorn-built vessels in the Liverpool shipping registers is that of the brig *Cooper* launched in 1778.[1] She was a square stern craft of 70 tons. A number of vessels named *Runcorn* appear in various registers in the 1780s but their place of build is not recorded. For instance in 1780 an Admiralty pass was issued for the sloop *Runcorn* of fifty tons for a passage to Leghorn in Italy whilst Lloyd's register for 1781 mentions another 'Runcorn', a sloop of 30 tons which was built in Wales in 1775 and which was engaged as a Liverpool privateer. Another 40 ton sloop is listed in the supplement to Lloyd's register in 1783 and her name appears as "Rencorn", a vessel which was trading between Bristol and Dublin.[2] A scrutiny of the Liverpool registers has produced only the *Cooper* as having been built at Runcorn before the *Royal Charlotte* of 1791.

From the end of the eighteenth century the larger sea going vessels with a loaded draught of ten feet and upwards began to trade into Runcorn and some precise marking of the channel would have been essential. It may be said that from this time Runcorn had become more than a landing place where the occasional sea going ship discharged its cargo. The town had become a minor port within the Customs port of Liverpool.

As might be expected in a small township of less than 1500 inhabitants Runcorn's merchant class was minute but the Liverpool Registry of shipping for 1787 gives the names of four local men as being the owners or part owners of small vessels which traded from Runcorn. John Fryer, merchant, is named as the sole owner of the *Fox* a 71 ton flat which had been launched in Northwich in 1786. The Duke of Bridgewater's agent at Runcorn, Samuel Wylde, and James Riding, both described as merchants, together with John Gilbert, the Duke's principal agent and another important official of the Bridgewater undertaking, Benjamin Southern, formed a business association with two Worsley men. In the register they are named as the co-owners of seven small ships trading out of Runcorn. Four of the vessels were two masted 'galliots'. They were the *Industry,* the *Navigator,* the *Dublin* and the *Betsey.* All of them were about 73 tons and all were built in Northwich between 1784 and 1787. The other three vessels were single mast flats; the *Runcorn,* the *Sly* and the *John and Nancy.* In the maritime records there exist undated affidavits signed by Samuel Wylde which state that *Navigator, Runcorn* and *John and Nancy* were lost at sea with their crews.[3]

By 1802 James Riding and Samuel Wylde were part owners with others of the flat *Bettys* which was built in St. Helens in 1784 and both had financial interests in the Chester built flat *John.* The two men were in partnership with Worsley merchants as co-owners of the 140 ton barquentine *Sampson* which was launched in Runcorn in 1798. Riding and Wylde and their partners also had the 'snow', *Mary,* 111 tons which was built in Warrington in 1800. (*Mary* was to have an interesting career. She was taken by the French as a prize of war but was recaptured in 1804 and by 1807 she was registered at the port of Whitehaven).[4] Samuel Wylde and James Riding also owned the large sailing flat *Royal Charlotte* which was built in a local yard in 1791. Riding's name which was prominent in the first registers does not appear after 1802 for in that year he was declared bankrupt. John Gilbert, the engineer who supervised the construction of the Bridgewater Canal and who may have been responsible for planning much of the undertaking, died in 1795 but in 1802 another John Gilbert of Clough Hall in Staffordshire had shares in a number of small craft based at Runcorn.[5] Together with John, Thomas and Cornelius Bourne and Edward Mason, merchants of Liverpool, Gilbert had *Clough Hall,* 70 tons and *Chatwell* 70 tons, both of which they used for salt and coal carrying. The partners had four smaller vessels of up to 40 tons as well as three boats of 15 tons which operated "within thirteen miles around Runcorn".

Many local men of modest means were prepared to invest their savings in shipping.[6] Kerfoot Janion, coal merchant, and John Janion, farmer, had the 58 ton square stern flat *Glory* which was built in Chester in 1782 and which was rebuilt in a Runcorn yard in 1803. They also owned *Tom* a flat launched in Northwich in 1769. Two local shipwrights William Wright and Charles Hickson built and operated the flat *Sarah.* They also launched the flat *Hannah* of 59 tons in 1803 and they shared the ownership with William Greenwood, a Runcorn grocer. Hickson and Wright and another local grocer, Thomas Hazlehurst, owned the *Ranger* which was built at Zetland in Scotland. The two shipwrights had considerable investment in small vessels. They owned *Friends,* a galliot built in Frodsham in 1793 and lost off the Welsh coast in 1806 and also the flat *John and Thomas* which was built in Northwich in 1793.

Other vessels in the ownership of local men included the *Sutton* built at Frodsham in 1787 and partly owned by John Fryer and the *Alice and Ann* built at Frodsham Bridge in 1802 in which William Kirkham, grocer of Runcorn had shares. Thomas Sothern and James Adam of Runcorn and Barker Chifney, a Liverpool merchant, owned *Ann,* a snow which was launched in Runcorn in 1802. Richard Cartwright, another local man, was both master and owner of the little flat *Ann of Runcorn,* 31 tons.

At the time of his death in 1803 the Duke of Bridgewater possessed sixty flats and three larger vessels. The latter were locally built craft, the *Worsley,* a square stern schooner of 130 tons and the barquentines *Rochdale* 133 tons, and *Manchester* of 139 tons.

From the last years of the eighteenth century there appeared more local merchants and tradesmen who were prepared to invest in shipping as a secondary interest. The Duke of Bridgewater and later, his Trustees, encouraged independent carriers to use the canal and the docks and local men availed themselves of the business opportunities that were offered. The resulting increase in maritime trade at Runcorn brought about the establishment of the shipbuilding industry. Whereas previously the slips had been occupied mainly with repairs and the rebuilding of river craft, from this time on the town began to acquire some reputation for the building of not only river craft·but also for the construction of the larger sea going ship.

The Duke of Bridgewater had boat repairing facilities at the end of his line of locks at Runcorn and the repair of canal boats soon developed into the construction of river flats. But the ambitious building programme at Runcorn in the last decade of the century was but a part of a regional expansion in shipbuilding for the industrial north west was experiencing the boom of the Industrial Revolution. Sailing flats were launched at Sankey Bridges, Warrington, Northwich, Winsford and Frodsham in increasing numbers as the river and canal commerce of the region expanded. Vessels were built in unlikely places. For instance twenty craft totalling 1,485 tons were constructed at St. Helens on the Sankey Canal between 1786 and 1805 and others were launched into the Bridgewater Canal at Worsley near Manchester.[7]

A glance at the baptismal registers of the parish church of Runcorn indicates the growing importance of shipbuilding in the Regency period. The proportion of fathers who were employed as carpenters is unusually large when compared to men engaged in other trades. "Stonegetters" (quarrymen), "flatmen" and labourers' names monopolise the entries but among the many fathers entered as carpenters, ten give their precise occupation as "ship's carpenter" or "shipwright". Other maritime occupations include sailmakers, rope makers and block makers.

The Port of Frodsham in the Eighteenth Century

Although information concerning Runcorn-built vessels which were constructed before 1790 is apparently non-existent more knowledge is available on Frodsham where shipbuilding was long established. The first Frodsham launch to appear in the records is that of the 40 ton *Armitage* built in 1728. The *Ann,* a 35 ton brigantine was launched in 1737 and the 50 ton brig *Benin* in 1746. The voyages made by these tiny craft was astonishing. *Ann* is recorded as having arrived at Lancaster from Barbados in 1741 and she appears in the registers again when she left Liverpool for a voyage to Virginia in 1747. The name *Benin* suggests that this vessel was a slave ship or she was a tender to slave ships which were operating on the West African coast. *Benin* was registered at Liverpool and she was lost as a prize of war at an unrecorded date.[8]

Eighteenth century Frodsham was a place of some importance. From Elizabethan times Cheshire cheese had been despatched down the Weaver to Liverpool to be transhipped to the London market[9] and salt in ever increasing quantities was sent to Liverpool from the Frodsham refinery.

The demand for salt led to the improvements of the river Weaver in the 1720's and also brought into being the fleets of Weaver sailing flats. Frodsham and Northwich were natural centres for building barges. The proximity of Delamere Forest assured, for some years at least, a ready supply of timber which was suitable for ships' frames. The river at both places was sufficiently deep and wide to permit launches and there existed a local population large enough to supply labour for the yards. Frodsham bridge, which carried the main Chester to Warrington road, effectively decided the limit of sea going navigation. It was possible for small craft to unship their masts to pass under the low arches of the bridge in order to proceed upstream but the bridge designated the siting of facilities for the discharging and transhipment of cargoes on its down stream side. Here there also came into being a modest shipbuilding and ship repairing industry. The capacity for ship construction was small but when the demand for small craft was acute during the Napoleonic war, the Frodsham builders, in 1802, succeeded in launching four vessels from their slips. This was not typical for it was to be another fifty-six years before they managed another four launchings in one year and again this was due to an extraordinary demand for small vessels in order to satisfy the needs of the booming mid-Victorian alkali industry of the region.

In 1793 the Frodsham builders launched three small craft but they were mainly concerned with ship repair for in the 134 years between 1728 and 1862 the names of only fifty-eight Frodsham-built vessels have been discovered in shipping and insurance records.

Frodsham had some traditional maritime trade. An early reference to a Frodsham vessel appears in the Quarter Sessions records at Chester for 1710 where it is stated that the *True Love* of Frodsham was lost in the Irish Sea with her cargo of 807 bushels of salt.[10] There was some foreign trade at Frodsham. In 1706 several Danish vessels put into Liverpool and sent lighters to Frodsham Bridge to collect 1250 tons of salt.

Among the wills deposited at the Cheshire Record Office are those of Frodsham men, Richard Norman, mariner, who died in 1725 and Thomas Morris also a mariner who died in 1740. William Tomlinson, merchant of Frodsham Bridge had shares in six small vessels in 1786.[11] They were the flats *Amity* 70 tons, *Mary* 53 tons, *John* 60 tons, *Pattys* 70 tons, *Glory* 49 tons, and the 74 ton galliot, *Betties*. Charles Buchanan and William Horabin of Frodsham owned the 71 ton flat *Mentor*.

In a register of vessels using the rivers and inland waterways of Cheshire in 1795 William Crosbie and John Urmson of Frodsham are named as the owners of seven flats, *Hornet, Ant, Bee, Fly, Wasp, Frodsham* and *John and Thomas.* The first two were over 70 tons displacement and the remainder were between 50 and 60 tons. All were engaged in the coal and salt trade between Northwich, St. Helens, and Liverpool.[12] Other Frodsham owners were Wharton Grayson with *Richard* 45 tons, Samuel and Ralph Manley with *Windmill of Runcorn* 57 tons, John Hazlehurst with *Frodsham Trader* 40 tons and Thomas Hazlehurst who owned *Compleat* of 50 tons.[13] By 1795 Catherine Horabin, widow, owned three flats *Mentor, Diligence* and *Liberty.* All these craft were registered for use on the Weaver and the Mersey but one or two of the larger flats went further afield. John Pickering, William Hayes, and William Mills of Frodsham used *Mills* 73 tons, in the salt trade but she was also registered for the slate trade to Bangor and Caernarvon. William Hayes and Andrew Ellis of Frodsham held shares in *Vine* which was also engaged in carrying slates. Hayes and Ellis were also part owners of *Betsy* and *Dido.*[14]

With the rise of traffic on the Weaver, Frodsham became increasingly a centre for the building of small craft. All the vessels built during the eighteenth century were less than 100 tons displacement and with few exceptions the names of the builders are not recorded but Isaac White, William Hayes and John Urmson were building vessels at Frodsham Bridge at the beginning of the nineteenth century.

The Appendix contains the names of vessels built at Frodsham. Most were built specifically for the Weaver salt and coal trade to operate the short distances between the Cheshire Salt field, the Sankey Canal and the refineries at Dungeon Point, Hale, and Liverpool. From all registry sources figures of ship launches show that Frodsham was the prominent local building centre between 1790 and 1810. For the next two decades it appears that the Runcorn and Frodsham yards built a similar number of craft but after 1830 Runcorn yards launched more ships of greater tonnage and Frodsham declined rapidly until the ship building tradition at Frodsham Bridge became extinct in 1862.

The rise of Runcorn's ship building and repair facilities can be attributed to the increase of river traffic in the vicinity. By 1804 there were two canals with outlets into the river Mersey at Runcorn and the Runcorn Gap Railway from St. Helens to Widnes together with the extension of the Sankey Canal to Widnes in 1833, enhanced the prospects for greater trade. Complementary factors were Runcorn's alkali and soap manufacturing industries which were growing in national importance by 1830 and also the town's quarries were in full production supplying stone for dock extensions at Liverpool.

But Runcorn's beginnings as a port of some consequence in the first half of the nineteenth century must be attributed to the development of the steam tug boat. The Mersey reaches above Garston had always been a barrier to maritime trade but the highly manoeuvrable paddle boats could make best use of the tides in the devious sailing channels to convey long trains of barges safely up river. It is a matter of no surprise, therefore, that Runcorn business men perceived the advantages of steam tugs and that they financed and built the first steamers to be used successfully on the Mersey.

The Early Steam Boats on the Upper Mersey

It is generally accepted that the world's first practicable steam boat was the famous *Charlotte Dundas* built by William Symington in 1802 and used for towing barges on the Clyde-Forth Canal. However, five years before this event a steamer had crossed the Mersey from the Sankey Canal to Runcorn and then had proceeded up the Bridgewater Canal to Manchester. In June 1797 this little steam boat, built by an unknown mechanic named John Smith was demonstrated on the Sankey Canal. The scene is described in a local newspaper cf the time.[15]

> A vessel heavily laden with copper slag passed along the Sankey Canal without the aid of haulers or rowers, the oars performing eighteen strokes a minute by application of steam only. On enquiry made since, it appears that the vessel, after a course of ten miles returned the same evening to St. Helens, whence it had set out. The form and motion of the oars is not easily described, but it bids fair to be ranked among the most useful of modern inventions.

Another eye witness described the scenes of excitement and curiosity as the little steam boat made its canal journey to Manchester.

Smith had bought his boat in Liverpool and he informed the previous owners that he intended to fit an engine in her. It is recorded that he was "treated as an insane person. He was laughed at by one, insulted by another and was pitied generally". Undaunted by their remarks Smith replied: "Those may laugh who will but my opinion is, before twenty years are over you will see this river (Mersey) covered with smoke.[16]"

Little more is known of Smith. His was one of the earliest steam boats to be invented. Even the name of the little vessel has been forgotten and her subsequent history is unknown but Smith's prophecy was more or less accurate, for, twenty years after his boat had crossed the Mersey to Runcorn another paddle steamer had appeared on the upper river. The second steamer was the wooden paddle boat *Elizabeth* said to have been the first vessel to have been fitted with a marine engine specifically designed for her. The engines of boats built before *Elizabeth* do not come into this category.[17]

The *Elizabeth* was forty tons displacement, fifty-nine feet long with a draught of four feet and she was built on the Clyde in 1813 by John Wood of Port Glasgow to the order of John Hutchinson, a local brewer. She was fitted with a ten horse power engine by John Thompson of Glasgow which gave the boat a top speed of nine knots in ideal conditions. *Elizabeth* was propelled by two side paddle wheels and she had a square sail fitted to a spar on her funnel.[18]

31

For a year *Elizabeth* provided a passenger service between Greenock and Helensburgh and Glasgow and in 1815 she was purchased for £1200 by a syndicate managed by Lieutenant Colin Watson of the East Yorkshire Militia to provide a passenger service on the Mersey between Liverpool and Runcorn. According to an account in the *Liverpool Mercury* of the 30th June 1815 the proprietors also intended to use *Elizabeth* for occasional journeys as far as Warrington.

But the voyage to Liverpool was to prove an ordeal for the primitive little boat and its crew. Lieutenant Watson and his cousin, a Lieutenant Hargrave R.N., with only a boy to help them encountered a storm off the Galloway coast and they "endured twelve hours of great peril". Then they "suffered an accidental throwing off one of the paddles" which necessitated repairs at Ramsey in the Isle of Man. They were also "deceived by the compass" and found themselves off the Welsh coast. Once again the paddles failed them and *Elizabeth* drifted almost to the Irish shore before they were able to make temporary repairs to enable them to reach Liverpool late on the night of June 27th.

Mr. Thompson, *Elizabeth's* first owner, has left us an interesting account of the boat.[19] She had two cabins, one forward and the other abaft of the engine house. Her after cabin was twenty-one feet long and eleven feet wide with a height of seven feet four inches from the floor to the ceiling. She was comfortably furnished with the cabin seats and a settee upholstered in crimson plush and there was also a red plush carpet. There were six small windows on each side and they were made to slide up and down like the windows of a coach. The windows were curtained with a red material with pelmets and tassels. The cabin had a large gilt mirror and the cornices of the cabin were also gilded. Two bookcases filled with current literature were provided and newspapers were available. According to the *Liverpool Mercury, Elizabeth* could accommodate a hundred passengers.

For a year the *Elizabeth* plied regularly between Runcorn and Liverpool but she was uneconomical and her machinery was unreliable and she was sold in 1816. Two years later the engine was removed and she was provided with a treadmill which was worked by up to four heavy carthorses.[20] In June 1818 the public were informed that the horse packet, *Safety* was providing a service between Runcorn, Weston Point and Liverpool.[21] This would most certainly have been the newly converted *Elizabeth* and the change of name to *Safety* suggests that passage on the former paddle steamer had been a source of anxiety to the passengers. Unfortunately the horse packet proved to be unsatisfactory as the horses became ill with the constant rolling of the boat so the paddle wheels were removed and *Safety, ex Elizabeth* was converted into a sailing barge.

The *Elizabeth* had been a limited success but she had aroused local interest. The little steamer could make progress against wind and tide - a fact which would have made her useful if she had been employed as a tug boat for sailing vessels. In fact the proprietor of the *Liverpool Mercury* in an article in his paper in September 1815 had advocated the use of steamers to tow sailing ships out of the Mersey and into favourable winds at sea. He noted that *Elizabeth* had been very useful as a tug when she had come upon the Runcorn sailing packet which was becalmed. The steamer had towed the packet for ten miles to Runcorn.[22]

It was a group of perceptive Runcorn tradesmen who first recognised the potentialities of the steamer to increase trade in the difficult upper reaches of the river and they were to finance and build the first paddle steamers to be built on the Mersey.[23] In 1816 two wooden vessels, the *Prince Regent* and the *Duke of Wellington* were completed in local yards for local men. The *Prince Regent* which was owned by a schoolmaster, an inn keeper, a waiter, a butcher, a seaman and a cabinet maker was built by William Rigby and the *Duke of Wellington* by William Wright.[24] Both men appear in the town books as being prominent in the management of Runcorn township in the early years of the century.

The dimensions of the steamers were almost identical, the length of each being sixty-nine feet and they had a beam of thirteen feet nine inches. The *Duke of Wellington* was the first to be launched and she appears to have been most successful. The *Liverpool Courier* of 3rd July 1819 carries an account of her activities.

> The perfection to which the navigation of steam boats has been carried and the celerity with which they sail will be evidenced by the history of one of the Runcorn Steam Packets.

> The *Duke of Wellington,* steamer, left Runcorn on Sunday last at four o'clock in the morning and arrived at this port (Liverpool) at seven. She sailed thence with passengers at about eleven o'clock and landed them at Runcorn. She departed from Runcorn for Warrington where she arrived at two o'clock. She left it again at 2.30 for Runcorn where she landed her passengers and, having taken a fresh cargo, sailed for Liverpool and arrived there at 7.30 in the evening. The whole distance she sailed in the course of the day was upwards of eighty miles, a distance we may imagine, which no vessel ever performed in the same time on this river.[25]

Little information is available on *Prince Regent* but it seems that she operated on the river for six years until she was sunk in a storm off Ellesmere Port in 1822.[26] She was raised and towed to Runcorn but no further history of her has yet come to light.

There is a brief but interesting description of the early steam boats in the journal of Ellen Weeton who 'discovered' the watering place of Runcorn in her travels in the north west in the early part of the last century. Miss Weeton sailed from Liverpool to Runcorn on a steamer in the summer of 1817 and in her *Journal of a Governess* she wrote that the steamers — "make a rather laughable appearance. They go puffing and blowing and beating their sides and labouring along". She added her opinion that it was unusual for steam boat passengers to be sick.[27]

There is no doubt that the little paddle boats were successful but inevitably the early steamers had their problems. Engine failure sometimes resulted in the boats drifting on to sandbanks and the passengers would have to wade ashore to wait until the next tide freed the vessel. Nevertheless the steam ferry service had proved profitable and by 1819 the road between Runcorn and Northwich had been turnpiked so that within a few years of the introduction of steam a regular coach service between the bottom locks and Northwich had been established.[28]

Soon other steamers came into service on the passenger run. In 1819 the former Parkgate to Bagillt packet *Ancient Briton* was acquired for the Liverpool to Runcorn ferry service. She was described as being the fastest packet boat on the river and her passengers were given reassuring information about her safety features. According to Gore's *Advertiser:*

> Her engine is constructed so that it cannot possibly be forced past its usual speed. The only communication with the safety valve is a chain instead of a rod therefore no weight can be placed upon it to prevent the overplus of steam escaping.[29]

Although this innovation is difficult to understand, the possibility of accidents to the boilers of the early steamers was very real. The boiler of the Runcorn packet *Earl of Bridgewater* burst in 1824 killing two passengers and injuring others.

It seems that the operators of the early steamers had good cause not to rely completely on the efficient performance of the engine. Contemporary illustrations and prints of the steam boats of the 1820s and 1830s show the spindly-funnelled vessels equipped with furled sails ready in case of mechanical failure and it was to be some years before the paddle boats were reliable enough to dispense with their stand-by sets of sails.

The increase in canal trade and the rivalry between the canal companies did not bring about an immediate development of towage facilities on the river although the question of tug boats had been considered by the Mersey and Irwell Company as early as 1815. The directors believed that if they did not provide an efficient towage service then private operators would. The directors realised that "certain adventurers will be attempting to put steam paddle packets on the old river to the prejudice of this company"[30] But in spite of their foresight it was to be more than ten years before the company did own steamers to work the Mersey-estuary.

As far as can be ascertained the first steamer to be regularly employed as a river tug was the paddle boat *Eagle*.[31] In 1824 she was used to tow flats from Queen's Dock, Liverpool to Runcorn from where the barges were horse drawn via the Duke's Canal to Manchester. The following extract from *Wheeler's Manchester Chronicle* of 1824 advertises the service.

> Queen's Dock to Eagle Quay, Manchester. A new method of carrying by water by means of a steam boat has been started. These leave Liverpool to arrive at Manchester the day after. Manchester and Liverpool merchants of all classes should avail themselves of this new mode of transport.

Unfortunately no details of the *Eagle* are available but a contemporary print shows her to be a typical early steamer with a large square sail fastened to a spar on the funnel in case of mechanical failure or perhaps because of a reluctance to break with traditional maritime practice.

All the early paddle steamers were made of wood and as suitable timber for ship's frames was still available locally, the Runcorn shipbuilders were ready to meet the demand for the new paddle boats when it arrived.

"An Astonishing Place of Business"

The volume of Liverpool-Manchester trade passing through the Bridgewater docks and canal and through those of the Mersey and Irwell Company expanded dramatically in the first two decades of the nineteenth century. Trade expanded because the Manchester cotton industry took advantage of the new techniques in weaving and the improvements in machine spinning to create a mechanised factory system which demanded ever increasing quantities of raw cotton. From about 1800 Liverpool had displaced London as the leading port for the import of raw cotton[32] and the two canals at Runcorn became the main supply routes by which the Manchester region obtained its cotton, raw wool, hemp, flax and dyewood. Other cargoes destined for Manchester via the inland waterways included timber, roofing slates, bricks, grain, flour, tea, sugar and rice. The Bridgewater system also carried an increasing volume of pottery materials destined for Stoke-on-Trent as well as a growing reverse trade in crated pottery.

The increase in business showed no sign of slackening and in June 1825 the Mersey and Irwell Company announced their intention to facilitate trade by constructing a large dock at Old Quay in Runcorn. The finished work was impressive and the improvements were described by Mr. Fowler in his *Visitor's Guide to Runcorn*. There were two sets of locks into the river, one used by incoming craft and the other by vessels leaving the canal. Mr. Fowler described the massive tidal gates into the river from the new basin and he gives an account of the new graving dock. He records:

> When a vessel requires to be repaired it is first hauled into the dock then two slides to which are attached very strong chains are let down under its keel and, by means of a powerful machine it may be drawn out of the water and placed on the stocks within the space of half an hour.[33]

This slip could accommodate a ship of two hundred tons and further improvements at Old Quay in 1829 allowed vessels drawing sixteen feet of water to enter the docks at Spring tides. In this year additional warehouses were built on the quay.

Runcorn was becoming a port of some prominence but it remained part of the port of Liverpool. However, a report of 1817 records some relaxation in the regulations concerned with the export of dutiable goods from the docks.

The great connection which Runcorn forms between the coasting and inland trade gives to it all the bustle of a considerable port and a supervisor is now established here for whom a suitable office or customs house has recently been built on the wharf. The privilege of clearing out certain commodities from here without touching the great port of Liverpool has recently been granted by the Commissioners of Customs.[34]

Within the seven years from 1816 to 1823 the Bridgewater trade increased from 76,000 tons to 118,000 tons, six sevenths of this being cargo carried to Manchester. The Mersey and Irwell's trade had also experienced a considerable boom growing from 90,000 tons to 135,000 tons over the same period[35] and this increase in maritime trade is reflected in the rise of Runcorn's population. From 1801 to 1821 the township increased in population from 1470 to 3103 inhabitants and it was heavily dependent upon the waterways for its revenue. In 1821 the properties of the Trustees of the Duke of Bridgewater accounted for no less than eighty-six per cent of the rateable value.[36]

Urban Development 1820-1840

Throughout the first forty years of the century maritime trade at Runcorn and the brisk canal traffic on both lines of the inland waterways continued to grow. The small area of housing which had comprised the original township had quadrupled between 1801 and 1831 and new streets of small houses had almost linked the old village of Runcorn to the houses at the Bridgewater Docks by 1841. The hamlet had by then grown into a bustling little industrial town with a population of 7000 inhabitants. But the Duke's canal formed an effective barrier to the further expansion of housing to the south of the town and new building was confined to the narrow strip of land running east-west between the Bridgewater Canal and the river.

The first major industry in the area was Thomas Hazlehurst's soap works which, from small beginnings as a resin and turpentine works in 1816, had grown into a large concern by the middle of the century producing a variety of basic chemicals in addition to the soap. In the decade beginning in 1830 there was the soapworks of Messrs. T. and J. Johnson, two tanneries, a slate works, an acid works, a steam flour mill and timber yards.[37] Because of the excellent facilities provided for the carriage of stone by water the Runcorn and Weston quarries were busy in supplying stone for dock works and public buildings over a wide area. Mr. Tomkinson's Weston quarries were extensive for, according to a county directory, they regularly employed 150 men but there were times when the workforce rose to 500 employees. The stone from these quarries was conveyed by means of tramways down the steep hillside to the river at Weston Point.

Runcorn's increased population of 6950 inhabitants in 1841 had arrived by short distance migration with only 27.8 per cent of them being born outside Cheshire. The town's rateable value was £14,433 of which industry represented £5,376. A town hall was built in the centre of the township in 1831 on land provided by the Trustees of the Duke of Bridgewater. A second Anglican church was erected in 1838 as well as a number of chapels one of which was intended for the use of the town's seamen and flatmen. The Runcorn Gas Company was founded in 1837 and by 1840 the place had become a thriving canal port and the centre of the commercial activity of the area.

The manufacture of chemicals had become of major importance by 1845. Runcorn's geographical position was ideal for the siting of the alkali industry. Equidistant from the Cheshire saltfield and Lancashire coal pits with easy and cheap communications by water to both sources of supply, the town soon acquired a reputation for severe atmospheric pollution and in spite of strong local opposition the fields to the south of the Duke's canal began to be used as the sites for the dumping of chemical waste.

Although the port was growing in importance its Customs House, which was built at the east end of the Duke's Gut, was so unimpressive that it was hard to find:

> and when found excites no ordinary degree of surprise, that so paltry a place should be used for so important a purpose; it really is a disgrace to the town. The Customs House (so called) consists of one small room which is occupied jointly by the Principal Coast Officer and his assistant and the Receiver of Liverpool Town and Light Dues.[38]

Another, more persistent cause for complaint was the ancient ferry across the river to Widnes. In the first decade of the century the ferry was leased to a Mr. Peter Brown at a yearly rent of £20 and later to a Mr. Gilbert at the same rent. By 1826 the ferry was a profitable concern and the local agent for the Mersey and Irwell Navigation Company secured the lease for £50 per year.[39] The improvements which had been made by the Old Quay Company at the terminus of their canal in 1828 had partly enclosed the Boat House Pool and the Duke of Bridgewater's Trustees had acquired the remainder for a boatyard. This site had been the public landing place and there had been some opposition to the enclosures. An observer noted that "The town was therefore excluded from the said creek which some persons complain against".[40] A new ferry crossing was established half a mile down river near to the parish church.

The primitive ferry service in the 1830s and 1840s was inadequate in every respect. There was no ferry slip or accommodation for waiting passengers at Runcorn and travellers were landed with their luggage on the muddy beach. Sir George Head gives his personal experience of a crossing in 1836.

> In the first place the public are ferried across by a couple of men who are not always to be found at a moment's warning. Next, the landing place at Runcorn is at all times extremely incommodious and thirdly that on the other side is still worse. In fact at low water the passenger here steps out of the boat on a plank, lands on mud and sand, and after walking on this compost upwards of a hundred yards to the ferry house he then has to walk a mile to proceed at all events whether bound for the establishment of the St. Helens Railroad or towards those of the proprietors of the Sankey Canal.[41]

After the opening of the St. Helens to Runcorn Gap railway in 1833 the river crossing assumed a greater importance as more travellers from Runcorn and the surrounding districts used the ferry in order to reach Liverpool, Manchester and St. Helens. A train left Runcorn Gap station in Widnes twice a day for St. Helens and intending passengers were advised to cross the river three quarters of an hour before the train was due to leave. When it was low water two ferry boats were required for the passage across the four hundred yards of river and passengers had to disembark on the mud in mid river and cross to a second boat in order to reach the opposite bank.

Yet another source of irritation was the fact that Mr. William Hurst of West Bank House, Widnes, the owner of much of West Bank, received payment for all goods landed there by ferry passengers and traders and he and his tenants had free passage across the ferry.[42]

Although for the first decade of its existence the St. Helens to Runcorn Gap Railway was overwhelmingly concerned with goods traffic rather than with passengers it was obvious that both the railway and the developments at the Widnes dock of the Sankey Canal extension would soon bring about an upsurge in the number of passengers crossing the river. Sir Richard Brooke of Norton Priory anticipated the difficulties which would occur at the ferry. When the Sankey Navigation was extended to Widnes in 1833 Sir Richard required the company to construct three wharfs or landing places and also to build a small basin capable of receiving small vessels of eighteen tons burden on his Cuerdley estate.[43] The facilities were for the exclusive use of Sir Richard's tenants and they also guaranteed him a convenient crossing between the Norton Priory estate and his Lancashire properties. In addition Sir Richard and his heirs were given the right to toll-free transport on the canal for the produce of the Cuerdley farms and for the carriage of any building materials that were required.

While Runcorn was expanding apace in the 1830s, Weston Point was also experiencing some growth. In 1810 the Weaver Trustees completed a canal from Frodsham to Weston Point in order to avoid the difficult entrance at the Weaver mouth. The canal had a sea lock and a small basin and from 1817 to 1820 piers were constructed. The new works stimulated traffic so that in the 1830s and 1840s further dock facilities were added together with new sea walls, warehouses and houses for the employees.

The rivalry between the Weaver Trustees, the Mersey and Irwell and the Bridgewater Trustees was keen and competition for business was beneficial to the three systems in that it promoted improvement and renovation. A proposed development by one company usually spurred the others into activity and delapidated sections of the three waterways were renewed and enlarged in the first three decades of the century. On one issue only were the three companies in agreement — they resented the interference of Liverpool in upper Mersey affairs and they kept vigilant watch in case the aspirations of the Liverpool Council should bring further encroachment in mid-Merseyside.

The Ship Builders

From its late eighteenth century beginnings Runcorn's shipbuilding activity became a permanent industry which was to gain something of a national prestige for the building of small coastal craft. Before 1790 ship launches had been an occasional event and the vessels on the slips were mainly river craft but at the turn of the century the local builders were launching genuine sea going ships.

It is not easy to reconcile the growth of shipbuilding with the fact that the river was not always ideal for launches. The natural deep could wander away from the shipyard sites and not return for some years. This migration of the channel and the problems caused by silting influenced the fortunes of the yards and decided the size of vessels that could be built. Nevertheless, the yards were busy. North American and Baltic timber imported into Liverpool was easily obtainable and by 1816 there was an ancilliary supporting industry of pump makers, block and spar makers as well as small rope and sail making establishments at Runcorn.[44] Even more important there was a growing number of merchants and tradesmen who were willing to invest in shipping. Furthermore Liverpool's immense increase in maritime trade resulted in her ship owners placing orders for new ships at the Runcorn yards.

The Runcorn ship builders did not acquire the necessary expertise and skills over night and it may not be unreasonable to assume that as Frodsham's shipbuilding decreased the shipwrights and carpenters looked for employment in Runcorn where they might expect to find more secure occupation. Indeed, Runcorn was fortunate in possessing men who were innovators (the building of Merseyside's first paddle steamers is an illustration of the inventiveness and business acumen of the ship yard owners) — and who required their own vessels in order to carry on their primary commercial interests in slate, coal, stone and salt carrying.

Despite this surge in ship construction it is difficult to find documentary evidence for the first half of the century. The yard books do not appear to exist even for the end of the nineteenth century and as the registers of British shipping up to 1824 do not usually include the builder's name, information is scarce. But occasionally clues do appear. At the time of a vessel's first registration "shipbuilder" or "shipwright" might appear amongst the owners' occupations but arduous scanning of registers often fails to provide knowledge of the builder of a particular vessel.

At Runcorn by 1803 William Wright and Charles Hickson were partners engaged in ship building and by 1816 William Wright was building under his name alone.[45] In a Cheshire directory of 1828 William Evans and William Martin are listed as shipbuilders but research has produced no further reference to them and it would appear that their business was slight and of brief duration. Among the merchants listed in the directory appears the name of Dennis Brundrit whose occupations were druggist and stone merchant. In 1816 Brundrit married Elizabeth, the daughter of William Wright, shipbuilder, and the Mersey Street shipyard passed to Dennis Brundrit at the death of his father-in-law. Brundrit was a man of considerable talent and he possessed wide interests. His business skills made him the town's best known personality and he was the most successful of the new merchant class.

Dennis Brundrit was born on 17th July 1796 at Stretford near Manchester. His parents had settled in Runcorn at a time when an increase in trade and employment at the docks had attracted many of the Duke of Bridgewater's Manchester employees to the town. By the time of his marriage the young Brundrit owned a druggist's shop which was situated at the junction of High Street and Bridge Street and in 1823 he entered into partnership with Philip Whiteway in the business of stone merchant and shipbuilder.[46] Brundrit, who owned the Stenhills quarry at Runcorn realised the potential uses of the stone from the Penmaenmawr granite[47] quarry in North Wales. He bought the mineral rights and the Penmaenmawr quarry proved to be a valuable investment because the expanding towns in the Merseyside region required a hard wearing stone for surfacing the streets and the squared or rectangular blocks or setts made of Welsh granite met this requirement and gave a longer life than any other road stone used in the region. As heavy merchandise was transported in horse drawn, iron-tyred carts and waggons many of Lancashire's industrial towns were paved with the durable Penmaenmawr setts and many of the roads were made of Macadam, that is the chippings of the same stone. A sett paving was needed between and on both sides of the tramlines when they were laid down later in the century. Brundrit and Whiteway supplied channels, curbs and crossing stones to local authorities over a wide area and the demand for the firm's hard wearing products lasted until well into the twentieth century.

The Brundrit and Whiteway Company needed vessels to bring the Penmaenmawr stone to Runcorn. They built their own boats for their purpose and they also catered for other business men who required vessels which carried similar heavy cargoes. The slate merchants and the carriers of salt and coal needed sturdy coasting craft and many of these were constructed at Brundrit and Whiteway's yard.

In the early years when ship construction first became established in Runcorn, the craft were built under very primitive conditions as indeed were the great number of coastal schooners and barges built in creeks near to fishing villages all round the coast of the British Isles. Old photographs of Runcorn's Castlerock and Belvedere yards taken during the 1860s show that the builder's yard consisted simply of a cluster of huts, a saw pit and an area set aside for the seasoning of timber. In the early years of the century drawings and ship models were rarely used. The vessels were built relying on previous experience and they were constructed to the satisfaction of the owner and the manager of the yard.

Under the supervision of the manager the shipwrights constructed the vessel using proven traditional methods. The sawyers fashioned the oak frames from irregular timbers which when shaped were assembled on the slipway. The seasoned planks needed for the hull were then cut to size and put in the steam oven. When ready the hot planks were hastily wrapped in sacking and rushed to be clamped into position. One end of the plank was secured and the carpenters would heave and strain it firmly into place as holes were cut so that the iron fastening bolts or wooden tree nails could be driven home.[48] Speed was essential and the rapidly cooling planks were forced into position using a simple Spanish windlass of twisted ropes which was operated from the unfinished deck.[49] Once the hull was complete the planks were adzed smooth and chamfered to the curve of the hull. Deck planks were secured with spikes and the deck was planed off to a smooth surface and the vessel was ready for caulking. The caulkers used pitch and oakum to make the ship watertight and the hull was smoothed until it was almost impossible to feel the individual planks.

The blow of a caulking mallet produced a musical note and each mallet was notched to give it its own distinct sound. The caulkers often worked in rhythm, the 'clop' of each mallet contributing to a musical round and the ring of the blacksmith's anvil joined in to give the characteristic sound familiar in the small shipbuilding towns of the time. The yards had their own particular odour, a blend of linseed oil, pitch, paint and sawn timber and the sight of a vessel surrounded by wooden scaffolding was an everyday scene in the three little shipyards which were situated along a half mile stretch of the river's strand.

The rate of shipbuilding increased in the 1840s and it is noticeable that the ships were of larger tonnage. Most of the newly launched vessels were either river flats or coastal schooners but the building of schooners now predominated and this suggests that local vessels were required for longer voyages. The flats rarely exceeded 65 tons and it can be assumed that they were still considered to be essentially river craft with design characteristics necessary for navigation in the upper Mersey's shallows.

By this time Runcorn shipyards had sufficient experience and skills to build ships which met the demanding requirements of Lloyd's assessors and more vessels were built for service in tropical waters. The brig *Rosalie* of 1847 and intended for the Liverpool to West Indies trade was felted and yellow metalled.[50] By this process the hull below the waterline was tarred and then felt sheets which had been soaked in tar were pressed against the planking. Thin yellow metal sheets (an alloy of copper and zinc usually in the proportion of about 63% copper and 37% zinc with phosphorous added for greater durability) were then nailed over the felt and the hull was finished by painting it with a green copper anti-fouling compound such as "Mr. McInness's Patent Insoluable Soap of Copper". This treatment was expensive but it was essential for all wooden ships trading in Mediterranean or in tropical waters as the activities of the wood boring worm would quickly ruin the timbers of the unprotected vessel.[51] Sometimes zinc sheets were substituted for yellow metal without the vessel losing status in Lloyd's assessment. Because yellow metal in contact with sea water eventually destroyed the iron fastening bolts of a wooden ship, gutta percha pads were used to protect the iron parts of a vessel. Although the zinc sheets did not possess the antifouling properties of the copper in the yellow metal, zinc sheets were often preferred as they did not generate the galvanic action which eroded the iron bolts. The Runcorn built *Reviresco* a brig of 114 tons and *Anne Walker,* schooner 128 tons, were both felted and zinc clad and they were listed in Lloyd's registers as ships which had been built to the highest specifications of the time. It was believed that by soaking a ship's timbers in brine the life of a wooden vessel could be prolonged and salt was often forced into the joints between the members in order to prevent rot setting in. This method of salting wooden ships was recommended by Lloyd's and by adopting the process the builders secured an additional year to a vessel's classification. *A.M. Brundrit* built at Runcorn in 1878 and the schooners *Alert, Sunbeam* and *Snowflake* were vessels salted in this way.

Of the four shipyards which were in operation in the 1830s there appears to be no surviving documentary material whatsoever. The only evidence available is a single ledger which contains plans of the various sails used by ships which were built locally at the end of the century. However, it is known that the Castlerock shipyard was established about 1800 and it may have been the first to be in use. By 1840 it was owned by John Anderton. In 1834 there were the shipyards of the Bridgewater Trustees, the Old Quay Company, another was owned by a Mr. W. Evans and there was also a yard owned by Messrs. Okell and Webster.[52] In a survey of the Port of Liverpool which was completed in 1839 for the Corporation of Liverpool, the ownership of all the properties which abutted the Mersey as far up as Warrington was recorded. In that year the land immediately to the east of the present railway bridge was in the ownership of Dennis Brundrit who had "shipbuilding and other yards" on the site. Further along the river's edge, below the present Belvedere buildings there were coal and timber yards belonging to Messrs. Brundrit, Whiteway and Forster. The survey also gave the Trustees of the Duke of Bridgewater as being the owners of a stone loading wharf, a coal yard and shipbuilding and repair facilities adjacent to the Boat House Pool.[53] Shortly after 1840 the Belvedere yard was owned by Samuel Mason, a Worsley man and at about the same time Messrs. T. and J. Johnson soap and alkali manufacturers, had a small shipyard near to the steam flour mills in Mersey Street.

The Brundrit firm had become the largest of the shipyards by 1848. From its beginnings as William Wright's yard, Brundrit and Whiteway's expanded rapidly in the 1840s and larger vessels were constructed. Many of the bigger sea going craft are listed in the Lloyd's Registers with the symbol of a Maltese cross against the ship's name.[54] This sign acknowledges that the vessel was built to the highest construction standards of the day and the coveted symbol denotes a ship of superior build. Without doubt the Runcorn shipwrights were widely esteemed for their expertise even though it had been barely fifty years from the time when the launch of a river craft had been an occasional event.

Although river conditions at Runcorn never allowed the launch of a ship of more than 500 tons, the builders were versatile and after the construction of the first wooden paddle steamers in the early years of the century they built screw steamers and one or two iron vessels. The shipyards were small and they were badly sited against an unpredictable river channel and yet'many first class sailing vessels were built to trade on the longest ocean voyages. It was the ubiquitous wooden schooner which was to carry the name of Runcorn to a great part of Europe and to North and South America.

Notes

1. The Wool Register 1778, H.M. Customs and Excise, Liverpool.

2. Supplement to *Lloyds' Register* 1783.

3. Craig, R. and Jarvis, R., *Liverpool Registry of Merchant Ships,* Chetham Society, Vol. XV, 3rd Series, 1967, p.187.

4. Liverpool Shipping Registers.

5. Register of barges and wherries used on Navigable Rivers and Inland Navigations, 1795, Cheshire C.R.O. QDN 4/1.

6. Details Liverpool Shipping Registers.

7. Craig, R. and Jarvis, R., op.cit., p.187.

8. Details Liverpool Shipping Registers

9. Fussell, G.E., "Cheshire Farming Systems", *Transactions of the Lancashire and Cheshire Historical Society,* Vol. 106, 1954, p.60.

10. Chester Quarter Sessions 1559-1760, *Records Society of Lancashire and Cheshire,* Vol. I, 1940, p.203. Barker, T.C., "Lancashire Coal, Cheshire Salt and the Rise of Liverpool", Transactions of the Lancashire and Cheshire Historical Society, Vol. 103, 1951, p.92.

11. Craig, R. and Jarvis, R., op.cit., pp.209-234.

12. Register of Barges and Wherries, 1795. Cheshire C.R.O., QDN 4/1.

13. Ibid.

14. Ibid.

15. Harris, J.R., "The Early Steam Engine on Merseyside", *Transactions of the Lancashire and Cheshre Historical Society,* Vol. 106, 1955, p.109.

16. *Liverpool Mercury,* 7th Aug. 1832.

17. Millar, W.J., *The Clyde from Its Source to the Sea,* Blackie, London, 1888, p.173.

18. McQueen, A., *Echoes of Old Clyde Paddle Wheels,* Cowans and Gray, Glasgow 1924, p.16.

19. Ibid. p. 14.

20. Simpson, John, A Description of Runcorn about 1750, Ms., c1860, Runcorn Local History Collection.

21. Aspin, C., *Lancashire: The First Industrial Society,* Helmshore Local History Society, Preston, 1969. p.12.

22. Harris, J.R., *Liverpool and Merseyside,* p.176.

23. Eastham Ferry Steamers, *Cheshire Sheaf* Vol. 38, 1943, p.108.

24. Duckworth, C.L. and Langmuir, G., *West Coast Steamers,* Stephenson, Prescot, 1966, p.26.

25. Liverpool Courier 3 July 1819, quoted by J.R. Harris, *Liverpool and Merseyside,* pp. 176-177.

26. Darbyshire, H., Manchester Ship Canal Tugs Past and Present, *The Gog,* Vol. 4 No.2 1955, p.18.

27. Berry, R.J., "Ellen Weeton 1776-1850", *Transactions of the Lancashire and Cheshire Historical Society,* Vol. 106, 1955, p.162.

28. Timetable Steamer *Duke of Bridgewater.* 1828.

29. Duckworth and Langmuir, op.cit., p.26.

30. Mersey and Irwell Minute Book. Quoted in Hadfield and Biddle, Vol. 1, op.cit., p.95.

31. Darbyshire, H., op.cit., p.18.

32. Edwards M. M., *The Growth of The British Cotton Trade 1780-1815*, Manchester University Press, 1967, p.llO.

33. Fowler, G., op.cit., p.37.

34. *Runcorn Weekly News*, June 17th 1910 quoting 'Hanshall' of 1817.

35. Mather, F.C., op.cit., p.61.

36. Leathwood, W., "Workshop of the World", *Port of Manchester Review*, 1976, p.21.

37. Nickson, C., op.cit., p.l85.

38. *Handbook and Directory of Runcorn and its Vicinity*, Walker, Runcorn, 1846.

39. Simpson, John, MSS., Runcorn Library circa 1860.

40. Boult, J., Littoral Survey of the Port of Liverpool, op.cit., pp.20~207.

41. Head, Sir George, *A Home Tour through the Manufacturing Districts of England*, Murray, London, 1836, p.6.

42. Boult, J., op.cit., p.218.

43. Priestley, J., *Priestley's Navigable Rivers and Canals 1831*, David and Charles reprint, Newton Abbot 1961, p.561.

44. Baptismal Register, Parish Church Runcorn for 1816.

45. Details Liverpool Shipping Registers.

46. Information: Dr. Dennis Brundrit, Kelowna, British Columbia.

47. Davies, J.E., "The Penmaenmawr and Trevor Quarries", *Caernarvon Record Office Bulletin No.6*, 1972.

48. For details of wooden ship construction see Basil Greenhill's *The Merchant Schooners*, Vols. I and II, David and Charles, Newton Abbot, 1968.

49. Information: Late Mr. F. Stubbs, shipbuilder, Runcorn.

50. Lloyds Register 1848.

51. Mercer, N. "On the Protection of Wood and Iron Ships to Prevent Fouling", *Transactions of the Lancashire and Cheshire Historical Society*, Vol 2, 1861, p.81.

52. Fowler, op.cit., p.37.

53. Boult, J., op.cit., pp.204-207.

54. Details of individual ships from Lloyds Register of the year subsequent to launching.

4
Competition from the Railways

Within a few years of the opening of the Liverpool to Manchester Railway in 1830 the intense public interest in the railway movement resulted in pressures being brought to bear on the canal companies. The railways represented formidable competition and the threat caused urgent consideration of schemes to improve the waterways. Sir John Rennie in 1838 recommended to a "Committee of Warrington Gentlemen" the construction of a ship canal, sixteen feet deep between Liverpool and Warrington which he said could be extended to Manchester without serious difficulty and in 1840 Mr. H.H. Palmer, the Vice President of the Institute of Civil Engineers, proposed a ship canal with five locks between Liverpool and Manchester for vessels up to 400 tons.[1]

Palmer's proposals were embodied in a report made at the request of the Mersey and Irwell Company but his plans had little chance of being implemented for the psychological impact of the railways, and the hope that they would provide cheap and quick carriage of goods, occupied the public mind.

Nevertheless, there were men of vision who remained convinced that Manchester would benefit enormously from a ship canal and in 1841 a deputation presented a petition to the committee of the proprietors of the Mersey and Irwell signed by "upwards of 700 of the most respectable and influential firms of bankers, merchants and manufacturers of Manchester and other commercial towns" proposing the construction of a canal which could accommodate ships of 600 tons.[2] The petitioners declared that Manchester was destined to be a bonding port and maritime town and they pointed out that John Selden, who was the M.P. for Lancaster in 1622, had produced a chart of the ports of Britain in which Manchester was listed as a port whilst no mention was made of Liverpool or Warrington. Once built the canal would "render Manchester not only the first Provincial City of the Empire but the Commercial Emporium of the World".

The massive engineering problems that such a scheme would encounter received scant attention from the promoters of the plan. They simply proposed that

> artificial means be used for confining the tidal waters within the estuary so as to give the greatest facility for the tidal waters to flow and that the present contractions at Runcorn Gap be removed.

It was even suggested that the finished canal would attract a vast holiday traffic with pleasure steamers plying to the estuary. It was declared that this summer trade would bring considerable revenue to the region and it was pointed out that the strollers and holiday makers of London spend more money in the mere item of steam boat excursions in one summer than would pay all the clergy of the Metropolis for three years!

All the grandiose schemes came to nothing. The 1840s were the years of railway mania and the plans for a seaway to Manchester were forgotten when the Bridgewater Trustees purchased their old rivals, the Mersey and Irwell Company in 1844.

But the sailing flats continued to use the old Mersey river to Warrington. In 1830 it was estimated that the sailing barges made 7000 passages through the difficult channels between Runcorn and Warrington. At this time it was accepted that 40 tons was the limit for vessels reaching Warrington by this route but vessels of 100 to 120 tons and drawing 7½ to 8 feet could reach Bank Quay at Warrington on spring tides.[3] In 1836 some 60,000 tons of toll free traffic came to Warrington by the river although most craft proceeding to Bank Quay required two tides as they were usually grounded when short of their destination.[4]

A number of Warrington corn merchants used the river extensively and the Liverpool Shipping Registers give some detail of their transactions as well as information of the vessels used by them.[5] The 56 ton flat *Hero* which was launched by William Hayes of Frodsham in 1844 was built for Joseph Forest, corn merchant of Warrington. In 1847 Forest sold sixteen shares in the vessel to John Hobson, miller, ten to James Sheppard, maltster, and ten shares to James Fairclough, miller, of Newton-le-Willows. Forest and Hobson also held sixteen and twelve shares respectively in *Briton,* a 53 ton flat built in Frodsham in 1837. Another shareholder in this vessel was Joseph Crosfield, soap manufacturer of Warrington. Crosfield was, in 1841 the sole owner of the flat *Mary* which was built in Frodsham in 1818.

Other Warrington merchants and tradesmen had small craft on the Mersey. In the 1830s and 1840s John Ellison, linen draper and Thomas Ellison were equal partners in *Frances* a 94 ton schooner which was built in Frodsham in 1831. Thomas Ellison also had a financial interest in the 63 ton flat *Jane* and he had twenty-one shares in the flat *Sparling* of 61 tons with Thomas Wilkinson, inn-keeper of Liverpool holding twenty-one shares and Joseph Wagstaffe of Warrington, gentleman, holding the remaining twenty-two shares.

All the vessels using the river to Warrington were locally built and they were specifically designed for service on the upper Mersey. The largest vessel operating to Bank Quay was *Frances* which had a cargo hold seven feet nine inches in depth. Undoubtedly the physical appearance of small craft was influenced by the tonnage laws. Registered tonnage was based upon a measurement of length and breadth only and upon this basis the ship owners had to pay port duties but deepening the hold of a vessel could increase the cargo carrying capacity without increasing its taxable dimensions. The tonnage laws brought about a general type of vessel. In his study of the

Liverpool registers, Mr. F. Neal found that practically all vessels registered from 1815 to 1835 were less than 100 feet long, the breadth being about one third of the length and the hold was half the breadth of the ship thus producing the squat sailing vessel which appear in prints of the period.[6]

The notion that the Liverpool to Manchester Railway was a response to inefficiency and monopoly by the waterways is described as a myth by Charles Hadfield and Gordon Biddle in their study of the canals of north west England. The authors point out that both the Mersey and Irwell Company and the Bridgewater undertaking had improved their lines and both had provided improved warehouse services. They had reduced freight charges and neither company was a monopolistic carrier on its own waterway.[7] However, complaints about delays in transporting goods by both canals were frequently made particularly during the winter months when ice slowed traffic. Congestion at Liverpool docks and the pressure on warehouses resulted in further delays. Increased shipping to Runcorn docks brought problems with berthing. An example of serious dislocation of the movement of goods was experienced during the winter of 1824-1825 when a consignment of timber had to wait for four months on the quay at Liverpool before a start was made to tranship it to Manchester.[8]

The 1830s saw mid Mersey river trade increase substantially and there was steady pressure on dock and canal facilities at Runcorn. The Sankey Canal extension and the completion of the St. Helens to Runcorn Gap Railway early in 1833 prepared the way for a great increase in coal getting in the St. Helens coalfield. Up to about 1830 most of the coal had gone to the Cheshire saltfield but after this date a demand arose to load coasters with coal for Ireland. The increase in Runcorn's commerce was noted by the directors of the Runcorn Gap railway who commented in their annual report of 1832:

> There has been a rapid increase in coasting trade at Runcorn which has nearly doubled in the last three years and proposals have already been made to land coal at the dock as back freight for the Irish market.[9]

The railway company's dock at Woodend, Widnes, is believed to have been the world's first purpose-built railway dock for, although the Stockton to Darlington line was operating from 1831, cargoes were shipped from staithes and it was not until 1839 that the dock was complete.[10] The new canal dock at Widnes was side by side with that of the railway thus the railway lost the advantage of better tidal conditions at Widnes over those formerly available to the canal at Fiddler's Ferry. The canal now entered the river more than three miles down river from Fiddler's Ferry and the new extension did much to prevent the nuisance of delays of which the coal proprietors had previously complained.

The improved means of transportation between the coalfield and the Mersey led to a marked expansion in the coal trade as the competition between the railway and the canal led to cheaper tariffs. In the first year of operation the railway carried 5,200 tons of coal and the canal 150,000 tons but four years later the railway tonnage had risen to 130,000 tons as against 170,000 tons carried on the canal. However, by 1845 the canal had massively increased its coal trade to 440,700 tons with the railway also transporting a substantial increase at 252,000 tons.[11]

In the early 1830s the Bridgewater Trustees exported coal from their Worsley mines to Ireland via Runcorn. The return cargoes were mainly grain and flour. Although this trade fell away during the next ten years the Old Quay Company continued to send St. Helens coal to Ireland through their docks at Liverpool. The Mersey's new steamboats seeking to avoid the high port charges at Liverpool also found coal readily available at Runcorn and they began to arrive with Irish cattle to return laden with coal.[12]

The steam tug boat appeared to be the answer to the problem of speeding barge traffic through the difficult channels between Garston and Runcorn and paddle boats began to appear on the upper river in increasing numbers. There was a building boom in the 1820s with *Egerton* (1824), *Earl of Bridgewater* (1824), *Manchester* (1825), *Eclipse* (1828) and *Duke of Bridgewater* (1828) all working to the Bridgewater or Old Quay Docks at Runcorn. Railway competition stimulated the building of more steamers, *Rival* (1834), *Tower* (1836) and the *Duke* of 1839. Runcorn's own shipyards were responsible for *Manchester, Rival, Tower* and *Duke*.[13]

By 1830 steam towage between Liverpool and Runcorn was being operated by the St. George's Steam Packet Company of Liverpool and by a number of smaller operators but the Old Quay and Bridgewater companies did not own steam boats. The Bridgewater Trustees hired steamers and they were forced to pay exorbitant fees.[14] But it was not long before both companies became aware of the growing competition from the Liverpool to Manchester Railway and as the Manchester merchants were constantly demanding a quicker and more efficient service it became vital that there must be a rapid turn round of flats and barges. In 1831 the Mersey and Irwell decided to build three small steamers and by 1833 the Bridgewater Trustees began using the paddle boats *Alice* and *Blanche* on the tideway. The Mersey and Irwell Company operated *Rival* and *Tower* and also *Hercules* (1830), *Mallory* (1831) and *Pilot* which was built in 1832. *Mallory* was a hasty conversion from a barge. She was inefficient and so dangerous that her crew would not work the vessel and she was scrapped.[15] These early paddle steamers were notorious for their avaricious consumption of fuel and they could easily become overworked and mechanically unreliable. In 1831 the Old Quay Company informed its tug masters that towing should take place only in cases of necessity and flats with sails should not be towed if they could proceed to their destinations unaided. The management stated that engines were strained unnecessarily and that the tugs consumed too much fuel when they were at the beck and call of every vessel seeking a quick passage.[16]

The possibility of quickening Liverpool to Manchester trade by introducing steamers on to the Bridgewater Canal had been explored as early as 1797. The experimental steam boats used at that time hauled their boats at a pace no greater than that of horses and because of the belief that the paddles' wash would damage the canal banks the steamer projects were abandoned. However, the idea of steamers on the inland canals received consideration again in 1831 when William Fairbairn of Manchester built a canal steamer.[17] His *Lord Dundas* was an unusual vessel with a single paddle wheel of nine feet diameter and with a width of nearly four feet placed aft of midships to work at fifty or sixty revolutions per minute. The vessel was known as a twin boat though it had a single hull which, in effect, had a trough in which the wheel revolved. The *Lord Dundas* was not a success for she produced too much bow wave to allow her to operate on the canals but her river trials from Warrington to Runcorn were entirely satisfactory. On the river she achieved a speed of ten miles an hour but in the canal a speed of six miles an hour produced an unacceptable wash.

There were casualties among the river steamers. The *Duke of Bridgewater* sank at her moorings in the hurricane of 1839 and the *Earl of Bridgewater* suffered a serious boiler explosion in 1824 but was repaired to remain in service for a few more years.[18]

The 1830s saw the beginning of what was to become an immense barge traffic upon the upper river and from this time many of the sailing flats were dismasted to become "dumb" towing barges and soon steamers were being built which were capable of towing up to twelve loaded flats. To aid navigation by night two lighthouses were built in 1838, one sited on the Lancashire shore at Halehead and the other at Ince on the opposite shore.[19] There was satisfactory growth in up river trade and for the first dozen years of its existence the Liverpool to Manchester Railway did not appear as a serious threat to the waterways. Indeed the railway remained more frightened of price cutting by the waterways than the other way around.[20] Such was the impressive growth in up river trade the Mersey and Irwell Company toyed briefly with the idea of cutting a ship canal from Garston to Runcorn Gap to enable vessels of over 150 tons to proceed to the Old Quay Dock but the idea was abandoned in 1841 as being impracticable.[21]

From statements given in evidence before Parliamentary Committees on the Preston Brook and Runcorn and the Aston and Huyton branch of the Grand Junction Railway it is possible to discern some idea of the development of the port of Runcorn between 1835 and 1845. During the ten years the number of vessels leaving the port trebled. The following table indicates the increasing volume of traffic.[22]

Vessels Cleared Outwards From The Port of Runcorn 1835-1845

Year		Vessels
1835	-	509
1836	-	526
1837	-	409
1843	-	1319
1844	-	1029
1845	-	1527

Vessels Arriving At The Port of Runcorn 1842-1845

Year	Vessels	Tonnage
1842	2259	180,720
1843	2569	205,520
1844	2786	222,880
1845	3022	241,760

Volume of Traffic at Runcorn

Table 4:1

The vital growth of Manchester (which was linked in 1837-38 to Birmingham and London by the opening of the Grand Junction and the London and Birmingham railways) had a profound effect upon Runcorn's trade. For raw cotton alone there was an average of 55,000 tons per annum passing through the Bridgewater locks in the years 1840 to 1842.[23] Sir George Head writing in 1836, included a description of the busy Bridgewater docks in his *Tour of the Manufacturing Districts of England.* He was impressed by the volume of trade and also by the attractive appearance of the wharfs.

The adjacent paths are covered with red burnt shale from the founderies and the economy of space preserved in the premises appropriated to the quays and warehouse is very remarkable. The latter is a striking object on the bank of the river, exceeding in size most other buildings in this country of like description and as the canal communicates by a cut of four miles with Preston Brook, bearing by that route the vast freight of the Potteries and the Metropolis, the general indications of traffic especially the former, are on an extraordinary scale. The enormous heaps of material piled up ready for embarkation would be sufficient, one would think to freight all the barges on the line for months to come, consisting of the substances used in the manufacture of British china such as flints from Kent and Sussex, pipe clay from Devonshire and Dorsetshire, besides a soft stone containing an abundance of mica from Cornwall and Wales. At the same time, so perfect in the allotment of space, that the whole extent of ground is laid out with the care and order of a pleasure garden; the enormous heaps of flints and other materials, each neatly piled and labelled with the owner's name, being interesting by highly kept walks, while the red shale aforesaid is, in colour and consistence, better suited to the purposes of use and ornament than any kind of gravel whatsoever.[24]

The railway soon monopolised the Liverpool to Manchester passenger carrying business but the waterways had not neglected the opportunity to put passenger services on the Mersey estuary. During the 1830s the *Duke of Bridgewater* and the *Eclipse* sailed daily to Runcorn from George's Dock at Liverpool. The former carried passengers to the Duke's Canal and the latter sailed to the Mersey and Irwell's basin at Old Quay. The passengers landing at Old Quay for Manchester were fortunate because *Eclipse* berthed conveniently alongside the canal packet boat which would convey them to their destination but those who preferred to travel by the *Duke of Bridgewater* were not so lucky. They had to toil up the slope from the river to Top Locks carrying their baggage before they began their canal journey to Manchester.[25] The Old Quay Company made much of their easy connection at Runcorn and a *Liverpool Mercury* advertisement of 1st May 1840 promised their passengers that the journey by *Tower* provided a "delightful and healthy excursion . . . avoiding the inconvenience of passengers removing their luggage and having to walk nearly half a mile in all states of weather at Runcorn as these packets always come alongside one another".

There were two classes of accommodation on the passenger steamers; the "best apartment" and the "second apartment". On board *Eclipse* in 1838 the fare from Runcorn to Liverpool was one shilling and six pence in the best apartment and one shilling in the second. The introduction of steamers had actually brought about a reduction in ferry fares. Thirty-five years before in 1803 the charges in the sailing packet were two shillings and one shilling and sixpence. Throughout the summer months *Eclipse* took excursion parties around the *Comet* lightship off Hilbre Island and also to the North Wales coast.[26]

The short journey to Liverpool by steam packet often left much to be desired both in comfort and in the time spent on the journey. One Bridgewater official was appalled by the standard of service given to the public in the 1830s. His appraisal was scathing:

It is so ill constructed that it is impossible for persons of respectable character to feel at ease in mixing with the low society on board, who are allowed to drink, smoke, swear etc. and the voyage took two hours instead of one.[27]

A contemporary timetable of the steamers gives the names of Runcorn's packet houses. They were Mr. Wilson's Hotel in Bridge Street, Mr. Rigby's "Boat House Inn", Mr. Percival's "Lord Nelson" tavern, Mr. Bolton's "Castle Hotel" in Halton and in Weston Point, Mr. Baynes' "Weaver Hotel". The timetable advertised that the Northwich coach met "Eclipse" on her arrival at Runcorn.[28]

By 1841 the time taken by the canal packets on the Bridgewater Runcorn to Manchester run had been reduced by half an hour to seven and a half hours[29] and the receipts from the passenger boats had risen in spite of the Liverpool to Manchester Railway. Nevertheless railway competition necessitated the introduction of a new type of packet — the swift boat. The swift packets were constructed using light gauge iron and they were introduced by the Bridgewater Trustees in 1843. The new boats completed the 28 mile canal journey from Runcorn to Manchester in four hours.[30] Pulled by two horses at a gallop *Swallow, Dolphin, Eagle* and *Waterwitch* provided a twice daily service except for Sundays. The Mersey and Irwell Company also provided swift boats which kept to a strict schedule.[31] The boats on both waterways had priority passage when passing other traffic and in order to keep to the severe timetable the horses were flogged from one stage to the next and their working lives were greatly shortened by the cruel treatment.

By the 1840s the commercial and industrial growth of Runcorn had expanded due to a number of factors all of which depended upon efficient transportation by water. Salt and coal were brought easily and cheaply to the soap and chemical works, the trade on both lines of the inland waterways continued to grow, the river's natural deep was favourable for the launching of larger ships and the quarries were in full production. But the tidal Mersey continued to present serious problems and there was still no central authority which was responsible for the maintenance of the navigable channel above Garston. None of the companies or local authorities which benefited from upper Mersey traffic was willing to finance the conservancy of the river. Liverpool Corporation prepared a Parliamentary Bill in 1837 which would have given the Corporation control of the upper reaches but the bill failed as did another in 1841.[32] The Liverpool Town Council which had developed the Port of Liverpool during the eighteenth century saw only too clearly that it was becoming necessary to construct larger docks for the bigger ships which were then being built but such an undertaking would have been pointless if silting prevented ships from getting into the docks. A hydrographic survey of Liverpool Bay carried out for the Admiralty in 1836 reported that there was "the danger of the estuary being closed from the sea by the deposit made by every tide". The Admiralty's report was the prime agent in promoting an Act "For better preserving the Navigation of the River Mersey" which was passed in 1842. Thus the Mersey was unique in having its own Conservancy Commissioners who were appointed by Act of Parliament and also were charged with the conservation of the river channels, the control of works abutting the river, and who were to authorise dredging and the removal of obstructions to navigation or the flow of the river.[33] The first Acting Conservator was Captain Robert Fitzroy of *H.M.S. Beagle* fame.

Piecemeal methods had been used in order to arrest the erosion of the river's bank between Runcorn and Weston Point. Throughout the 1830s wooden piles had been driven into the sloping bank in order "to prevent the wasteful and injurious wearing away of the land".[34] To improve and deepen the river channel at Runcorn, Mr. Bateman the Bridgewater Trustees' engineer, suggested in a report of 1840 that a larger volume of water should be channelled through the Duke's Gut but his idea was not implemented and the difficult sailing channel remained a factor limiting the size of heavily laden sea going vessels which could reach the Bridgewater Docks.[35] Improved dock facilities were also needed and between 1841 and 1843 a new dock named Francis Dock was constructed two locks up from the tideway on the new line of locks on the Bridgewater Canal.

In spite of the fact that Runcorn town and docks were inaccessible by rail (it was to be another quarter of a century before they were) business bowled along merrily. The coal trade was of particular importance and in 1842 John and Thomas Johnson, soap manufacturers of Runcorn, bought into the St. Helens coal trade.[36] They succeeded in obtaining a contract for supplying naval vessels at Liverpool with coal. Also about this time Samuel Stock, who owned a colliery at Blackleyhurst near St. Helens was exporting 16,000 tons of coal to Ireland. Stock had his own private railway line from his mine to the Sankey Canal [37] and he transported his coal in his own flats and schooners some of which he launched at Widnes.[38]

Runcorn had become the most important outlet for coal from the St. Helens mines and by 1845 the direction of the coal trade had changed. Up to about 1830 most cargoes had been shipped to the Cheshire saltfield but in 1846 the secretary of the new amalgamation, the St. Helens Canal and Railway Company, estimated that of 693,000 tons of coal from St. Helens 183,000 tons went to the Cheshire saltworks and 440,000 tons went down the river for export or for the coastal trade.[39] At Liverpool the Duke's Dock was improved in 1845 and a basin was constructed to enable the coal flats to leave on the half tide on the same day and the entrance was made wide enough to admit coasters from Ireland.[40] The coal for the Duke's Dock had come from the Bridgewater Trustees' Worsley mines via their docks at Runcorn.

The railways posed a threat to Runcorn's trade in 1847 when the new railway port of Fleetwood began to attract Scottish pig iron cargoes which had previously been landed at Runcorn for distribution via the inland waterways. Three years before this date the Grand Junction Railway Company had considered a scheme to bridge the Mersey at Runcorn in order to improve its access to Liverpool. The railway company proposed to construct a bridge at such a height so as not to obstruct the passage of sailing vessels.[41] For some reason the plans were not carried out and it was to be another thirty years before the Runcorn Bridge became a reality and before the Bridgewater docks had a rail link.

In the meantime the Trustees established a rail link to their waterway at Norton about four miles from Runcorn. Here, in 1853 a short branch line was constructed from the Chester to Warrington line of the Shrewsbury and Chester Railway to the canal side warehouses at Preston Brook where the Duke's canal joined the Trent and Mersey Canal. It was anticipated that canal flats towed across the Mersey estuary from Liverpool would discharge into railway waggons to bring new business but from the start the venture appears to have been of little consequence due to the high freight charges imposed by the railway company[42] and the line remained little used in the forty years of its existence.

Notes

1. Tracey, W.B., *Port of Manchester,* Hind, Hoyle, Light, Manchester, 1901, p.4.

2. Suggestions for the Improvement of the Navigation of the Rivers Mersey and Irwell for Sea-going Vessels to Manchester, Mersey and Irwell Navigation Company, 12.5.1841, Central Library, Manchester.

3. Hadfield, C. and Biddle, G., *Canals of N. W. England,* David and Charles, Newton Abbot, Vol. I, pp.120-121.

4. Liverpool Shipping Register.

5. Details of ownership from Liverpool Shipping Registers.

6. Harris, J.R., (ed.), *Liverpool and Merseyside. Liverpool Shipping in the Early Nineteenth Century,* Cass. London, 1969, p.171.

7. Hadfield, C. and Biddle, G., Vol. 1, pp.107-108.

8. Jackman, W.T., *The Development of Transportation in Modern England,* F. Cass, London, 1966, p.520.

9. Barker, T. and Harris, J., *A Merseyside Town in the Industrial Revolution.* St. Helens.1750-1900, F. Cass, London, 1954, pp.195-196.

10. Moorsom, N., *The Stockton and Darlington Railway,* Peckston Ltd., Middlesbrough, 1975, p.70.

11. Russell, R., *Lost Canals of England and Wales,* David and Charles, Newton Abbot, 1971, p.210.

12. Mather, F.C., op.cit.

13. Duckworth and Langmuir, op.cit., p.24.

14. Mather, F.C., op.cit. p.108.

15. Corbridge, J., *A Pictorial History of the Mersey and Irwell Navigation,* Morten, Manchester, 1978.

16. Mather, F.C., op.cit.

17. Haldane, J.W., Origin and Development of Steam Navigation, *Transactions of the Warrington Literary and Philosophical Society, 1897,* pp.11- 13.

18. Duckworth and Langmuir, op.cit., p.24.

19. McRoberts, J., "The Mersey Lighthouses", *Sea Breezes,* Vol.47, No.336, 1973.

20. Hadfield, C. and Biddle, G., Vol. 1, p.121.

21. Tracey, W.B., op.cit., p.4.

22. *Handbook and Directory of Runcorn and its Vicinity,* Walker, Runcorn, 1846.

23. Mather, F.C., op.cit., p.5.

24. Head, G., *A Home Tour through the Manufacturing Districts of England in the Summer of 1835,* London, p.3.

25. "Diary of Richard Lea. What was Runcorn Like in 1838?", *History of Holy Trinity Church,* Centenary Publication, 1938, Runcorn.

26. The Bridgewater Trustees, Timetable of River Steamers 1839.

27. Mather, F.C., op.cit., p.108.

28. The Bridgewater Trustees, Timetable of River Steamers 1839.

29. The Bridgewater Department Handbook M.S.C. 1968, p.38.

30. Mather, F.C., op.cit., p.109.

31. Slater's Directory of Manchester and Salford 1845, p.462.

32. Hadfield, C. and Biddle, G., Vol. I, op. cit., pp. 1 12-113.

33. Rear Admiral Sir Edmund Irving, Acting Conservator of the River Mersey, *Port of Manchester Review,* 1980, p.22.

34. Fitzroy, Robert, Report on the Navigation of the River Mersey, Mersey Conservancy Board, 1842.

35. Mather, F.C., op.cit., p.182.

36. Hadfield, C. and Biddle, G., Vol. 1, op.cit., p.126.

37. Barker, T.C. and Harris, J.R., op.cit., p.197.

38. Liverpool Shipping Registers.

39. Hadfield, C. and Biddle, G., Vol. 1, op.cit., p.145.

40. Mather, F.C., op.cit., p.182.

41. *Runcorn River Crossings,* Cheshire Education Committee, 1975, p.5.

42. Mather,.F.C., op.cit., p.250.

5

Runcorn, an Independent Customs Port 1847-1850

Runcorn's growing importance was recognised on the 5th April 1847 when the town was designated an independent customs port and certain wharfs were declared to be "legal quays" where dutiable goods could be landed.[1] The new customs port extended from Warrington Bridge to include both shores of the Mersey to a point on a line from Eastham Church to Chapel Farm House on the Lancashire side of the river. The shores and waters of the river Weaver to Frodsham Bridge also came within the boundaries of the new port of Runcorn. In keeping with its changed prestige the town now needed a more dignified Customs House and a new one was built between the old line of locks and the old coach road.

The register of local shipping for Runcorn's first brief period of independence from the port of Liverpool offers some insight into the business ventures of a number of the town's prominent citizens.[2] Dennis Brundrit and Philip Whiteway appear as merchants who had considerable holdings in maritime trade. They are usually described as "gentleman" or "merchant" and in addition to their shipbuilding activities they feature as ship owners. The schooners *Sarah, Philip, Julia, Ellesmere* and *The Port* and the flat *Edward* were vessels which were built and owned by the partners. They possessed equal shares in the vessels and they held forty-eight shares in the schooner *John* with the remaining sixteen shares in the vessel belonging to Robert Owen, her master. On his own account Philip Whiteway owned a number of small vessels and the register records him as the sole owner of the flats *Glory, Brothers* and *Roche Light*.

Some of the other local shipbuilders owned vessels. John Anderton of the Castlerock shipyard built for his own use the schooners *Emperor* and *Empress* and he and John Crippin of Runcorn were the co-owners of the flat *Nettle*. Crippin had a wide variety of interests. In some local directories he is described as millwright and iron founder of the Bridgewater foundry, in others as "salt and coal merchant" and he was also agent to the Bridgewater Trustees. Crippin was a perceptive man who had an eye for business. During the 1840s he had offered towage facilities to the owners of sailing vessels and by 1850 he was a partner in the Rock Ferry Steam Packet Company. He owned the schooner *Elfleda* and he was part owner of the schooners *St. George* and *Princess Royal*.

Samuel Mason, shipbuilder of the Belvedere yard was another builder who launched vessels for his own use. He owned the flat *Thomas* which he launched in 1838 and he held sixteen shares in *Thomas Mason* a schooner built in his yard that same year. Some of the smaller craft were owned by tradesmen. A draper, a waterman and a master mariner had the flat *Mary and Ann* whilst James Janion, an inn-keeper and William Janion, master mariner, were the owners of the flat *Caldwell* which was built at Witton, Northwich in 1830. James Janion also owned the Manchester-built flat *Joss*. William Clarke, rope maker, had *William Court*, a schooner which was lost in the Irish Sea in 1853, whilst Samual Whinyates of Runcorn owned the flat *Jenny* built in 1755 and wrecked off Hilbre Island eighty years later.

William Hazlehurst, a coal merchant of Sutton, Frodsham had a thriving business. He owned the Frodsham-built schooners, *Pearl, Mary Ann, Waterloo* and *Sarah* and also the flat *Hannah* which was built at Sankey Bridges in 1807. William Hazlehurst, with his brother Charles, also owned the flat *John and Ann* which was launched in Runcorn in 1811. Mr. T. Rigby of Runcorn was another salt and coal merchant who had substantial assets in local shipping. He had *Laurel* a brigantine of 111 tons which was built in Hillsburgh, Nova Scotia, in 1844 and also the schooners *Mersey* and *Rigby*. Thomas Rigby and William Ravenscroft of Frodsham had equal shares in the schooner *Lyon*. After Rigby's death his widow Elizabeth added to the fleet with *Ann* a 54 ton flat, *Theodore*, a brigantine which was built in Annan in 1824 and also *John Knox*, a Dumbarton built schooner which had, by way of a figurehead a carving representing the reformer. Samuel Stock, the colliery proprietor of Blackleyhurst, St. Helens, was one of a number of local ship owners who preferred to leave their vessels registered at the port of Liverpool for in 1849 he had only the flat *Helen* registered at the new customs port of Runcorn. Ten years later Stock's fleet had grown to include the schooners *Try, Eva, Maud* and *Janie* and the flats *Flora, Lilly, Hind, Dora* and *Rush*.

Some names appear briefly in the registers as vessels changed owner-ship. Mr. John Wright, tanner, owned the locally built flat *Susannah* 45 tons, and the small schooner *Dee*, 40 tons, ws owned by a Mr. T. Clough in 1849. *Maria*, a flat built in Runcorn by John Weedall, was owned by Mr. J. Ryley whilst the flat *Dido* belonged to William Raynes, a man who was to increase his holdings in shipping considerably in the next twenty years.

Only one steamer was registered at the port of Runcorn. She was the propeller driven *Die Schoene Mainzen* of 108 tons, built in Warrington in 1845 and sold to foreign buyers two years later.

The introduction of steamers providing free towage to and from the Runcorn docks, the buoying of the sailing channels and the building of two lighthouses at Ince and Halehead served to attract more shipping to Runcorn. Most of the incoming cargoes consisted of potter's materials, slate, pig iron and pit props and outgoing cargoes were mainly crated pottery, coal, salt and building stone. Besides the dressed stone to be used in buildings and public works, the Runcorn and Weston quarries also produced quantities of quarry waste which was suitable for road making but which also made ideal ballast material for Liverpool's ocean-going sailing ships. This by-product from the quarries was loaded into flats at the stone wharfs in Runcorn and the river steamers regularly towed ten or a dozen flats at one time to Liverpool docks.

In 1842 the Bridgewater Trustees had two steam vessels, the *Alice* of 1839 and *Blanche* completed in 1842. Both vessels were intended for service as passenger packets but they "had liberty to tow which was greatly exercised"[3], When the Bridgewater Trustees purchased the Mersey and Irwell Company in 1844 they acquired four more paddle boats and increasing business caused them to hire the *Earl Powis* and the *Clive* from the Ellesmere Canal Company. The four vessels owned by the Mersey and Irwell Company were doubtful assets as they were inferior in performance to *Alice* and *Blanche* and they were also in poor mechanical order.[4]

In 1847 the Bridgewater Trustees attempted to revive their Irish coal trade and in that year 42,000 tons of coal were exported through their Runcorn docks. However, this business could not be maintained because of the competition from Welsh and Cumberland coal on the Irish market and also because of the impossibility of obtaining back cargoes of grain during the period of the Irish famine.[5]

The Board of Trade's tables of statistics for the years 1847 to 1850 indicate the volume of trade at the various ports of the north west and the amount of coal shipped coastwise for each year is as follows:

	1847	1848	1849	1850
Runcorn	63,766	64,777	61,941	117,209
Liverpool	14,830	18,393	25,871	
Chester	89,326	100,340	93,149	95,970
Preston	33,511	49,314	31,332	43,602
Lancaster	4,324	4,793	3,488	3,764
Fleetwood	-	-	16,130	18,819
Whitehaven	308,846	295,565	330,495	350,458
Maryport	195,159	183,239	197,061	190,640

Tonnages of Coal Shipped Coastwise at Various Ports[6]

Table 5:1

The Customs Bills of Entry of Imports for the port of Runcorn from 1847 to 1849 show what may be described as traditional cargoes arriving from traditional sources. A typical sample of cargoes landed can be ascertained from the following list for the three days from the 11th to 13th April 1849:

From	Ardrossan	50 tons pig iron	London	140 tons flints
	Aberdovey	15 loads propwood	Swansea	55 tons pig iron
	Barrow	80 tons iron ore	Troon	60 tons pig iron
	Cardiff	119 tons bar iron	Wicklow	105 tons pyrites

| Carlisle | 120 tons alabaster | Fowey | 75 tons china stone |
| Glasgow | 108 tons pig iron | | |

Runcorn's direct coal trade to foreign countries and to British possessions overseas was practically non-existent. In 1847 only 110 tons of coal were exported, 39 tons in 1848 and 589 tons in 1849. In the same three years Liverpool exported abroad 112,625 tons, 64,529 tons and 151,976 tons respectively. Of course much of the coal exported from Liverpool had arrived there in flats from the Bridgewater, Old Quay and Widnes docks.

Foreign business at the new customs port of Runcorn was trivial. Customs duties received in 1847 were negligible falling away to almost nothing in 1849. The table below shows the gross amount of revenue collected at each of the six ports of the region.

	1847 £	1848 £	1849 £
Runcorn	2,551	1,599	588
Liverpool	3,230,921	3,481,796	3,474,202
Chester	90,231	83,945	83,234
Preston	77,312	78,891	87,655
Lancaster	32,658	32,058	30,736
Fleetwood	-	-	1,757

Gross Customs Duties Received 1847-1849[7]
Table 5:2

From the beginning it was obvious that the customs port of Runcorn would not be a success. Few large sea going craft were registered during its three years of independence. The average displacement of vessels registered was 70 tons and none exceeded 120 tons. During this period few ships were transferred from the Liverpool register and on 12th April 1850 the Customs Port of Runcorn was abolished and the boundaries of the Port of Liverpool were amended to include all the waters of the rivers Mersey, Weaver and Irwell.[8]

Thus the independence of Runcorn was short lived. One or two foreign vessels had arrived bringing cargoes of oats from Denmark and oak bark from Ostend for the local tanneries,[9] but the high hopes of developing international trade were not realised. The reasons for the failure are not difficult to discern. First there was the difficult channel, adequate for coasting craft but not for vessels of deeper draught. The plotting of the channel and the approaches were unsatisfactory and the town's docks were designed for the 70 ton sailing flat and they could not cope with vessels of much larger dimensions. Then there was a woeful lack of warehouse facilities and the absence of a rail link. In addition to these handicaps there was the overwhelming success of the port of Liverpool.

At the very time that Runcorn's prospects as a minor port were at their lowest trade began to grow as a new commodity started to arrive in quantity. Cargoes of pyrites, a raw material required by mid-Merseyside's alkali industry for the manufacture of sulphuric acid, were discharged at Runcorn from Wicklow and Arklow.[10] Sicilian sulphur had become too expensive for the manufacturers so the newly established chemical works at Widnes began to take pyrites as a satisfactory substitute. By 1847 John Hutchinson had built the first chemical works in Widnes on land adjacent to the terminus of the St. Helens Canal and Railway Company. Hutchinson realised that he had an ideal site for his factory with Cheshire salt and St. Helens coal being easily available. He planned to use the Mersey in order to import his raw materials and to ship his manufactured chemicals to Liverpool. When Hutchinson arrived in Widnes he found a population of 2,200 in the area. By 1851 this had risen to 3,200 which he claimed was "owing to my works alone"[11].

The success of Hutchinson's "No. 1 Works" attracted other entrepreneurs and among the first to arrive was William Gossage who established a small chemical works on the opposite side of the St. Helens Canal to the Hutchinson works. Gossage was interested in copper smelting and in addition to his experiments in obtaining sulphur from copper ores he successfully recovered copper from burnt pyrites which was the waste material which was discarded after burning iron pyrites in order to obtain sulphur dioxide for sulphuric acid manufacture. Unfortunately for Gossage, the owners of the pyrites mines discovered what he was doing and they removed the copper from the pyrites before delivering it. This was the start of a trade in "purple ore" — the residue of the burnt pyrites after the copper had been extracted. As this material was almost 95% iron oxide it was valuable as iron ore.[12]

Before 1850 practically all the cargoes unloaded at Runcorn were destined for the manufacturing centres which were connected to the town by the inland waterways — such cargoes as whitening, flints and clay for the Potteries, propwood for the Lancashire coal mines, pig iron for the Lancashire and Midlands foundries and slates and stone were distributed by the canals. Now there was some change in the nature of trade. The establishment of the alkali industry in Widnes and Runcorn brought new business. As the Widnes works developed at an astonishing rate so the Customs Bills of Entry for the port of Liverpool began to list chemical ores among the traditional cargoes being landed at Runcorn.

As salt was required in large quantities in the Leblanc process of making chemicals so the barge traffic to the Widnes works on the St. Helens Canal grew as new factories proliferated. There was a need for more shallow draught vessels for the transportation of chemicals, salt and coal and the Runcorn shipwrights were handily placed to benefit from the demand for sailing flats.

The Appendix (p.193) indicates a building boom in small craft construction which began about 1850 and which continued until the 1870s.

Thus in spite of its loss in status in losing its independence as a customs port Runcorn's prospects began to brighten and from 1850 the town's trade and commerce were enhanced by the rapid growth of industrial Widnes. Yet another heartening event occurred in 1848 when Runcorn's prestige as a port was declining. The Bridgewater Trustees made an agreement with the Winsford salt producers by which salt was to be sent to their Runcorn docks in the hope that it would become the practice to export cargoes through the Bridgewater docks rather than through those in Liverpool.[13]

More important was the fact that at the moment the bonded port of Runcorn failed the Navigation Laws were repealed. The laws had laid down that all goods leaving Britain had to be carried in British ships whilst goods coming into the country had to be carried either in British ships or in the vessels of the country where the goods had been produced. The laws were repealed for ocean shipments in 1849 and those which had reserved the coastal trade for British ships were repealed in 1853. The abolition of the Navigation Laws was to have a profound effect on the future prospects for the Runcorn docks and in the next decade small foreign vessels began to arrive in numbers to load salt for the fishing industries of France, Holland, Germany, Belgium and Denmark.

Notes

1. H.M. Customs and Excise, Limits of Port and Legal Quays, Runcorn, 31st March 1847.

2. The Runcorn Shipping Register, 1847-1850, Customs House, Liverpool.

3. Kelly's Directory of Cheshire 1857.

4. Mather, F.C., op.cit., p.272.

5. Ibid. p.310.

6. Statistics of the Trade and Shipping of the United Kingdom. Coals, Cinders and Culm Shipped Coastwise. Board of Trade Reports, 1847, (p.28); 1848 (p.73); 1849 (p.79); 1850 (p.81).

7. Ibid., Customs Duties Collected in the United Kingdom, 1847 (P.2); 1848 (p.27); 1849 (p.28).

8. Annulment of the Port of Runcorn 12th April 1850. H.M. Customs and Excise.

9. Customs Bills of Entry for the Port of Liverpool. 1847-1850.

10. Ibid.

11. Hardie, D.W., *A History of the Chemical Industry in Widnes,* I.C.I., 1950, p.25.

12. Ibid., pp.25-37.

13. Mather, F.C., op.cit., p.190.

6

The Expansion of the Shipbuilding Industry

The Iron Ships of Warrington

The uncertain conditions which prevailed in the shifting channel along the Cheshire shoreline at Runcorn limited the size of the ships which could be launched from the local shipyards in the nineteenth century. The largest vessels built were two wooden ships of just over 450 tons which left the slipways in 1853 and 1856[1] at a time when the natural deep appears to have been unusually favourable for ship launches. However, these two vessels were the exceptions and the next largest ship displaced only half their tonnage.[2]

Although Runcorn-built vessels were of modest dimensions, iron ships of far greater size were built in Warrington from about 1840 and as Warrington was within the customs port of Runcorn for thirty-five years of the last century, an account of the Bank Quay and Warrington Bridge vessels is a relevant chapter in the history of local shipbuilding.

It had long been argued that if Britain was to maintain her supremacy as a maritime nation then iron must replace wood in ship construction. By the end of the eighteenth century the oak forests had been drastically thinned to provide timber for ships and for house building and the hedgerows and woods were becoming denuded of their highly prized trees.

By the middle of the 1850s Warrington's railway network was almost complete and the coal and iron necessary in heavy engineering were available from Lancashire mines and Staffordshire iron works.[3] Iron barges had been used on the Mersey from the 1830s and in 1840[4] the 100 ton iron steamer *Warrington* was launched by the Warrington Bridge Foundry Company. She was registered at Liverpool and the record states that she was "propelled by steam" — probably by means of paddles although details are not given in the original or in later registrations. *Warrington* was schooner-rigged having two masts, standing bowsprit and with a square stern. The first owners were Lee Watson of St. Helens and George Sanderson, iron founders, together with John Tompson and James Tompson, both of Wigan. The four partners traded under the name of the Bridge Foundry Company. They did not keep *Warrington* for long for they sold the vessel to a Joseph Coyne of Liverpool in 1844 and in 1846 she was sold to foreign owners.[5] After *Warrington* the next recorded launch of an iron ship at the Bridge Foundry was that of the brig *John Wilson Patten* in 1841 followed by the square stern iron schooner *Libya* 125 tons, of 1842.

As vessels of astonishing tonnage were subsequently built at Warrington it is of interest to note Sir John Rennie's observation of the maximum draught of vessels which could proceed to Warrington. Sir John surveyed the upper

Mersey with the intention of exploring the possibility of constructing a ship canal to Manchester and in his report of 1840 he stated:

The largest vessels which can navigate the Mersey from Liverpool to Bank Quay, Warrington draw about eight to nine feet of water and are eighty to a hundred tons burden but vessels of this class can only come up to Bank Quay at high water of spring tides and even then unless assisted by a favourable wind or steam tug they cannot get from Liverpool on one tide.[6]

Yet within thirteen years of Sir John Rennie's report a ship of nearly 1,800 tons and which had a cargo hold twenty-eight feet in depth was launched from the Bank Quay shipyard.[7]

It was in 1847 that George Sanderson entered into partnership with Edward Tayleur and the Bank Quay foundry was extended in order to manufacture shot and shells and heavy castings for bridges. The site was also expanded to permit the construction of large ocean going ships of extra-ordinary size.

Tayleur, an iron ship of 1,979 tons, launched in 1853 was the largest of the Warrington vessels and she was to have a very short life. This clipper ship was 230 feet long with a breadth of forty feet and her cargo carrying capacity was said to be nearly four thousand tons.

From the beginning *Tayleur* was an unlucky ship and misfortune occurred even before her launch when her master, Captain Noble, fell into the hold and was remarkably fortunate in escaping serious injury.[8]

On completion the ship was handed over to her owners, Messrs. Charles Moore and Company, and she was towed carefully down river to Liverpool. To edge the great ship past the sandbanks at Fiddler's Ferry was an extremely hazardous task but it was accomplished without mishap and as *Tayleur* passed Runcorn there was a tremendous display of interest and enthusiasm from the watching crowds.

The Bridgewater Trustees had been responsible for guiding the ship down river and the Bank Quay Foundry readily acknowledged the efficient way she had been handled. In a public notice printed in the *Warrington Guardian* and addressed to the Trustees the shipyard management said:

We have the greatest pleasure in thanking you for the kind way in which you lent us Captain Foulkes (The Trustees' Superintendent of Lights and Buoys) and the men with him. Captain Foulkes has most successfully accomplished the delivery of the ship "Tayleur" in Liverpool. The practical manner in which he buoyed the river, made arrangements with the steamers and conducted the whole of the preparations cannot be too highly spoken of.[9]

The *Tayleur* was built for the Australia run and the White Star Line owners were proud of their new gold rush clipper. They boasted:

This truly splendid vessel just launched and the largest merchantman ever built in England, will undoubtedly prove the fastest of the Australian fleet as she has been constructed expressly with the object of attaining the very highest speed.[10]

The ill fated *Tayleur* which was lost in the Irish sea on her maiden voyage to Australia in 1854.

Runcorn's waterfront in 1880.

On Thursday January 19th 1854 *Tayleur* left Liverpool for Melbourne with 488 passengers and 71 crew members. She encountered heavy weather as soon as she emerged into the Irish Sea. Visibility was too thick to allow observations to be made and it was also found that the compasses were inaccurate and the steering defective. New ropes were stiff in the blocks and the Chinese and Lascar members of the crew were inexperienced and inclined to panic. *Tayleur* ran on to rocks at Lambay Island near Dublin and 290 persons were drowned.[11] A week later sad wreckage was washed ashore near Maryport and on 8th February divers reported that "Tayleur is parted at the stern, and the decks abaft burst up, the cargo being strewn about the bottom". Beds, barrels, empty casks and prepared boards drifted ashore on the west coast of Scotland for weeks after the disaster.[12]

In recent years the wreck has been discovered by the Irish sub-aqua club and today souvenirs of the *Tayleur* — such as glassware, pottery and cutlery are to be found in many homes in Dublin.[13]

The catastrophe prompted the weird legend that sea sprites had enticed the ship ashore in order to favour the Carpenters' Society whose members looked askance at the use of iron instead of the traditional oak in ship construction. But the Bank Quay yard continued to build iron ships and in June 1853 *La Perlita* was launched. An awkward vessel, schooner rigged with two masts and paddle wheels, *La Perlita* was built to the order of the Pacific Steam Navigation Company and she too was not destined to last long for, three months after her launch, the Liverpool register records that she had been lost at sea.[14]

The disasters did not slow the building of iron ships at Bank Quay and in 1855 the *Startled Fawn* a clipper ship of 1,165 tons was built for G.H. Fletcher and Company of Liverpool. She lasted a little longer but within two years of her launch she was sunk in collision off Dungeness.[15] Another unlucky Warrington ship was *Sarah Sands* which was completed in 1857. Before the year ended she was burnt out when under charter to the East India Company.

The Warrington yard enjoyed a spectacular building boom and large iron vessels which were destined for long ocean voyages left the slips in quick succession. *Lady Octavia* of 1,132 tons was completed in 1854 for Messrs. Adams of Greenock for their Liverpool to Australia service and the following year *Sarah Palmer* of 1,325 tons was launched.[16] This ship nearly came to grief a couple of miles from the builder's yard when she ran aground at Fiddler's Ferry and she had to wait for the next tide before she could be freed and towed to Liverpool. The *Medora,* an iron barque of 357 tons was completed in 1854 for G.W. Turner, ship owners of Liverpool,[17] to be used between Liverpool and South America and in the same year *Liverpoolania,* a clipper of 800 tons was launched. Other Warrington ships included the iron schooners *Neptune* and *Enterprise,* both of which were built for the South American trade. The *Deerslayer,* a barque of 390 tons, was ordered by Swansea owners to run between South Wales ports and South America[18] and on the slips at the same time was *Retriever,* a 500 ton screw steamer.[19]

A large vessel provisionally named *Golden Vale* was nearing completion in 1854. She was "constructed of the best Staffordshire iron and the best Moulmein teak with a foremast of iron and a wooden mizzen mast". In addition she had "a noble figurehead — a full length female bearing in her hands the produce of a fertile land".[19] As *Golden Vale* does not appear in either the Lloyds Shipping Registers or in the Liverpool Shipping Register she was almost certainly renamed to become *Sarah Palmer* launched in August 1855.

Warrington is a most unlikely centre for large ship construction but in the mid 1850's it bustled with remarkable energy. In a local newspaper article of 1854 it was reported that besides *Golden Vale* which was nearing completion, two other vessels each of 500 tons were on the stocks and a further two ships of greater tonnage were to be started that year. An optimistic editorial proclaimed that Warrington "would become a first rate building place and a port capable of receiving large vessels to load and unload".[20] But within a year the same newspaper when reporting the launch of *Sarah Palmer* in August 1855 concluded the account by stating — "We regret to observe that no other keels are laid in the Bank Quay yard"[21].

The era of the iron ships of Warrington was spectacular but of short duration and by 1857 the venture was at an end. The advertisements of "Premises to Let" for the Bank Quay Foundry appeared in the press for November 1857 and from then until January 1860 the shipbuilding equipment and machinery were sold off.[22] The reasons for the brief attempt to establish a shipbuilding industry at Bank Quay can be attributed to a number of factors. Warrington was well served by its railway network and the builders were able to receive the necessary materials easily at a time when there was a demand for iron ships from all the major ports of Britain. The district was also fortunate in possessing the expertise necessary for the construction of iron vessels. Even as early as 1830 iron barges had been built locally[23] and they and the iron coasters of the 1840s had proved to be very serviceable. Ship owners were prepared to invest in iron ships. Furthermore the upper reaches of the Mersey were unusually favourable at Warrington and Runcorn during the 1850s.

Of course the Bank Quay company's success depended upon the enterprise of its proprietors and Tayleur and Sanderson were energetic pioneers but the rapid decline of the yard was due to causes beyond the control of the management. Other, more suitable shipbuilding centres were established when ships' dimensions increased. The upper Mersey was too unreliable for building these new vessels. When the Crimean war ended there was a recession in armament manufacture and this brought about a rationalisation of the works and shipbuilding ceased at Warrington.

The Wooden Ships of Runcorn

The notoriously capricious Mersey deep channel which favoured the Warrington shipbuilders during the 1850s also provided ideal conditions at Runcorn for the launching of much larger vessels than had been possible for many years. An official report of the state of the Mersey compiled by Rear Admiral George Evans, the acting conservator for the Port of Liverpool described the sea channels and the channels of the upper river in 1858 as being "in a most satisfactory state"[24]. For about ten years deep water lay along the Cheshire shore at Runcorn and it was during this period that Brundrit and Whiteway's shipyard built their largest vessels. The *Dennis Brundrit* of 462 tons was the largest ship ever to be built at Runcorn.[25] She was 141 feet long with a beam of 27 feet and she must have caused some anxiety at her launch because of her size — the depth of her hold was 18½ feet. Claimed to be the smallest full-rigged ship of her time the launch of *Dennis Brundrit* aroused considerable interest locally and the carnival atmosphere which prevailed on the day of her launch in September 1856 is described in a local newspaper:

> On Tuesday Runcorn was the scene of unusual gaiety, the greater part of the resident gentry of the neighbourhood and others interested in nautical matters from Liverpool etc. having met together to witness the launch of the largest vessel ever built in Runcorn.
>
> The streets were hung with banners, which, with packets and boats floating on the river, glittering with decorations and thronged with spectators in their best attire, together with the thousands that crowded the shore on both sides of the river, rendered the sight most animating and beautiful.
>
> About one o'clock the stately craft was seen to glide nobly into the water amid the booming of cannon and the hurrahs of admiring thousands. Mrs. Robert Cheshire Whiteway, in the centre of a circle of friends, performed the ceremony of christening.
>
> The vessel will carry 800 tons and is of the model and to the lines of Mr. James Boot, the talented manager of the builders Messrs. Brundrit and Whiteway, and was pronounced by competent judges to be an exceedingly superior ship.[26]

The "competent judges" were correct in their estimate of the quality of *Dennis Brundrit's* construction. She was employed for many years in the trade between Britain and the Falkland Islands. In May 1879 the ship survived a storm to reach Stanley from Cardiff in a derelict condition and with her mainmast, foretop gallant mast, yards and sails lost and with the mizzen mast sprung. On October 2nd 1879 she was sold by public auction to George Dean of Stanley, Falkland Islands for £355.[27] After refit the *Dennis Brundrit* was rerigged as a barque and she lasted until 1892 when she was wrecked on Centre Island, San Salvador, Falkland Islands as she was loading wool, hides and tallow for London. Her fourteen crew members were rescued and part of her cargo was salvaged.[28]

The *Anne Chesshyre* a ship of 451 tons was launched from the Brundrit and Whiteway yard in 1853. Like the *Dennis Brundrit* she was felted and yellow metalled for service in tropical waters and she was recognised by Lloyd's assessors to be a vessel of superior build. *Anne Chesshyre* was owned by a French firm when she went out of the registers in 1891.[29]

The schooner *Redtail* on the stocks at Blundell and Mason's
Belvedere yard in 1867.

The launch of the last Runcorn built schooner, *Despatch,* about to take
to the water from Brundrit and Hayes' yard on the 4th May 1886.

Thus by 1850 Runcorn builders had proved that they could construct ships to the highest standards of the day. The mid century demand for new ships and the fortunate channel along the Cheshire bank resulted in increased activity in the shipyards. *Anne Chesshyre* and *Dennis Brundrit* were the exceptions in that they were by far the largest vessels built at Runcorn. The majority of the sea going vessels were schooners — coasting vessels of from 70 to 100 tons displacement and all were of wood construction. Some schooners which were built in the first half of the century were very small indeed. *William Court* of 1849 was a mere 56 tons and *Thomas Mason* of 1838 only 62 tons. Other tiny two masted schooners were *Emmeline* of 1851 at 70 tons, *Margaret* of 1841 at 64 tons and the oddly named *The Port* of 1847 which displaced 65 tons.[30]

The Runcorn yards enjoyed a high reputation for building ships of quality. *Barlochan,* a barque of 227 tons and *Eva* a brigantine launched in 1853 were vessels listed as having been built to the most exacting requirements. Both were metal clad for service in tropical waters. *Barlochan* was trading to China in the 1860s and *Eva* served Mediterranean routes.[31]

Of course ships which traded solely in northern waters did not need to be metal sheathed but even some of the smaller locally built schooners appear in Lloyds registers with the prestigious Maltese Cross symbol against their names. They include *Cheshire Lass* 1857, *Rival* 1862, *Harvest King* 1879, *Snowflake* 1880 and *Despatch* of 1886.

The rise in shipbuilding activity at the port of Runcorn was due to a number of reasons the most important being the vast increase in Liverpool shipping. The Liverpool register of merchant ships shows that her merchants were ordering new vessels from Canada, from the major shipbuilding centres of the United Kingdom as well as from minor centres such as Anglesey, Whitby, Scarborough, Runcorn and Sankey Bridges. The magnitude of Liverpool's commercial expansion was such that all kinds of vessels were in demand including the small coastal schooner and the sailing flat. The local yards were helped by the decline of shipbuilding at Liverpool. In 1850 a Committee of Enquiry was held at Liverpool to investigate the causes of this recession and the findings suggested that the Corporation's policy to dock building was causing a contraction of the area available for shipyards. The shipbuilders also claimed that the Corporation's practice in granting short leases did not allow the yards to install expensive equipment as the builders could not get full benefit from new investment before the lease expired.[32]

As long as the river's channels scoured the Cheshire shore at Runcorn the three little shipyards prospered but if the channel was to move across to the Lancashire side then the construction of the larger vessels would become impossible but for nearly thirty years from 1840 river conditions remained satisfactory and the slipways were occupied by new vessels or by those under repair. While things remained in this happy situation the builders made good use of their opportunities knowing full well that the feckless channel could just as easily move away or silt up to leave them in desperate circumstances.

Notes

1. Lloyds Registers 1854, 1857.

2. Appendix, p.210.

3. *Warrington Guardian,* 6th May, 1854.

4. Ibid., 17th October 1853.

5. Liverpool Shipping Register.

6. Norton, P., *Waterways and Railways to Warrington,* Railway and Canal Historical Society, 1974, p.53.

7. "Tayleur" 1853.

8. Boscow, H., *Warrington. Its Heritage,* Teare, Warrington 1947, p.40.

9. *Warrington Guardian,* 15th October 1853.

10. Anderson, R., *White Star,* Stephenson, Prescot, 1964, p.111.

11. *Lloyds List,* 22nd January 1854.

12. *Lloyds List,* 10th February 1854.

13. Anderson, R., op.cit., p.111.

14. Liverpool Register 1853.

15. Lloyds Register 1857.

16. Ibid., 1855.

17. Ibid., 1856.

18. Ibid., 1847 and 1854.

19. *Warrington Guardian,* 29th April 1854.

20. Ibid., 6th May 1854.

21. Ibid., 4th August, 1855.

22. *Warrington Guardian,* 14th November 1857.

23. *Warrington Guardian,* 29th April 1854.

24. Annual Report of the Conservancy Board of the Port of Liverpool, (G. Evans), 31.1.1859.

25. Lloyds Register, 1854 and Dennis Brundrit, "Those Far Seeing Brundrits of Runcorn", *Mond Mail,* May 1976.

26. *Warrington Guardian,* 20th September 1856.

27. Mercantile Navy List. Lloyds 1879.

28. Lloyds Court of Enquiry Report No. 4592. 1892.

29. Lloyds Registers 1854 and 1891.

30. Lloyds Registers, 1838 to 1851.

31. Lloyds Registers, 1853 and 1854.

32. Harris, J.R., *Liverpool and Merseyside,* F. Cass and Co., London, 1969, pp.171-172.

7
Expanding Maritime Trade and Industrial Restraint, 1850-1865

When Runcorn's short lived prestige as an independent customs port ended on 16th April 1850 its status was reduced to its former state, that of a creek town within the port of Liverpool but in spite of this set back trade continued to improve with the number of ships using the docks increasing from 935 in the first six months of 1850 to 1328 in the corresponding period of 1851.[1] The arrangements at the docks proved to be inadequate and in 1851 the volume of shipping was such that many vessels seeking to discharge cargoes could not be accommodated and they had to berth on the foreshore. The problems caused by the growth in business also resulted in difficulties on the Bridgewater Canal when the Duke's Trustees could not find enough canal boats to clear the accumulation of cargoes on the quayside.[2]

It was expected that since the town no longer had customs authorities foreign trade would not be attracted to the Bridgewater and Old Quay Docks but the opposite occurred with ships arriving from foreign ports in increasing numbers. They by passed Liverpool in order to load salt, Staffordshire earthenware and manufactured iron goods.

The table on page 221-223 of the Appendix indicates the sources and the volume of imports into Runcorn for 1852. The nature of these caroges landed on the quayside shows the significance of the town as a canal port for, in addition to goods passing between Liverpool and Manchester without the necessity of transhipment at Runcorn's docks, all the major items of commerce — potters' materials, iron ore, pig iron, roofing slates and pit props were distributed to centres of industry via the inland waterways. The raw materials of the pottery industry predominated with 70,000 tons of potters' clay, china clay and flints being landed in 1852. Iron ore and pig iron from Scotland and north Lancashire totalled 58,000 tons whilst 42,000 tons of slates arrived from North Wales ports. The shipment of pyrites was already a major trade and 20,000 tons were imported from Arklow and Wicklow with smaller quantities arriving from Padstow and Conway. John Hutchinson had financial interests in pyrites mines in Spain and by the late 1850s new trade routes had become established with cargoes arriving from Huelva and Bilbao. The trade in propwood and in oats and meal from Ireland had been long established and in 1852 over 8,000 tons of oats and meal, 6,000 tons of pit props and 3,600 tons of copper ore were discharged on to the Runcorn wharfs.[3]

Of course much of the freight on the upper river was transported by barge from Liverpool and, as most of this trade passed through Runcorn and into the inland waterway system without the necessity of unloading at the port, the tonnage is not included in the figures. F.C. Mather has estimated that in 1851 eighty per cent of this Liverpool to Manchester canal traffic consisted of three main categories of goods — raw cotton, sawn timber and grain and flour.

It is somewhat surprising to see that no record of the considerable quantities of Welsh road setts and Macadam chippings were included in the port statistics for that year and yet Brundrit and Whiteway's had been importing Penmaenmawr stone since the 1840s.

The beginnings of a trade which was to become one of some consequence within twenty years is noticeable in the figures of 1852.[4] Among a miscellany of cargoes there was a consignment of 210 tons of animal bones from Dublin which were probably destined for the bone grinding mills at Runcorn. The mills were established in 1843[5] and they supplied sulphate bone manure to farms over a large area of Lancashire and Cheshire.

The amount of "glass blower's sand" arriving at Runcorn in 1852 was small with 419 tons coming from Yarmouth. The St. Helens Crown Glass Company (later Pilkington Brothers) built their first glass house cone close to the Sankey Canal and although they used mainly local sand they always had alternative sources of "white" sand which was brought to the Mersey by coaster from Kings Lynn or the Isle of Wight to be transported in barges up the Sankey to St. Helens.[6] From the mid 1850s regular cargoes of sand were despatched from France and Belgium and the Liverpool Customs Bills of Entry list regular 150 ton cargoes arriving at Runcorn from Antwerp and Rouen.[7]

As more alkali works were established in the region there was a demand for firebricks for furnace linings and regular shipments were despatched from Chester. Over 3,500 tons of firebricks arrived at Runcorn in 1852[8] and this trade was to remain lively for the next thirty years. Other incoming cargoes required for local use included 2,500 tons of railway lines from Newport, oak bark from Ostend and small consignments of gun powder for the Runcorn and Weston quarries.

The upsurge of maritime trade on the upper Mersey was in response to a number of simultaneous economic developments. The expansion of industry and population in the locality coincided with the enlargement of the pottery industry of Staffordshire and also with an increased demand for raw cotton from Manchester textile manufacturers. Canal traffic was busy and the Mersey was favourable with the river steamers providing free towage between the town's docks and the Sloyne anchorage off Tranmere. Coasting vessels entering Runcorn were always assured of a return cargo of coal for delivery to Ireland, North Wales and to Cornwall and Devon. Salt was now a principal export commodity and the increase in trade was impressive. In eight years from 1846 to 1854 the salt shipments out of Runcorn had increased five fold to 83,000.[9] Salt was an ideal ballast material and Liverpool sailing vessels carried it to the Baltic and to North America to return with timber some of which was used in the Lancashire collieries which supplied the fuel for salt refining.

The pressure of increasing business forced the Bridgewater Trustees into putting dock improvements in hand and in 1853 an Act of Parliament was promoted by the Earl of Ellesmere for making a short canal from the Francis dock, which connected with the Bridgewater Canal at Runcorn, to join the Weston Canal of the River Weaver Navigation near Weston Point. The new cut was called the Runcorn and Weston Canal and its main purpose was to provide a sheltered waterway for small craft which brought salt from the Weaver to the Runcorn docks. The Bridgewater Trustees were anxious to see the canal finished as they feared the Weaver Trustees would build warehouses at Weston Point and the salt transhipment would then take place there instead of at Runcorn. Work commenced on the new undertaking in 1857 but it was not until 25th February 1860 that the Trustees were able to advertise that the canal was open for traffic.[10]

Not all the Bridgewater enterprises were successful in the 1850s for the swift boats on the Duke's canal became casualties of railway competition. There was a continuing falling off in the number of passengers using the boats between Runcorn and Manchester and the service was withdrawn and the packets were sold in 1855.[11] In the early months of that year the weather had shown how vulnerable was the canal traffic to stoppages caused by ice. The frost in February was so severe that it was described as being "greater than the memory of the oldest inhabitant can furnish with a parallel instance". Thirty horses failed to haul four flats along the four mile stretch of the Bridgewater Canal from Preston Brook to Runcorn and the canal was closed. In spite of the severe weather the old Mersey and Irwell Navigation remained open as the ice "was passed through weirs and the water from the higher levels was used to flush the ice down the canal from Warrington to Runcorn where it was raked into the river".[12]

Although the Bridgewater Trustees had reason to be satisfied with the business on their undertaking they must have viewed with some anxiety the major dock construction which was taking place on the opposite side of the river at Garston. At the time the Trustees were promoting their Bill for the Runcorn and Weston Canal, the St. Helens Railway Company opened the Garston dock. The railway company's Widnes dock had proved incapable for increasing coal exports because of the problems caused by neaping at Woodend and by 1853 both the canal and the railway to Widnes were each transporting over half a million tons from the St. Helens coalfield.[13]

The new Garston dock was equipped with modern coal drops which could load over a hundred tons an hour and this was a faster rate than at any dock on Merseyside. At first there were problems for the Garston dock proved too difficult for sea going vessels of deep draught but improvements carried out during the following twenty years resulted in the dock becoming a rival for Liverpool's coal trade and by the end of the century it had succeeded in taking fifty percent of the city's coal exporting business.[14]

Undoubtedly the developments at Garston had prompted the Bridgewater Trustees to construct the Runcorn and Weston Canal. They knew from experience that the new railway ports were formidable opposition. As the Runcorn docks did not possess a rail link it was necessary to exploit the canal system to the utmost.

Whilst it was true that the Bridgewater Trustees had made considerable improvements to port facilities at Runcorn they were accused (with some justification) of hindering the growth of the chemical industry of the town. In 1854 the Trustees refused Messrs. Haddock and Parnell's application to have land from them for the purpose of building a chemical works. Lord Ellesmere of the Trustees wanted to avoid trouble with Sir Richard Brooke of Norton Priory whose estate had been noticeably affected by the alkali fumes emitted by the primitive processes at the Leblanc chemical factories in Widnes. As the 1860s approached the problem became intense and Sir Richard alleged that his trees were damaged, his crops wilted and he could not fatten his cattle on pastures which had been polluted by industrial fall out.[15]

With the Trustees' refusal to release land for factory sites industry stagnated and employment opportunities in Runcorn were reduced. From 1855 Widnes expanded rapidly at Runcorn's expense and the growth of the latter, which had been rapid during the previous twenty years, now slowed down and the Trustees were held to blame for the town's inability to grow at the same rate as Widnes. The *Chester Courant* of 27th October 1858 observed that:

> Widnes was indebted for its existence to the course pursued by the Bridgewater Trustees in refusing to lease on reasonable terms land for the erection of factories and chemical and other works for which Runcorn is more elegibly situated.

The *Courant's* view was not entirely correct for other circumstances had helped to make Widnes a more favourable proposition for the siting of new chemical works. When the St. Helens Railway Company expanded their lines to Garston they needed capital to finance the new project and to do this they raised the freight charges on the St. Helens to Widnes line and also on their canal by nearly fifty per cent. The coal owners at St. Helens escaped the new tolls because they were closely connected to the directors but the St. Helens chemical manufacturers had to meet the new charges in full. They therefore turned away from St. Helens and the new works were built at Widnes where coal could be transported at the old rate and without charges being incurred in carrying the raw materials and products of the chemical industry on the railway or canal.

But although the expansion of the chemical industry at Runcorn suffered a restraint in the 1850s the ancilliary trades which were required to maintain and supply local shipping proliferated. The town had a nautical atmosphere with ship building at the Castlerock yard of John Anderton, at Brundrit and Whiteway's Mersey Street slips, at the Belvedere shipyard of Samuel Mason and at the smaller establishment of T. and J. Johnson in Mill Street.[16]

By 1859 there were twenty-three master mariners resident in Runcorn and there were six sailmaking establishments, four rope making concerns, six ship broking companies and four ship chandlers. A local directory for 1857[17] lists a number of small businesses which were connected with shipping. John Stubbs and Sons of Percival Lane were shipwrights, block makers and makers of masts and spars. John Rawlinson of Top Locks was a pump maker. He also fashioned the hard wood blocks needed for ships' rigging, making their casings of elm and the sheaves of lignum vitae. Such items as chemicals, dairy produce and liquids were transported in barrels and casks and there were four cooperage businesses. Mr. J. Ravenscroft of Church Street and Samuel Mason of Belvedere Building advertised that they were "ship and anchor smiths". Some tradesmen showed their versatility by conducting a number of enterprises simultaneously. William Robinson was a man of many parts for he combined the businesses of "sailor's outfitter, auctioneer and eating house keeper" at his premises in High Street and Gilbert Street whilst William Bate was a flat and boat builder, coal merchant and a dealer in building and moulding sand. Among the more unusual occupations was that of Francis Gallagher of 58 Ashridge Street who gave his profession as "marine artist". It is difficult to determine whether he made his living with canvas and oils or by decorating and gilding ships' figureheads. Another small industry which depended upon the slate trade of North Wales was that of Dutton and Company of High Street who were manufacturers of school writing slates.

Slater's Directory for 1855 gives the following description of Runcorn.

> Of late years Runcorn has become a place of resort for salt water bathing, while the purer air, the pleasantness of the neighbourhood, the fine views (particularly from Halton Castle) with the exhilarating effects derived from the busy scene upon the river, constitute auxiliary benefits to those produced by the baths. The accommodation for visitants is provided by respectable inns and lodging houses.[18]

As the contemporary prints of Runcorn show that there was considerable industry along the river front, one suspects that the directory for 1855 was in need of revision. Certainly the view into Lancashire was becoming a prospect of unpleasant industrial features. The Mersey was no longer pure and Runcorn could not be regarded as a watering place to which invalids came to benefit from the clean air. The description of Runcorn by Nathaniel Hawthorne who was the United States consul at Liverpool from 1853 to 1857 is nearer to reality. He said that the town had:

> two or three tall manufacturing chimneys with a pennant of black smoke from each, a church or two and a meagre uninteresting shabby brick town with irregular streets — not village — like but paved and looking like a dwarfed stunted city.[19]

Transport and Religion

The efforts by the various religious denominations to provide spiritual and welfare amenities for seamen and watermen seems to have begun about 1830. In the first thirty years of the century Sunday working on the canals and on the river became common because of the growth in traffic. Sabbath working was necessary because the consequences of not taking advantage of the Sunday tides could mean a congestion of shipping at the docks and in the shipping channels. It was held that there was little religious feeling among the seamen and flatmen and it was said that they were "of a low and debased standard". By 1840 there was nationwide pressure on canal and railway companies to end Sunday working. At a "very numerous and respectable public meeting" which was held in Runcorn in 1839 the following resolution was carried:

> That this meeting, deeply feeling the importance of the due observance of the Lord's Day, as connected with the glory of God and the good of man, beg most earnestly, to solicit the proprietors of the several navigations in the parish of Runcorn, as well as the different companies trading upon the same, to make such arrangements as may secure to the flatmen and boatmen the privileges of the day of rest. That the sailing of packets is especially offensive to Almighty God and injurious to the morals of the community, causing disorder, confusion and gross irregularities on the day set apart for divine worship and the performance of other duties enjoined by our holy religion.[20]

As a result of the new attitude to Sunday observance the Trustees of the River Weaver Navigation Company in 1841 built a church at Weston Point for their employees and their families. The Trustees were generous for they built a vicarage, paid the vicar's stipend and also made allowances to the church cleaners and choiristers. A school was provided for the boatmen's children and a house was built for the schoolmaster whose salary was paid by the Trustees.[21]

The parish registers of Christ Church, Weston Point record its nautical connections. The entries include such occupations as "boatman" (narrow boat man), "waterman" (river flat man), and pilot. It is said that during the evening service in winter months in later years the Church blinds had to be drawn in order that the church lights should not be mistaken for that of the nearby lighthouse.

The pressure which some congregations had brought to bear on the canal companies had its desired effect, for, on 12th August 1839 "great joy was expressed by the Reverend John Davies and the Holy Trinity congregation" in Runcorn when the Weaver Trustees ended Sunday working and "granted the boatmen the Sabbath to its full extent".[22]

In Runcorn township private generosity enabled the church to found a Mariner's Mission. Through the liberality of the Countess of Ellesmere the seamen and flatmen of the Old Quay Docks were provided with a mission church in 1834. One of the earliest Welsh religious centres on Merseyside was the Welsh chapel in Back King Street, Runcorn which was established in 1829.

The Welsh community in the town grew quickly during the first three decades of the century as seamen, dock workers and quarry men from Wales settled in Runcorn. The minister at the Welsh chapel was the Reverend John Jones and in two letters published by him in *Y Drysorfa* in 1843 he reviews six years of his ministry from 1837 to 1843.[23] Mr. Jones said that his congregation numbered fifty to sixty "of Runcorn people alone" and seamen, sometimes more than eighty of them, swelled the congregation on occasions. Before 1826 sailors from Wales were given credit for beginning a religious movement among Welsh people in Runcorn when they held prayer meetings aboard a barge in "chapel basin". The Duke of Bridgewater's Trustees contributed £10 per annum towards the cost of the venture but nothing more is known of its subsequent history.[24] A Welsh chapel was built in Rutland Street in 1856 and in its early days the congregation received support from Canon Barclay, the vicar of Runcorn.

The Welsh community in Runcorn was considerable. According to customs officials half of the 4,418 ships to visit the port in 1865 were Welsh vessels and the essay prize at the Welsh Eisteddfod held in Caerleon in 1866 was the gift of Welshmen living in Runcorn. The first recorded formal Methodist Chapel meeting in Widnes occurred in 1863 and here again the initiative came from Welsh seamen.[25]

The Bridgewater Trustees encouraged church missionary activity at their docks and in the late 1850s they provided a floating church. The church seems to have been adapted from an old barge. Originally it had been moored at the Top Locks later to be moved down the line of the old locks to a new berth near to the river. Services on board the strange craft appear to have been well attended. Canon John Barclay writing in 1864 stated that the average attendance for the 129 services held during the previous year was ninety which must have meant near capacity congregations for the barge church.[26]

The minister of the floating church for the first years of the mission's existence was the Reverend E.D. Garven, M.A., and the Bridgewater Trust Mission, of which the church was the nucleus, eventually included a Sunday school and a day school for the children of boat people. In addition to providing the floating church the Trustees paid part of Mr. Garven's stipend of £110 per annum and they also gave financial support to the day school. When in 1866 the timbers of the barge-church were found to be rotten the Trustees provided a building to serve as St. Peter's Mission Church and the first service was held in December of that year.

When trade was flourishing in the 1860s Sunday working on the river and on the canals became the rule once more and the committee of the Mersey Mission to Seamen approached the Earl of Ellesmere of the Bridgewater Trust drawing his attention to this undesirable practice.[27] A reply to the committee's protestations was received in February 1870 from the Bridgewater agent who stated the company's regulations on Sunday sailings. He pointed out that vessels leaving Liverpool on Saturday when tides occurred between

4.00 p.m. and 10.00 p.m. were to proceed to Lymm where they were to remain between 5.00 a.m. and 6.00 p.m. on Sunday and then go forward to reach their destinations in Manchester in time for business on Monday morning. Vessels sailing from Liverpool after 10.00 p.m. on Saturday:

> were to remain at Runcorn until 6.00 p.m. on the Sunday and then go forward except those laden with cotton or other competitive traffic (in which case the Liverpool station will issue a speed note to each flat) when they must proceed to their destination without stopping.

The committee of the Mersey Mission got little satisfaction from this as the Trustees were not prepared to stop much of their Sunday traffic. The reply concluded with the vague statement that:

> all vessels will be required to tie up between 6.00 a.m. and 6.00 p.m. on a Sunday except those laden with down goods and such as may be from Liverpool carrying speed notes.[28]

The transfer of the Bridgewater undertaking from the Trustees to a limited company in 1872 seriously curtailed the missionary work in the docks and it brought about the end of the Floating Church Mission. The directors of the new company discontinued the payment of the minister's stipend and they refused to make any contributions whatsoever towards the maintenance of the church and the day school. The Mission attempted to carry on after the Trustee's contribution had ceased but eventually services were discontinued and the establishment was closed. The Mission's activities for the temporal welfare of seamen and boatmen's families in times of hardship also came to an end.[29]

The cessation of church missionary work at the Bridgewater docks was not of long duration for it is known that a lay preacher was working among the flatmen and their families about 1873[30] but nothing is known of his activities and it was not until 1875 that the Committee of the Mersey Mission to Seamen founded a Seamen's Mission headquarters in the town. The man they appointed to establish the new headquarters was Mr. William Shaw who arrived in the town without detailed instructions or money to begin his life's work among the town's seamen and their dependents. Mr. Shaw was still actively engaged in serving the maritime community nearly fifty years later when he was over eighty years of age.[31]

The new missioner made his headquarters the old mission building which had not been used since the Floating Church Mission had closed and his early reports illustrate his devotion to his work. With the assistance of four boys and three girls Missioner Shaw visited boatmen and seamen in their homes and on flats and ships. In one year his visits totalled 7,447. There were thirty-three Band of Hope and Temperance meetings and seventeen open air meetings conducted aboard ships and at the docks. In order to counteract the attractions of the many public houses Mr. Shaw provided a bowling green, a skittle alley and a recreation field for seamen as well as a recreation and reading room. He was even instrumental in providing a seamen's grave in the town cemetery for those who died locally but who came from all parts of the world. At the time of Missioner Shaw's retirement in 1921 forty-seven seamen had been buried in the grave. The stone commemorates seamen from Dublin, Anglesey, New Brunswick, Bordeaux, Norway and the United States.[32]

Throughout a period from about 1877 to 1910 the local press frequently reported on the Mersey Mission to Seamen's attempts to relieve distress during periods of unemployment or during times when work on the canals was stopped because of ice. Typical of the reports is the following from the *Warrington Guardian* of 17th December 1879.

> During the four days the soup kitchen connected with the Mersey Mission to Seamen has been open, no less than 468 meals have been given away. Mr. Shaw having announced that a free meal would be given away on Sunday morning there was a large muster and 128 children were regaled with tea and buns. Should the thaw continue the soup kitchen will cease its operations after this day.[33]

Coastwise Traffic and the Development of Foreign Trade 1862-1876

On 1st January 1862 Runcorn was once again appointed an independent customs port[34] with certain areas of the docks designated as legal quays and the Duke of Bridgewater's Trustees began determined efforts to attract new trade to the port. In April 1862 they established an agency in Dublin and they arranged a favourable through rate to be charged for goods sent from Dublin to Manchester.[35] Later in the year they made similar arrangements to allow Birmingham and Staffordshire iron goods and Staffordshire pottery to be transported at through rates to Le Havre, Rouen and Paris.[36] The Trustees' main efforts were to secure foreign trade and they sent two of their agents to develop trade links between Runcorn and various European ports. Mr. Howarth and Mr. Mitchell visited Le Havre, Paris, Nantes, Bordeaux, Cette, Marseilles, Santander, Bilbao and Bayônne and in spite of the fact that Hull was a serious rival to the Mersey for the export of iron goods and earthenware they met with some degree of success in their negotiations.[37]

From about 1862 Runcorn's trade showed a startling increase and on 12th April a local newspaper reported that:

> An unusually large number of vessels has arrived. Upwards of 110 vessels have entered the Bridgewater Docks, the Mersey and Irwell Docks and the Weaver Docks at Weston Point. This number was more than the present docks could conveniently accommodate and the extensive additions which are rapidly progressing and which when completed will carry the line of docks nearly to Weston Point will all be required to meet the increasing traffic of the port.[38]

In order to facilitate shipping movements a telegraph line was introduced in 1862. It connected the Trustees' offices in Hulme, Manchester to Egerton Dock in Liverpool and the line was erected along the Bridgewater Canal to Runcorn where it was suspended across the river at the Gap.[39]

The Alfred dock which was completed in 1860 was equipped with hydraulic cranes[40] and this together with the improved docks and the satisfactory river channels served to attract foreign shippng. But in 1862 the tonnage of shipping which was cleared from Runcorn to colonial and foreign countries was 16,000 tons compared to 145,000 tons cleared coastwise. By 1868 however, the colonial and foreign traffic had risen to 36,000 tons. The rise in the value of exports grew from £4,178 to £28,480 in 1867 and to £44,553 by 1871 and this represents a ten fold increase over the fourteen year period.[41]

In order to cope with the additional shipping the Bridgewater Trustees in 1867 began work on a new dock and at the same time they removed obstructions from the river. They deepened the Duke's Gut and they walled the outer face of Runcorn Island (Duke's Island) in order to assist the scouring action of the tide through the navigable channel.

By April 1863 foreign trade at Runcorn docks had become considerable. In that month vessels arrived from Dunkirk, Nantes, Rouen and Le Havre with cargoes of flour, from Bordeaux with pit props and from Antwerp and Rouen with glass sand. A number of Danish vessels arrived to discharge cargoes of oats from Odense, Kolding and Horsens to return with salt for their local fishing industries.[42]

Runcorn's foreign export trade in salt was well developed by 1870 with vessels loading for fishing ports in Russia, Germany, Denmark, Iceland, Norway and the Low Countries. Most of the cargoes were destined for obscure destinations and the names of more than fifty small creek ports in Northern Europe which were trading with Runcorn appear in the Customs Bills of Entry for the Port of Liverpool. In addition to Rotterdam, Ostend, Bruges, Riga and St. Petersburg, salt was despatched to Harlingen, Vardoe, Pernau, Termonde, Randers, Dordt, Aalborg and Zierickzee. During the summer of 1870 a dozen vessels carried salt to St. Petersburg and also in that year the first cargoes were loaded for St. Johns, New Brunswick and Gaspe and Yarmouth in Nova Scotia. This trans-Atlantic trade was to grow in importance in the latter part of the century when Runcorn-built ships were specifically built for the Newfoundland passage but from the beginning, some hundred ton schooners which were regarded as coasters, were engaged in supplying salt for the salt fish industry of Newfoundland.[43]

The efforts of the two Bridgewater agents who had visited European ports in 1862 soon proved to have been profitable and vessels arrived from ports which they had included in their itinerary.[44] By 1872 a very successful business had been established with La Rochelle, St. Nazaire, Cette, Nantes, Marseilles and Santander. In every case vessels leaving Runcorn for these places were loaded with cargoes of pitch. The quantity despatched to Cette was remarkable for in the first ten months of 1873 nearly 5,500 tons of pitch were sent there together with another 1,500 tons going to St. Nazaire.[45]

The trade in bones, horn piths and bone ash from Rio Grande had grown from a single cargo in 1870 to fifteen in 1873. The process of decomposing phosphate material such as bones and bone ash with sulphuric acid in order to produce super phosphate fertilizer was being used by James

Muspratt in his chemical manure works in Widnes.[46] Runcorn's bone mills had expanded to new premises at Sutton Weaver in 1864 and they required bones for glue manufacture and also for bone meal fertilizer. Some cargoes of bones were sent via the Duke's Canal to the potters of Staffordshire. The traffic in pyrites was well established by the 1860s and regular cargoes arrived from Huelva, Wicklow and Pomaron.

Foreign trade continued to grow steadily. Vessels loaded salt for Danzig, Stettin, Lagos, the Faeroes and the Channel Islands. Coal was sent to Gibraltar, to Pernambuco and to Iceland. Incoming cargoes included felspar from Bergen and Arendal in Norway, madder roots from Naples, manganese from La Lajaa and Lisbon and timber from St. Petersburg.

The satisfactory expansion of Runcorn's foreign business kept going until 1871 when the menace of shifting sands began to appear and serious silting began to occur in the channels and at the dock entrances. This prevented the larger foreign vessels from using the port and there was a noticeable falling off in overseas trade. The figures for foreign and colonial trade for the five year period from 1868 to 1872 are as follows:

| | Cleared | | | |
| | Foreign Trade | | Colonial Trade | |
	Vessels	Tons	Vessels	Tons
1868	267	35,894	6	409
1869	201	24,018	13	1,233
1870	244	28,457	24	1,965
1871	366	43,038	22	2,282
1872	193	25,979	21	2,530
	Entered			
1868	209	24,710	18	1,218
1869	203	23,599	22	1,299
1870	338	38,061	42	2,544
1871	275	30,442	29	2,104
1872	209	26,446	31	2,861

Number and Tonnage of Vessels Engaged in Foreign and
Colonial Trade at Runcorn from 1868 to 1872

Table 7:1

Runcorn's foreign export trade had grown from virtually nothing in 1845 to 43,000 tons of shipping in 1871 and in the same year the tonnage of vessels bringing cargoes from foreign ports totalled more than 30,000 tons. So many vessels came from France that the Annual Report of the Salt Chamber of Commerce for Cheshire and Worcestershire described Runcorn as "a small draft port . . . . chiefly frequented by French craft".[49]

The pressures created by rapidly growing trade during the 1860s and the promising outlook of further expansion in business brought about improvements to the Bridgewater Docks system. The tidal dock and the adjacent Alfred Dock which had been completed in 1860 was further improved in order to enable laden ships of 750 tons to reach Runcorn on some 300 tides a year.[50] Although the new docks were equipped with the latest hydraulic hoists the system did not possess the essential railway link and the Trustees began to lose business to Garston, Fleetwood and Preston all of which did have a connection to the main railway network. For over ten years Fleetwood had taken Runcorn's Scottish iron trade and further difficulties appeared when Birkenhead threatened to take Runcorn's traditional earthenware trade because Birkenhead docks could guarantee covered storage.[51] However, in 1869 events favoured the Trustees when the railway line from Weaver Junction to Ditton near Widnes was completed. The canal company welcomed the coming of the railway as they were able to reach agreement with the railway company in order that they could construct the vital stretch of branch line from their docks to the main London to Liverpool line[52] and from then on they were no longer at a permanent disadvantage to Garston and Fleetwood.

Not all the Bridgewater Trustees' enterprises were flourishing in the 1860s. The Mersey and Irwell canal had assumed a minor role and there had been no major dock improvements at Old Quay since 1829. The docks at Old Quay were constructed to enable vessels drawing sixteen feet of water to enter at spring tides but the various Bridgewater Superintendent's reports show that the river channels were always difficult in front of the entrance and the docks were never able to accommodate vessels of such large draught. The canal itself had become so neglected that where it was once possible for craft drawing five feet four inches of water to proceed to Latchford, by 1859 it was difficult for vessels with a draught of three feet six inches to manage the journey.[53]

Foreign traffic into the upper Mersey was seasonal in the 1860s and 1870s. Overseas trade fell away between October and February and the local docks were then used almost exclusively by craft which were engaged in coastwise trade. The few cargoes from foreign sources which did arrive during the winter months consisted of sulphur ore from Huelva and flints from ports in northern France. Although foreign business fell away in the autumn the coastal trade showed a steady gain with clay from Devon and Cornwall, slates from north Wales pyrites from Ireland and pig iron and iron ore from Scotland being the main commodities landed at Runcorn.[54] There was no variety in export cargoes. Practically every vessel leaving the port carried salt or coal. The daily departures show little variation throughout the decade

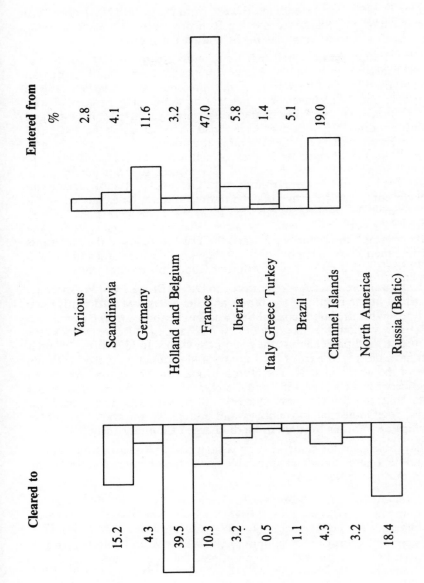

Entered from

	%
Various	2.8
Scandinavia	4.1
Germany	11.6
Holland and Belgium	3.2
France	47.0
Iberia	5.8
Italy Greece Turkey	1.4
Brazil	5.1
Channel Islands	
North America	
Russia (Baltic)	19.0

Cleared to

15.2	
4.3	
39.5	
10.3	
3.2	
0.5	
1.1	
4.3	
3.2	
18.4	

The Direction of Foreign Trade at Runcorn in 1881
Vessels Entered and Cleared

85

beginning in 1860. For instance in the week from 9th to 16th November 1870 of the twenty-eight coasters departing Runcorn twenty-six were carrying either coal or salt to destinations in the United Kingdom.[55]

The Duke's Trustees had made strenuous efforts in 1860 to recover some of Runcorn's trade in iron from Whitehaven, Barrow and Ardrossan which had been lost to Fleetwood and they presented attractive new rates to the Scottish and Whitehaven iron masters by subsidising cargoes of iron landed at Runcorn to be carried by the Bridgewater system to Manchester and Midland foundries. No dock dues were levied on vessels using the docks and basins unless the vessel remained for more than twenty-one days.[56] The new rates and the fact that back cargoes of salt were always available kept Runcorn's iron trade going in spite of Fleetwood's superior geographical position. Pig iron and iron ore from Barrow, Greenock, Glasgow, Irvine and Ardrossan continued to arrive but the trade could not be expanded and it never assumed the importance that it had in the 1840s before the railway network of the north had become extensive. When the carriage of iron by the railways overtook the water borne trade the Trustees renewed their attempts to increase their share of the business but they were unsuccessful and by 1875 the iron trade was a modest proportion of Runcorn's coastal trade.

Some iron ore was delivered directly to Ditton Brook Iron Works which had a wharf at the mouth of the brook and the water was sufficiently deep enough to enable the larger coastal flats and small schooners to land cargoes from Barrow without the necessity of first discharging at Runcorn docks for subsequent transhipment across the river to the works. In 1879 an explosion is said to have destroyed part of the foundry and production ceased with the closure of the works in 1881. The Ditton Brook Iron Works was advertised for sale between February 1881 and October 1883 and the advertisements indicate that the foundry was extensive with forty-two acres, six blast furnaces, four industrial locomotives and enough steam cranes to enable three ships of 150 tons burthen to be discharged simultaneously.[58]

The table gives the statistics for coastal traffic at Runcorn from 1868 to 1872 and the figures show an appreciable rise in the number of vessels using the port during the five years.

	Cleared		Entered	
	Vessels	Tons	Vessels	Tons
1868	1798	123,649	721	44,727
1869	1866	130,860	903	54,764
1870	1986	140,741	833	50,616
1871	2271	153,836	987	61,121
1872	2261	160,653	705	41,796

Coastal Traffic at the Port of Runcorn, 1868, to 1872
Table 7:2

The Irish trade into Runcorn consisted of pyrites from Kingstown, Wicklow, Skibbereen and Arklow with consignments of prop wood from Newry, Waterford and Wicklow. From the beginning of the century cargoes of oats from Drogheda, Newry, Westport and Dundalk had been landed for Runcorn millers. Messrs. Hardy and Wylde's six storey steam mills at Old Quay were a landmark in the district and on the occasion of a fire in 1857 a local account reported that there were "six stones which were at work day and night producing between 500 and 600 tons of oatmeal"[59]. The mills soon resumed production and in the 1870s a number of schooners which were intended for the Irish trade were built at Runcorn for Hardy and Wylde.

Exports to Ireland from Runcorn consisted almost entirely of salt and coal shipments and from 1862 much of the latter was sent through West Bank Dock at Widnes which was completed in that year and which was connected to the Warrington, Widnes and Garston railway.[60]

The table gives the numbers of vessels engaged in trade between various ports in the north-west of England and Ireland for 1872 and it gives some indication of Runcorn's share in the traffic.

	Vessels	Tonnage
Runcorn	873	62,188
Preston	164	10,505
Chester	332	24,624
Workington	313	32,352
Whitehaven	648	65,586
Liverpool	3,910	933,638

Vessels Engaged in Trade Between Various North West Ports
and Ireland in 1872
Table 7:3

The "Annual Statements of the Navigation and Shipping of the United Kingdom" for 1872 include a summary of the coastal trade of the six ports. The figures are given below:

	Entered		Cleared	
	Vessels	Tons	Vessels	Tons
Runcorn	705	41,796	2261	160,653
Preston	497	24,125	294	16,182
Chester	1,485	91,520	1528	97,037
Workington	279	21,616	849	74,704
Whitehaven	762	68,086	2570	231,404
Liverpool	7,139	1,684,401	8182	1,494,934

Coastal Trade at Various North West Ports in 1872[62]
Table 7:4

As stated previously the bulk of sea going traffic at the port of Runcorn throughout the last century consisted of small craft which were engaged in coastwise trade. The year 1872 is typical and of the 945 ships entering the docks, 705 were coasters and 2261 out of 2475 leaving the port in that year were carrying cargoes to places in the United Kingdom.

The table below shows the total movement of shipping both coastwise and foreign for the five years between 1868 and 1872. The figures show a steady rise up until 1872 after which there was a reduction in traffic when serious problems of silting began to effect trade.

	Entered		Cleared	
1868	948	70,655	2071	159,952
1869	1128	79,662	2080	156,111
1870	1213	91,221	2254	171,163
1871	1291	93,667	2659	199,156
1872	945	71,103	2475	189,162

Vessels (Steam and Sail) using the Port of Runcorn to and from Foreign Countries and British Possessions and Coastwise from 1868 to 1872[63]

Table 7:5

Some insight into the variety and volume of the trade through the upper Mersey wharfs in the 1870s can be deduced from the Register of Electors for the Upper Mersey Navigation Commission which was compiled in 1876. In the electoral roll are the names of 179 merchants and shippers who had landed or despatched at least 2000 tons of cargo at Runcorn, Widnes, Weston Point or at Garston Docks in 1875.[64] Most of the bulk cargoes consisted of grain, chemicals, ores, stone, potter's clay, coal, salt and timber. In 1875 there were nineteen timber firms, mostly from Manchester and Salford who between them imported 52,000 tons of timber through the port of Runcorn. Much of the timber was carried via the former Mersey and Irwell Navigation and contemporary photographs of the Old Quay Docks invariably show stacks of sawn timber on the wharfs awaiting transhipment to Manchester. Grain came into the port in some quantity and in 1875 some 54,000 tons were shipped via Runcorn to millers in Warrington, Manchester and Salford and not inconsiderable cargoes were carried to the Runcorn mills of Hardy and Wylde at Old Quay Docks.

By this date the railways were rivals for the carrying of Lancashire's raw cotton but the canals continued to transport considerable quantities and in 1875 some 60,000 tons of cotton bales came via the estuary to be taken by the two waterways to Manchester.[65] These cargoes passed through Runcorn from Liverpool in river craft and only a small proportion of the raw cotton was landed at the town's quays. Consequently the Commissioner's returns list only three Lancashire spinners each of whom took annual cargoes of more than 2000 tons from Runcorn docks in 1875.

West Bank Dock at Widnes was busy with over 175,000 tons of chemical ores and finished products being shipped in 1875. The names of the pioneer alkali manufacturers include Widnes Alkali Company which received and despatched 30,000 tons of cargo, the British Alkali Company's works of Sullivan and Company with 10,000 tons and Holbrook Gaskell, Henry Deacon, J.L. Muspratt and George Pilkington of the Mersey Chemical Works all of whom transhipped material in quantity through the St. Helens Canal at Woodend, Widnes. It is interesting to note that Mr. J. Mathieson, alkali manufacturer of Widnes, owned the largest vessel to be registered at Runcorn in the last century.[66] This was the full rigged ship *Annie Fleming* 911 tons, which was briefly registered at Runcorn from 1869. Because of her large dimensions it is certain that *Annie Fleming* never visited her home port.

By 1875 Golding Davis and J. Vickers who had established factories for the manufacture of chemicals and fertilizers in West Bank were importing their raw materials through West Bank Dock. The largest volume of trade was that carried on behalf of Charles Wigg, soap and alkali manufacturer of Old Quay, Runcorn who shipped 70,000 tons of freight through the Bridgewater, Old Quay and Weston Point Docks. Some Manchester chemical companies used Runcorn quays extensively. They included Peter Spence of Pendleton who carried 7,500 tons by way of the canals, H. Pochin and Company with 4,200 tons and J. Vickers and T. Roberts and Company each transporting in excess of 2000 tons of cargo annually by the Bridgewater system. The copper smelters J. Allen of St. Helens, J. Keates and Company of St. Helens and the Tharsis Sulphur and Copper Company between them imported 25,000 tons of copper ore through Widnes and Garston docks in 1875.

Besides the Ditton Brook Iron Company which used their own wharf at Ditton Brook to unload cargoes of iron ore for the foundry, William Baird and Company, ironmasters of George Street, Glasgow shipped 6,000 tons of pig iron to Runcorn in 1875 some of which was despatched to the foundry of Edward Maybury and Company in Manchester.

In spite of the fact that the channels to the St. Helens Canal at Widnes were persistently difficult there was considerable traffic on every tide. The Llandulas Quarry Company took 25,000 tons of stone on to the waterway and Gossage's soap works used the canal extensively with sailing flats discharging straight into the factory to return to Liverpool with boxes of soap. Substantial quantities of white sand for Pilkington's glass works at St. Helens arrived at West Bank dock from Kings Lynn and the Isle of Wight.

Among the industrialists using upper Mersey wharfs were the dyers and bleachers of Ratcliffe, Bury and Salford who, in 1875 landed some 7,528 tons of goods at Runcorn and Messrs. Sharpe and Galloway, sugar refiners of Manchester, who shipped 2,000 tons of sugar via the local docks. William

Ockleston, leather manufacturer of Runcorn imported over 2000 tons of material annually through the Duke's docks and John Brundrit was delivering his Welsh granite for road making over a wide area of Merseyside.

The largest single item of imported material was still potter's clay and 70,000 tons were landed at Runcorn and Weston Point. The largest shipper was Jonathan Samuder of Stoke whose cargoes for the year totalled 30,300 tons. Potter and Sons of Runcorn, carriers by canal, transported over 10,000 tons of pottery clay in 1875. Roofing slates accounted for much of the cargo tonnage landed with two Manchester companies, Richard Blackstock and Messrs. A.L. Whiting each receiving large consignments through the Bridgewater system. The Manchester firm of Boden and Company had the schooner *William Boden* built for the slate trade at Brundrit and Whiteway's yard in 1869.

Salt remained by far the main export commodity and in 1875 there were seventeen firms from Runcorn, Northwich and Liverpool named as major carriers on the waterways of the region. Total salt exports through Weston Point and Runcorn together with cargoes from the salt fields landed at Widnes wharfs amounted to nearly half a million tons. The largest of the carriers was John Davis of Runcorn whose business accounted for an annual total of 200,000 tons.

Garston had taken much of the coal trade from Widnes Dock but Samuel Stock of Blackleyhurst Colliery at St. Helens continued to despatch his coal through West Bank in his own flats and schooners. The St. Helens Colliery Company, Messrs. R. Williams of Liverpool and Levi Maiden of Stockport also exported coal through Runcorn. Manufactured iron goods were shipped out through Runcorn by Richard Curtis of the Phoenix Works at Manchester and by John Hetherington of the Vulcan Works in Manchester. Marston and Sharpe, hoop iron manufacturers of Manchester, sent their finished goods via the Bridgewater Docks as did the Astbury Company, railway carriage and wagon builders of Openshaw.

By this time Hazlehurst's soap works in Runcorn had developed into a major concern. Thomas Hazlehurst's sons developed the alkali side of the business and during the 1870s the firm did considerable trade in carbonate of soda with the United States.[67] This led to an export trade in soap from 1870 and Hazlehurst's pale, brown and mottled soaps became known world wide. Hazlehurst's relied on the Mersey's channels as the means of transporting their goods to and from Liverpool docks to the same extent as did their rivals, Gossage's of Widnes. Charles Hazlehurst owned a number of sailing vessels and when he died in 1879 his assets included five schooners and two flats.[68]

Because all the Runcorn factories and the early Widnes works were established on canal or riverside sites they relied on water borne carriage and it would be difficult to exaggerate the importance of the Mersey's sailing channels or the part played by the fleets of small craft which supplied industry on both sides of the river and which carried their products to Liverpool to be shipped all over the world.

Notes

1. Mather, F.C., *After the Canal Duke,* Clarendon Press, Oxford, 1970, p.258.

2. Ibid., pp.258-259.

3. *Warrington Guardian,* 22nd October 1853.

4. Ibid.

5. *Warrington Guardian,* 3rd January 1867.

6. Correspondence. P.A. Pemberton, Group Archivist, Pilkington Brothers, St. Helens, 1974.

7. Customs Bills of Entry. Port of Liverpool 1847-18S2.

8. *Warrington Guardian,* 22nd October 18S3.

9. Mather, F.C., op.cit., p.259.

10. *Warrington Guardian,* 25th February 1860.

11. Hadfield, C. and Biddle, G., *Canals of North West England,* Vol. 2, David and Charles, Newton Abbot, 1970, p.l33.

12. *Warrington Guardian,* 24th February 1855.

13. Russell, R., *Lost Canals of England and Wales,* David and Charles, Newton Abbot, 1971, p.210.

14. Hyde, F.E., *Liverpool. The Development of the Port 1700-1970,* David and Charles, Newton Abbot, 1971, p.33.

I5. Brooke of Norton Collection, Brooke v Mathieson 1863, Cheshire C.R.O. D/24/BI.

16. Bagshaw, *History Gazetteer and Directory of the County Palatine of Chester,* 1850, p.577.

17. Slater, *Directory of Cheshire,* 1855, p. l06.

18. Ibid., p. l06.

19. Dore, R.N., *Cheshire,* B.J. Batsford, 1977, p.68.

20. *The Chester Courant,* 2Sth May 1839.

21. Hadfield, C., *The Canal Age,* Pan Books, 1968, pp.126-127.

22. "Diary of Richard Lea. What was Runcorn Like in 1838?", Holy Trinity Church, Runcorn, Centenary Publication, 1938.

23. Evans, H., *Hanes Methodistiaeth Lerpwl,* Cyfol 11, 1932, p.72.

24. Mersey Mission to Seamen (Runcorn Branch) 187S-1921 Local Collection Runcorn Library.

25. Eames, A., *Ships and Seamen of Anglesey,* Anglesey Antiquarian Society, 1973, p.377.

26. Mersey Mission to Seamen (Runcorn Branch) op.cit.

27. *Warrington Guardian* (Supplement), 26th February 1870.

28. Ibid.

29. Mersey Mission to Seamen (Runcorn Branch) op.cit.

30. Correspondence L.M. Robertson, Secretary, Mersey Mission to Seamen, Liverpool 1973.

31. Mersey Mission to Seamen (Runcorn Branch), op.cit.

32. Ibid.

33. *Warrington Guardian*, 17th December 1879.

34. Port of Runcorn. Limits of Ports and Legal Quays, H.M . Customs and Excise, lst January 1862.

35. Mather, F.C., op.cit., p.284.

36. Ibid., p.284.

37. *Warrington Advertiser,* 12th April 1862.

38. Ibid.

39. Wheat, G, *On the Duke's Cut*, Transport Publishing Company, Glossop, 1977, p.29.

40. Morris and Co. Commercial Directory and Gazetteer of Cheshire 1874, p.559.

41. Board of Trade Annual Statement of Trade and Navigation of the U.K. for 1859, p.36; 1860, p.64; 1862, pp.393 and 418; 1868, p.457; 1868-1869 LVIII. For 1871, p.27; 1872, p.318;

42. Customs Bills of Entry of the Port of Liverpool. Central Libraries, Liverpool. 1863.

43. Anderson, J., *Coastwise Sail,* Percival Marshall and Co., 1948, pp. 1 and 57.

44. *Warrington Advertiser,* 12th April 1862.

45. Customs Bills of Entry, Port of Liverpool.

46. Campbell, W.A., *The Chemical Industry,* Longman, London, 1971, pp.75-76.

47. Details of foreign cargoes with their ports of origin and the destination of cargoes despatched to foreign countries have been obtained from Customs Bills of Entry of the Port of Liverpool.

48. Annual Statement of the Navigation and Shipping of the U.K. 1872, p.204.

49. Challoner, W. H. & Furnival, William, "H. E. Falk, and the Salt Chamber of Commerce", *Transactions of the Lancashire and Cheshire Historical Society,* Vol 112, 1961, p.122.

50. Hadfield, C. and Biddle, G., Vol. 2, op.cit., p.360.

51. Mather, F.C., op.cit., p.277.

52. Greville, M.D., "Chronological List of the Railways of Cheshire", *Transactions of the Lancashire and Cheshire Historical Society*, Vol. 106, 1955, p.136.

53. Mather, F.C., op.cit., p.289.

54. Customs Bills of Entry, Port of Liverpool.

55. *Warrington Guardian,* November 22nd 1870.

56. Morris and Co. Commercial Directory and Gazatteer of Cheshire and Stalybridge, 1874, p.559.

57. *Sheffield Daily Telegraph,* 28th February 1881 and *Colliery Guardian,* 19th October 1883.

58. Annual Statement of Navigation and Shipping of the U.K. Board of Trade. For 1868 and 1869, p.498 vol.1869. For 1870, p.482, 1870. For 1871 and 1872, p.ll9 vol.1872.

59. *Warrington Guardian,* 5th September 1857.

60. Hyde, F.E., op.cit., p.133.

61. Annual Statements of the Navigation and Shipping of the U.K. 1872, p.l19. 59.

62. Ibid.

63. Ibid., p.120.

64. Details from the Upper Mersey Navigation Electoral Roll, 1876.

65. Mather, F.C., op.cit., p.353.

66. Lloyds Registers 1869.

67. *The House of Hazlehurst 1816-1916,* Centenary Publication, Lever Brothers, Port Sunlight, 1916.

68. *Warrington Guardian*, 10th May 1879.

8

Trade Fluctuations and the Deteriorating Navigable Channel, 1859-1872

The Bridgewater Trustees' Superintendent of lighthouses, buoys and the lightship was required to submit a detailed monthly report on the state of the navigable channels of the river to the Steam Towage Committee.[1] The surviving reports begin in 1859 when James Foulkes reported that the channels were "remarkably good" and for the next two or three years his reports indicate favourable conditions for navigating sea going vessels to Runcorn.

In addition to the upper Mersey lighthouses at Hale Head, Ince and Garston the Trustees had a light vessel, the *Plutas,* which was stationed off Speke and they marked the channel from Runcorn to Garston with forty-three buoys and ten perches. In the autumn of 1860 *Plutas* was reported to be in a leaky condition and in December she was withdrawn from service to be replaced by a new light vessel, the *Rival.* The lightship had a crew of three and an inventory of her fittings shows that her crew lived an austere existence. Besides the equipment necessary to maintain the vessel and the lantern the value of the few domestic items is listed:[2]

"One form and table" .... £1 - 0 - 0
"Eight blankets" .... £0 - 14 - 0
"Four top coats" .... £2 - 10 - 0
"One frying pan" .... £0 - 1 - 0
"Two kettles" .... £0 - 6 - 0
"Four sauce pans" .... £0 - 4 - 0
and one ton of coal valued at ..... £0 - 10 - 0

The wages for the crew of the lightship in 1860 amounted to thirteen pounds a month and the pay never varied over the years. Eight years later the crew members were still receiving the same pay for their lonely and tiresome job.

Superintendent Foulkes' reports show that the sailing channels were good during the late 1850s but they also indicate considerable activity by the crew of the buoy vessel in plotting the frequently changing deep channel. The continuous migration of the channel demanded constant vigilance on the part of the Superintendent and his observations are a narrative of strenuous effort by the crew of the old paddle boat *Tower* to keep the passage marked. *Tower* was hired by the Trustees at an average monthly rental of £24 but this soared to £60 a month when the boat was needed for long periods during the winter. *Tower* was also used as a supply tender to the lightship.

Mr. Foulkes' monthly reports vividly describe how the scouring action of the tides altered the contours of the river bed, often with bewildering speed.

Channels which were sufficiently wide and deep to permit steamers and their trains of barges to proceed with confidence at night could, in a couple of months, become impassable for craft of any size. The Superintendent noted new ways opening up, carved through the sandbanks by the tidal scour. Sometimes the passage to Liverpool would become much shorter and safer because of a fortunate migration of the channel, but often the reports record the reverse situation when a safe, straight passage became a hazardous route through a twisting channel.

Severe weather hindered traffic on the tideway in December 1860 when Foulkes reported that masses of ice floating down river had severed some of the buoys from their moorings. He wrote that little could be done other than to replace the buoys with smaller, temporary ones until the ice had cleared away and the permanent buoys had been recovered. The buoys had to be resited to cope with the constant shifting of the channel. When the route was difficult the passage could become an obstacle course with shallows, rocks and tide levels all to be taken into consideration by the masters of the sailing flats. The monthly surveys of the state of the upper Mersey which were made by the Bridgewater Superintendent and later by the Upper Mersey Navigation Commissioners' Superintendent of Lights and Buoys, contain numerous references to vessels sunk in the river. When the passage was a tortuous one sandbanks could seize and quickly destroy any vessel which digressed a few yards from the marked channel in rough or foggy weather. At Hale there were dangerous rocks whilst the prominent Hurst Rocks and the Snig Pie Rocks at Runcorn Gap were an area of considerable menace until they were lowered in the 1860s.

Throughout 1860 the river channels remained "remarkably good" but in August 1861 the first signs of anxiety began to appear in Foulkes' comments when he observed:

> The channel is well lighted and buoyed but in some places it has become serpentine and bad to navigate heavy vessels at low tides particularly on the ebb tide.

Again in December he wrote:

> The channel to Old Quay is remarkably good but the channel at Woodend (Widnes) is not so good at this time.

The situation on the northern bank of the river deteriorated rapidly so that by April 1862 the Superintendent reported that the Woodend channel to the St. Helens Canal was completely sanded up. Silting at Weston Point was also becoming a problem and in December 1861 Foulkes observed that:

> Weston Point is sanded up and is very unfavourable for traffic to and from this place. The steamers of the Anderton trade from Liverpool cannot be navigated on low tides.

Foulkes was also becoming concerned about the channel along the Cheshire shore which was becoming shallow and narrow and trouble was developing opposite Hale lighthouse where the channel had become difficult for the navigating of large vessels.

The buoying vessel *Preston*

After the first three months of 1862 conditions at Old Quay suddenly deteriorated with a large sandbank quickly developing in front of the lock gates and extending towards the shipyard at Castle Rock. Foulkes reported a desperate situation in March 1863:

> Church Bank is increasing in height and breadth. The channel on the Cheshire side of the river is becoming very narrow and shallow.

By July the situation was even more serious and Foulkes stated that although the channel was usable it was only kept open by the water from the Old Quay locks. Soon Church Bank had increased so much that the channel from Castle Rock to the Old Quay steam mills was completely sanded up. The inexorable process of silting continued and a year later in July 1865 Foulkes declared that the way into the docks was closed and "All trade to the Old Quay has to be taken across the banks that come dry at low water". To add to Foulkes' problems work began in 1863 on the construction of the railway bridge between Runcorn and Widnes and the bridge works in mid river constituted a new danger to shipping. The superintendent noted that Admiralty lights were erected on the staging of the bridge and that the steel bells each weighing three hundredweights had been installed. They were tolled two hours thirty minutes before high water and for one hour thirty minutes after high water during foggy weather. The great lattice of staging and scaffolding erected during the bridge construction grew until it effectively barred the river's south channel to shipping. There were other hazards to navigation besides the bridge works. On the morning of March 7th 1864, as the brigantine *Kelly* was being towed up river by the steamer *Dagmar* belonging to the Bridgewater Trust, her top mast fouled the telegraph wire which was suspended across the river from Runcorn to Runcorn Gap. The wire was broken and *Kelly* lost her top mast.

Garston lighthouse ceased to function when the railway company acquired the site in July 1865. The lighthouses and the lightship were inspected every month when a careful examination was made of the lamps and their reflectors and also the state of the light vessel's hull. Foulke's report on Ince lighthouse shows a rapid deterioration of both the building and the lamps during the summer of 1864. His brief comments condemned both the lamp and reflectors and the lighthouse itself. He wrote "The lamp and the reflectors and the lighthouse are in bad condition". He repeated his warnings every month until June 1865 when the lighthouse was demolished and a new one was built.

Although even the slightest change in the channel from Old Quay to Garston was carefully noted in the records, the superintendent does not appear to have concerned himself with the stretch of river from Runcorn to Warrington. His comments vary little over the years. He simply repeated every month: "From Bank Quay to Runcorn the channel is narrow, shallow and serpentine".

The difficulties occasioned by the building of the railway bridge eased towards the end of 1867 when Edward Davies, the new superintendent of lights and buoys, was able to report that the mass of scaffolding had been removed from the bridge and the south channel was again open for traffic proceeding either to the Old Quay Docks or further up river. However, Davies recommended that as ships were forced to pass closer to Runcorn Island the dangerous rocks at the east end of the island should be lowered. But the newly opened south channel was still a difficult passage and in January 1868 Davies suggested that small craft from Old Quay Docks would be safer going through the Gut. There was a permanent bridge across the east end of the Gut as well as a boom and as the superintendent's recommendation required major works his idea was not implemented.

It was now that the deepest water lay along the Lancashire shore but this route could not be used because the channel was still closed by the piles and staging of the bridge works. These obstructions were finally cleared away in August 1868 and the sailing channels were at last free from encumbrances. The new bridge itself constituted a major problem for some ships' masters and the schooner *Dreadnought* appears to have been the first casualty. As she was coming up the river in April 1868 she collided with the bridge piers and her foremast was carried away.

By now the winding channel to Liverpool was marked by sixty buoys which were serviced by the crew of the *Preston*, a new screw steamer which replaced the worn out *Tower* in March 1867. The *Preston* was built by Brundrit and Whiteway of Runcorn and she commenced her long life as buoying vessel in April when the Trustees hired her at £2 per tide. Throughout 1867 they paid an average of £12 for the steamer's monthly hire.

A second lightship was required in 1867 when the river's currents exposed dangerous rocks near the navigable channel at Stanlow. The new superintendent suggested that shore lights and a fog bell should be installed near the danger and the Trustees responded promptly by equipping the flat *Lyon* as a light vessel. She was towed to her station off Stanlow and in his next report Mr. Davies observed with satisfaction that "The lightship is a great safeguard near this point". But new problems were being created by the capricious river and in 1868 features of river bed which had not been seen for many years appeared at low tide off Hale Head. This new danger was the area of "Seldom Seen Rocks" which quickly became a formidable barrier of rock jutting up from the bed of the river to a height of four feet.

Wrecks in the channel were a menace to navigation and they were not infrequent occurrences. The schooner *Catherine* which sank across the Garston channel in February 1867 was blown up by the water bailiff and her timbers were quickly pulled out of the way of passing ships. The flat *Gipsy* went down off Hale Head in February 1869 and the wreck greatly impeded traffic and the flat *Margaret* belonging to Messrs. Clare and Sons of Penketh sank near the same spot. Even steamers could be ensnared as in the case of the

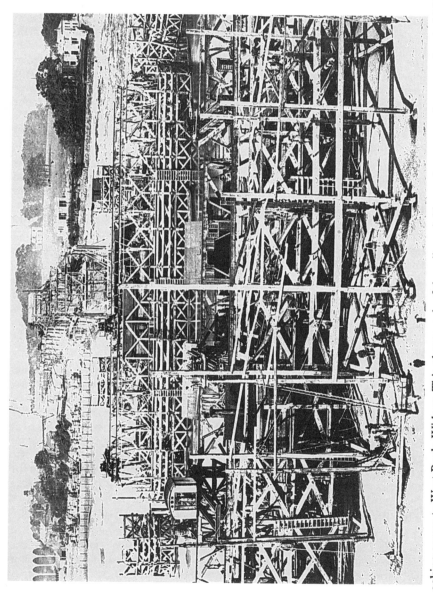

Looking across to West Bank, Widnes. This photograph of the railway bridge under construction was taken in 1865.

tug boat *United States* which ran aground off Otterspool in 1873. Strenuous efforts were made to get her free but these were unsuccessful and the tug turned over to become a total loss. The wreck defied the efforts of the water bailiff and the explosions left the shattered hulk embedded in the sand where she remained for some months a danger to passing shipping. The shifting channels sometimes revealed old casualties as in the case of the flat *Peggy* which sank off Stanlow to vanish below the sand in September 1866. *Peggy* suddenly reappeared four years later when she was washed into the sailing channel to become a nuisance to shipping. As up river traffic increased so did the number of wrecks. The owners were often able to salvage a sunken flat or her cargo between tides but if the vessel could not be refloated quickly she was blown up or pulled apart by the water bailiff. The superintendent was plagued by wrecks in the 1860s and the situation was to worsen in the next ten years when the upper river became very difficult for shipping.

Over the whole area of the upper Mersey in the 1870s the silting up of the sailing channels advanced remorselessly to the dismay of the merchants using the Port of Runcorn. The situation was assessed by Mr. Davies in his report at the end of 1875. His summary concludes:

> The channel from Liverpool to Runcorn is in a bad state for November and it is with great difficulty that the steamers and their trains (of barges) travel at low tides in bad weather.

The great migration of the river's channels continued throughout the 1870s and by 1876 the south channel past Stanlow and Ellesmere Port was fast closing up. The following year it was no longer navigable and in October the buoys were removed to the depot at Runcorn. As the river's deep channel now lay along the Lancashire shore additional aids to navigation were required there, and to help steamers which were towing by night, two shore lights were erected near to the decoy at Hale and the lightship *Rival* was removed from her station off Stanlow and placed on Oglet beach. Even the increased numbers of buoys could endanger vessels and the Upper Mersey Navigation Commission's list of wrecks and casualties records a number of small craft sunk as the result of being holed after colliding with buoys.

Conditions at the approaches to the Bridgewater Docks were becoming impossible for safe navigation by the middle of 1874. At Weston Point on 23rd November 1874 the schooner *Domitila* ran aground. As the tide ebbed she settled and broke her back. She then capsized and sank across the channel. Before *Domitila* could be blown up the flat *Jackal* sustained damage when she collided with the wreck. On the last day of 1874 Davies reported:

> The channel along the piers of the Bridgewater Docks is now banked up which impedes the working of craft to and from those docks very much.

To add to his difficulties the weather was bitterly cold and he recorded:

> A great quantity of ice has accumulated during the late heavy frost consequently we have been labouring for some time under great disadvantages.

Davies presents a vivid picture of the difficulties he was facing in his attempts to keep traffic moving through the unpredictable channels. In his report for 31st March 1875 he wrote:

> This day I noticed 43 flats and 11 coasting vessels aground between the pumping engine and the dock entrance and I also counted 35 vessels aground on the Lancashire side of the river between West Bank Dock and Widnes Dock.

Two months later the superintendent showed how desperate the situation had become:

> The bank along the pier of the Bridgewater Dock very much impedes the working of craft to and from the dock. Fifteen flats are employed in the river turning water to assist in scouring the channel and men are doing all that is possible to improve the approaches to this place.

But in spite of these efforts conditions at Runcorn did not improve and the superintendent recorded yet another astonishing scene. On 30th September he wrote:

> The approaches to Bridgewater Docks do not appear to have improved. On the 10th inst. I counted 73 flats aground outside of the docks, also "Preston" (the buoy boat) two canal tugs and five coasters below the bridge and twenty more flats aground above the bridge.

For the next three months a steamer was employed continuously working a rake in the river bed near the Bridgewater Docks and by February 1876 Davies was able to report that the approaches were "favourable". Fortune favoured him too, for, just when conditions had become impossible a dramatic change came about when suddenly the Duke's Gut began to function satisfactorily. The strong ebb tides were funnelled through the narrow passage and by May 1876 Davies reported that the water had scoured away the mud and sand at the dock approaches and by the end of the year he was able to report that the entrance was "tolerably good". The channel to Old Quay, however remained "very awkward".

The problems caused by silting had been desperate since the early 1870s and it had a serious effect on business. On February 17th 1876 the Bridgewater Company reported a decrease of 90,000 tons of shipping at the Port of Runcorn owing to the large sandbank which prevented vessels from entering the docks and it was reported by another source that:[3]

> A dangerous sandbank, nearly destroying the entrance to Runcorn docks has driven a large amount of trade to Liverpool in 1875.[4]

The unsatisfactory state of the river made necessary the quick turn about of ships in order that they could take advantage of high tides and the local press frequently reported "Quick despatch at the Port of Runcorn". In August 1873 for example, the steamer *Glenamor* of Glasgow discharged 250 tons of pig iron and sailed for Glasgow less than twenty-four hours after her arrival.[5] The unloading of the steamer *Roll Call* in 1879 appears to have been a record for she arrived with 200 tons of white glass sand from France on the morning of Friday, 25th July and sailed with a cargo of 285 tons of salt next day.[6]

The increase in the height of Church Bank from Old Quay to Castle Rock and the difficult channel which persisted during the 1870s at this point certainly resulted in a diminishing of Runcorn's ship building industry. Few vessels of any size were launched in the decade which began in 1870. In 1868 nine sailing ships and two small steamers had been launched from local yards. In the following year fourteen vessels, eleven of them sailing ships with three steamers, totalling 780 tons had been completed. During 1870 four sailing ships having a total tonnage of 484 tons left the slipways. The next twelve months saw the completion of another four vessels but they were small craft and the average displacement was only 61 tons. During the whole of 1872 there were no sea going vessels built at Runcorn.[7] Building recovered in the next twelve months but again the craft were small and the four sailing vessels and the steamer which was launched in 1873 only totalled 354 tons.[8] There was also a falling off in ship repair and within fifteen years the industry would become extinct leaving only a remnant of its expertise to be employed in barge building and repair.

The effects of silting were felt beyond Runcorn. At Warrington by 1860 there was an obvious dwindling of river traffic. The Bridgewater Trustees Superintendent's records show that trade had declined enormously since 1795 when John Aikin had declared "that Warrington could be considered a port town". In 1824 Baines had described the river traffic trading to Bank Quay as "incessant" and in 1832 there were about 100 vessels trading to Warrington but by 1860 there were only ten boats engaged in regular trade.[9] However, the toll free river remained very important to Crosfield's, the Warrington soap manufacturers and when the London and North Western Railway Company proposed in 1860 to build a bridge across the river at Fiddler's Ferry, Crosfields and other Warrington merchants combined with the Warrington Corporation in opposition to the Bill on the grounds that the bridge would impede traffic on the river.[10] The proposed bridge was to have a centre span eighteen feet above high water with a width of seventy-five feet and it was anticipated that the small vessels proceeding to Warrington would be able to lower their masts when necessary.

Crosfields claimed that 5,000 tons of their raw materials came by river from Liverpool docks with another 1,000 tons of limestone coming from North Wales each year. George Crosfield maintained that the river flats could work to his factory on 200 days in the year and if he was forced to use rail transport the additional charges would amount to £900 per year.[11]

Besides Crosfield's Mr. E. Robinson, glass maker of Warrington, used the river for the carriage of his flints and sand and two millers, Littons of Bank Quay and Messrs. Fairclough and Hale, were also operating boats to Warrington. Some cargoes of barley for Greenall's brewery came via the

Mersey and Mr. Tayleur of Bank Quay Foundry was also trading on the river.[12] However, the general pattern of up river traffic beyond Runcorn was one of decline and from 1860 the Bridgewater Trustees Superintendent's reports and later, those of the Upper Mersey Navigation Commission, show almost no expenditure of the lighting and buoying of the upper reaches to Warrington. Indeed the only references to this stretch of the Mersey are occasional accounts concerning a rowing boat and its equipment which occur in the annual inventories of the Upper Mersey Navigation Commissioners' lists of effects.

The Liverpool Town Dues. The Upper Mersey Navigation Commission

In addition to the natural hazards of entry to the Port of Runcorn the local merchants and shippers had long suffered the affliction of the Liverpool Town Dues. Before 1857 the Corporation of Liverpool under a title acquired through the Molyneux family which originated in an ancient royal charter, levied tolls called Town Dues on all goods imported into or exported from the port of Liverpool. The revenue from this toll was used for the general municipal purposes of Liverpool and, as Runcorn was part of the port of Liverpool, the town was obliged to pay according to the volume of trade entering Runcorn's docks. In 1836 Runcorn's share of the Town Dues amounted to £1,172 but as trade increased so did the levy and by 1855 it had risen to £3,182 for the year. The money raised was used by the Corporation of Liverpool for the benefit of Liverpool and little attention was given to the requirements of up river navigation which had provided the revenue. Those ship owners and merchants who were interested in the rapidly growing traffic on the river above Liverpool complained of dues being levied to benefit Liverpool docks (which were their rivals in trade) and they alleged that there was misapplication of funds because the monies raised should have been used within the vicinity of Runcorn. All vessels entering or leaving the Mersey paid dues for the cost of buoying, lighting and maintaining the channels from Liverpool to the sea but no expenditure was allocated from the Town Dues for buoying and lighting the Mersey above Liverpool. The costs of marking the upper river were met by the Trustees of the Duke of Bridgewater who were responsible for the greater part of the traffic on this stretch of the Mersey.

Controversy between the local interests and Liverpool Corporation had sparked for some years and things came to a head in 1857 when the docks at Liverpool and Birkenhead were transferred to a new corporation called the Mersey Docks and Harbour Board which for £1½ million bought out the Liverpool Town Dues. At that date the amount raised annually in Town Dues was about £150,000 and it was estimated that about nineteen twentieths was paid on cargoes carried into and out of the Board's docks and one twentieth or £7,500 per annum on goods landed or loaded at docks higher up the river beyond Liverpool. Besides the Town Dues, other dock charges were levied on vessels and cargoes using the Board's docks but Mersey shipping not using these facilities were exempt from these.

The aggrieved Runcorn and Warrington merchants introduced a Bill into Parliament in 1860 which required the Mersey Docks and Harbour Board to sell them the Town Dues on the up river traffic. In the passage of the Bill through Parliament it was arranged that instead of the charge being ascertained in direct proportion to the original £1½ million it should be fixed at £105,000. With the passing of the Act the money was raised largely by the parties who were engaged in up river traffic and they became Trustees for the purposes of the Act. The first of the Trustees included the chemical manufacturers David Gamble of St. Helens, John Hutchinson of Widnes, John Johnson of Runcorn, George Crosfield of Warrington with Arthur Sinclair of Garston, William Gill of Manchester and Thomas Hostage of Northwich. The dues were continued to be levied on upper Mersey shipping by the Trustees, the revenue at first being used in payment of the interest on the amount borrowed and then in gradual repayment of the debt.

In 1876 a further sum of £12,000 was paid by the Trustees to the Mersey Docks and Harbour Board for the inclusion in the up river area of the new dock which had been constructed by the London and North Western Railway Company at Garston so as to put this dock on the same footing as the docks which already existed at Garston at the passing of the Upper Mersey Dues Act of 1860.

The tonnage of vessels entering the Mersey but not using the docks of the Mersey Docks and Harbour Board in 1861 when the Upper Mersey Dues Trust was formed amounted to 335,481 tons. By 1877 when it had accomplished the objectives for which it was founded, the traffic to places beyond Liverpool totalled 554,029 tons.

Shortly before the Upper Mersey Dues Trust came to an end the Bridgewater Trustees who owned both the Bridgewater Navigation and the Mersey and Irwell undertaking sold these concerns to the newly formed Bridgewater Navigation Company. The purchasers did not care to continue the custom of their predecessors in bearing the expenses of buoying and lighting the upper Mersey. The reasonableness of their objections was conceded by others who were interested in up river shipping and in 1876 they promoted the Upper Mersey Navigation Act under which a Commission was constituted on whom was imposed the duties of lighting and buoying and who were enpowered to levy dues and to borrow money for the purpose of carrying out the duties entrusted to them. The upper Mersey was defined in the Act as being that part of the river between Bank Quay, Warrington and an imaginary line running from Eastham Ferry to Garston.

The Commissioners were appointed to the Commission for periods of three years by the following bodies: the Bridgewater Navigation Company, the Mersey Docks and Harbour Board, the London North Western Railway

Company, the Shropshire Union Canal, the owners of West Bank Dock Widnes, the owners of Ditton Brook Wharf and the Trustees of the River Weaver Navigation. Other members were nominated by the Mayors and Corporations of Manchester, Salford, Warrington and St. Helens, by the Widnes Local Board, the Runcorn Improvement Commissioners and by the South Lancashire and Cheshire Coal Association. Persons elegible to elect the Commissioners were enrolled on a Register of Electors, qualification for which required the person or body to be an exporter or importer of 2,000 tons of goods into or out of any upper Mersey dock in the twelve months prior to application.

The Commissioners were originally empowered to levy dues according to the following criteria. Owners operating a vessel within the upper Mersey limits paid five shillings per annum, those navigating craft in or out coastwise paid a half penny per registered ton and those vessels entering or departing to foreign countries paid one penny per registered ton. Owners could compound the payment of dues and vessels navigating to Ellesmere Port were subject to half dues and owners could compound at half rates.

The Commissioners were also given restricted powers to submit to the Mersey Conservancy Commissioners requests for the removal of rocks in any upper Mersey channel. If the Conservancy agreed the Mersey Dock Board was required to carry out the work to a limit of £500 per year.

Runcorn Ferry and the Coming of the Railway

From its earliest beginnings in 1847 the evolution of the chemical industry in Widnes was spectacular and by 1855 seven alkali works were clustered round the termini of the St. Helens to Runcorn Gap Railway and the St. Helens canal.[14] But although identical products were being manufactured on both sides of the river communications between Widnes and Runcorn remained as primitive as they had been in medieval times. The ancient ferry was still the only crossing available for the vastly increased numbers of passengers who were travelling to employment in the two towns and the ferry service was inefficient and irregular. Conditions became so bad that in December 1853 a meeting was held in Runcorn to discuss the situation in the hope of finding a remedy. The meeting was lively with searing condemnation being directed against the ferrymen and the owners of the ferry. A local newspaper account of the proceedings records the phenomenal growth of the ferry's importance during the previous fifty years.[15]

Runcorn Ferry

Yesterday week a meeting of the rate payers of Runcorn was held in the Town Hall for the purpose of considering the best means to be adopted to obtain a reduction in the charge for Runcorn Ferry. Mr. John Simpson Esq. one of the overseers for Runcorn presided. Mr. Varey said that he had been connected with Runcorn for upwards of forty years and therefore felt himself qualified to speak about the matter. The toll of two pence was unjust and unreasonable he thought — every exertion ought to be made for its reduction. He had been told that the ferry was let for £10 per year, now it was £400 and there was every possibility of its being let again for something like £1000 per annum.

Mr. S. Brown had occasion to speak feelingly on the subject. He thought it would be better if the town took it in hand. Better accommodation ought to be provided like a waiting room on each side of the river and that stated periods should be appointed for the boats to be passing and repassing similar to the railway companies. It was also highly dangerous at times to pass over the ferry as presently managed.

The ferrymen were severely criticised for their alleged inefficiency and avarice and they were condemned for their lack of public spirit.

Some few days ago a letter appeared in one of the papers respecting the conduct of the ferrymen. It had come to their knowledge and they suspected a certain person of being the author and they made very strong threats against him — nay they said if he was drowning in the river and putting out one of their oars would save his life they would not do so.

Mr. Singleton said it would take him from then until five o'clock to tell a thousandth part of the inconvenience and complaints he could make against the ferry. He had been on the banks for hours together and had to pay scores of times for drink for the ferrymen before they would bring him over, besides detaining his cattle on the Lancashire side many a time all night and putting him to great expense to find shelter for them.

A poor man unfortunately lost his wife and, not having the means to inter her, subscription was entered into by several charitable individuals for that purpose. She was brought to Runcorn Gap station. From the railway to the Ferry (less than a quarter of a mile) she was carried on a truck and Mr. Gerrard charged six shillings and eight pence and the ferrymen charged six shillings and eight pence for bringing the corpse across the ferry making it a charge of thirteen shillings and four pence from the railway to Runcorn. (Cries of "shame," "shame").

A committee was formed to memorialize the Marquis of Cholmondeley the lessor of the ferry for a reduction in rates of fare and for the better working of the ferry.

The results of the committee's efforts are not recorded but one month later on 31st January 1854 the Marquis of Cholmondeley granted the lease to Mr. (later Sir) Gilbert Greenall M.P. representing the directors of the St. Helens Railway Company. The terms of the new lease reflected the astonishing growth in the importance of the ferry between the two expanding towns on opposite sides of the river. From a meagre £10 a year at the beginning of the century the rental had increased a hundred fold in fifty years. The twenty-one year lease was granted at a rental of £920 per annum for the first term of seven years, at £1000 for each year of the second term of seven years and at £1,100 per annum for the third. The conditions of the lease required the lessee to repair and maintain the landing place and also to provide three boats and sufficient ferrymen to provide a regular service.[16]

Improvements in the ferry service were not immediately forthcoming and the local newspapers continued to clamour for better conditions. The railway company proposed the use of amphibious craft which would be equipped with wheels in order that they could be hauled across the sandbanks in the middle of the river. This curious innovation does not appear to have been tried and a newspaper comment stated:

> The railway company has been satisfied with ordering boats which would sail or run on wheels as required but the bankrupt workers have twice found the business unprofitable and amphibious machines have never seen the light.[17]

In order to quicken the passage of the ferry boats they had been equipped with sails, but these were reported to be "in a torn and delapidated condition and the sailing of the boats is very much impeded in rough weather and the passage is a matter of considerable hazard"[18].

Throughout the 1850s the Runcorn Improvement Commissioners attempted to get satisfactory accommodation for ferry passengers with suitable jetties on each side of the river. They had no success until a boat capsized in October 1858.[19] The five passengers were rescued but a number of farm animals were drowned and the accident prompted Lord Cholmondeley's agent to try to improve conditions. The *Warrington Guardian* had conducted a bitter attack on Lord Cholmondeley since the railway company had secured the lease of the ferry. In June 1858 the newspaper carried the following leader:

> Lord Cholmondeley by the good fortune having the St. Helens and Garston Railway made in his day now receives the sum of £900 for *allowing* the railway company to take passengers across the river in coble boats which often stick on the sand and mud the Mersey delights in leaving at Runcorn every tide. For a long time efforts have been made to get the ferry accommodation improved — improved is the wrong word for it — for it has never been anything but a hop, step and jump business over wet sand, onto slippery rocks and finally, a scramble with hands and feet. Well efforts have been made to get a jetty and a somewhat straight cut across at all tides. Hitherto, all efforts have been in vain.[20]

The matter of the vast increase in the rental for the ferry and also the attitude of Lord Cholmondeley's officials came under attack. It was claimed that "The august majesty of the leading official has snuffed out the patriotism of every deputation". The newspaper derived little satisfaction when the Marquis at last promised to take action but the writer did give credit to the Runcorn Improvement Commissioners for their dogged persistence:

> Mr. Cawley, like the widow in the Scripture story, by his continued coming has wearied them . . . . The nobleman who receives £900 a year for the *right* of ferrying across the Mersey at Runcorn is bound by law, by common sense and by equity to keep the river and the ferry and the means of crossing in such condition as £900 a year rental will justify.

At Runcorn the long awaited improvements included a waiting room and booking office with a notice board outside which gave the ferry charges and also the departure times of the trains from Runcorn Gap station in Widnes. From Waterloo Road a long narrow stone causeway was built across the mud and rocks to terminate in a flight of steps which led to mooring posts at the low water mark. By 1860 the improvements were complete[21] and George Wylde, the ferry manager advertised that boats left Runcorn Ferry for Widnes, Runcorn Gap six times a day.

Passenger traffic by the ferry soared in the next few years and in his petition against the proposed railway from Aston to Ditton the Marquis of Cholmondeley in 1861 claimed that: "Two hundred thousand foot passengers cross the river in the course of a year besides two or three thousand horses and other cattle"[22]. He stated that the boats used any part of the shores according to the state of the tide and the positions of the constantly shifting sandbanks. Lord Cholmondeley declared that a bridge would be a danger to the ferry boats because the buttresses would cause new sandbanks to form in the centre of the river. The Marquis's opposition to the railway company's plans to build a bridge across the Mersey could not succeed and in 1861 he proposed that the railway company should purchase then abolish the ferry and undertake to make the railway bridge available for pedestrians and that he and his lessee should have the benefit of the tolls from the bridge. Lord Cholmondeley's scheme did not materialise and the ferry remained for a further thirty-six years after the completion of the bridge.

The ferry continued to grow in importance and pressures were such that by 1865 boats were crossing every five minutes to and from Runcorn. In that year the lease on the ferry was assigned to the London and North Western Railway Company whose bridge works were already adding to the difficulties of operating the ferry crossing. A correspondent writing to the *Warrington Guardian* in 1864 outlined the dangers accruing from the construction works:[23]

> The current of the river always rapid past the town is more so now than ever owing to the obstruction of the new bridge works and many vessels have been injured and some sunk on the piles. A small steamer (in addition to the "Secretary" — which from its nominal service is termed "Honorary Secretary") has been provided to tow them through the passage gratuitously and it is undoubtedly fully incumbent on the parties causing the obstruction to assist the ferry boats with their living freight.

The writer went on to declare that it was the duty of the Runcorn Commissioners to watch over the interests of the town and to

> obtain such extra provisions for the security of passengers as will be urgently required during stormy weather, long nights and fogs of winter.

As Lord Cholmondeley had anticipated, the bridge works did cause sandbanks to form in mid stream and these were a nuisance to the ferrymen. The Reverend Joseph Dixon, Methodist minister of Runcorn, recalled that he had "many wonderful adventures in connection with the ferry and the sandbanks when the Runcorn Bridge was erected". Mr. Dixon was often late for services and he observed, "It is very trying to be stuck on a sandbank with the wind blowing strongly up river".[23] Two boats were necessary for the crossing with passengers embarking from the first boat to walk across the sand to the waiting boat to complete the journey. The ancient ferry was by now completely inadequate to cope with demands. After the opening of the Victoria Road Wesleyan chapel in Widnes some three hundred of Mr. Dixon's Runcorn congregation were stranded on the Widnes side of the river until late at night. As the Marquis of Cholmondeley had stated in his petition,

> The passage of foot passengers across the Ferry has greatly increased of late years in consequence of the increase of Alkali and other works on the Widnes side of the river

107

inasmuch as a large number of persons employed in such works reside at Runcorn and cross the river twice a day in going to and returning from their work.[24]

The new railway bridge had a footway and therefore the passenger traffic across the ferry diminished until one boat was sufficeint to cope with it and, just as at the beginning of the century, the service after 1868 became intermittent. The ferry boats were still used to carry farm animals across the river and they were quite unsuitable for this purpose. A letter in the *Widnes Weekly News* condemned the cruel treatment of terrified cows and sheep which were driven on to the boats by men using sticks and dogs.[25]

After purchasing the ferry the railway company "managed the crossing in such a way as to make passengers eager to travel by other means"[26] but the boats continued a spasmodic service long after the railway bridge was opened for rail and foot passengers in 1869. The ferry remained useful for the carriage of light freight between Widnes and Runcorn but fewer passengers used it even though it managed to survive until 1905.

With the opening of the Ethelfleda railway bridge the Bridgewater Docks acquired the vital rail link and the town at last lost its position of isolation. The steam ferry boat service from and to Liverpool continued for some months after the railway was completed and the Bridgewater Trustees steamer *Dagmar* carried passengers between Georges Pier, Liverpool and the Boat House Pier at Old Quay Docks at Runcorn.[27] But the railway soon monopolised passenger carrying and the Liverpool to Runcorn passenger service by river seems to have ended within a year of the completion of the line.

Notes

1. The details of the shipping channels from 1859 have been obtained from the monthly reports of the Superintendents of Lights and Buoys to the Bridgewater Trustees, the Bridgewater Navigation Company and the Upper Mersey Navigation Commission.

2. Bridgewater Trustees. Inventory of lighthouses and lightships (about 1865).

3. *Warrington Guardian,* 19th February 1876.

4. Ward, T., Salt and Its Export from the Mersey, *Proceedings of the Literary and Philosophy Society of Liverpool,* Vol. 30, 1875-6, p.182.

5. *Warrington Guardian,* 20th August 1873.

6. *Warrington Guardian,* 30th July 1879.

7. Annual Statement of Shipping and Navigation of the U.K. 1872, p.269.

8. Ibid., 1873, p.273.

9. Norton, P., *Waterways and Railways to Warrington,* Railway and Canal Historical Society, 1974, p.44.

10. Musson, A.E., *Enterprise in Soap and Chemicals, Joseph Crosfeld and Sons Ltd.,* Manchester University Press, 1965, p.94.

11. Ibid., p.94.

12. Details taken from ownership of vessels. Liverpool Shipping Registers.

13. The account of the history of the Liverpool Town Dues and the establishment of the Upper Mersey Commission is taken from a manuscript prepared by Commander Rossiter, Superintendent to the Commissioners. (Document circa 1932).

14. Smith, W., *A Scientific Survey of Merseyside,* Liverpool University Press, 1953, p.254.

15. *Warrington Guardian,* 17th December 1853.

16. *Warrington Guardian,* 4th February 1854 and Cholmondeley Papers, Cheshire C.R.O.

17. *Warrington Guardian,* 17th June 1858.

18. *Warrington Guardian,* 1st September 1860

19. *Warrington Guardian,* 12.12.1857, 19.6.1858, 6.11.1858, 13.11.1858.

20. *Warrington Guardian,* 19th June 1858.

21. *Warrington Guardian,* 5th September 1860.

22. Petition presented against "A Bill for enabling the LNWR Company to construct railways from Aston to Ditton 1861". Cholmondeley Papers, Cheshire C.R.O.

23. Rev. Joseph Dixon, St. Pauls Wesleyan Church Jubilee Publication, Runcorn 1917.

24. Cholmondeley Papers, Cheshire C.R.O., BRA 984 and DCH/2 92X.

25. *Widnes Weekly News,* 19th October 1878.

26. Porteous, J.D., *Canal Ports,* Academic Press, London, 1977, p.159.

27. *Warrington Guardian,* 13th March 1869.

9
The Schooners

Wrecks and Casualties

It was not until 1876 that a Parliamentary Bill gave powers of government inspection to ensure that all ships were adequately manned. At the same time owners were obliged to mark a vessel's hull showing the waterline at maximum safe loading. Before that date unscrupulous shipowners could send over-insured and over loaded craft to sea in the worst of winter weather.

Throughout the second half of the last century there appeared in the local press with awful frequency items which were simply headed "Loss of Runcorn Schooner". The brief reports often give no account of the drama which accompanied the sinkings for many vessels foundered without survivors or witnesses. It is not possible to compare losses among local vessels with those of similar small ports but there is a suspicion that the proportion of casualties amongst local shipping may have been heavier than that which could be accepted as inevitable.[1] A number of reasons might be advanced to support the belief that Runcorn shipping tended to have more than average losses. For instance all Runcorn vessels were small sailing craft of wooden construction. Cargoes were invariably heavy commodities with flints, iron ore, pig iron, china clay, coal, slates and salt predominating. According to Mr. M.M. Schofield a prominent feature of locally built craft was the wide hatches presumably introduced to allow easier loading and discharging of bulk cargo between a mass of standing rigging. There was another factor which could imperil the safety of the small coasting vessel. This was when the economics of the coastal trade resulted in schooners and flats being undermanned. Rarely did a coastal schooner have more than five crew members and often three men were considered to be sufficient crew for the short voyages to the North Wales slate ports. But the most dangerous practice of all was the tendency to change the rig of river flats into schooners and use them in the coastal trade. River flats had design characteristics eminently suited for navigation in the shallows of the Mersey but even the larger two masted "jigger" flats were not intended for the longer sea voyages. Nevertheless, many flats were to be converted into schooners with disastrous results for the extra canvas made such craft unstable in heavy weather. An example of this unhappy practice can be seen in a newspaper advertisement[2] for 1865:

For Sale

Flat "Rose Ann"

Of Warrington, 60 tons register carrying 120 tons of grain on a light draft of water. It is now lying in Old Quay Dock, Runcorn. Built of English oak and diagonally bound with iron. It is in first-rate condition and well found with sails, ropes and all requisite materials and could easily be made into a coasting schooner. For inventories and further particulars apply to:

John Anderton and Co.,
Castle Rock Yard,
Runcorn.

It is small wonder that the list of Runcorn vessels lost through shipwreck is a long one. *Mary Bollind,* schooner, 99 tons, launched in Frodsham in 1858 was lost off the Norfolk coast two years later.[3] The local newspaper does not give details of her end or of the fate of her crew but the account does record that the vessel was laden with coal and that her owner was insured.

The frequency of shipwreck was appalling. The flat *Bay* was lost with her crew of three off the Cumberland coast on February 1st 1859. *Edith* laden with coal, parted her anchor chain in a gale off Penmaenmawr and was swept on to rocks and sank drowning the master's wife. *Ino* schooner, 75 tons, owned by Brundrit and company, and bound from Penmaenmawr to Dublin with 135 tons of granite foundered in a force nine gale four miles off Beaumaris with the loss of her crew of three on 20th February 1877. *Olive* flat, 58 tons, owner Samuel Stock of Castle Rock wharf, Runcorn was lost off West Hoyle in November 1870. *Alma* was lost with her crew in 1879. *Lymm Gray* schooner, foundered off the mouth of the River Elbe in the same year. *Uncle Tom* flat was wrecked at Llandudno in 1861 and her crew were rescued. The *Ann,* a flat built by Isaac White in Frodsham in 1799 was wrecked on St. Tudwal's Islands on October 18th 1858. Her master cried for divine help at the height of the storm and his ordeal is still remembered by posterity for he became the subject of a folk song which is still sung in Welsh schools to this day. The schooner *Argus* of Runcorn was lost at sea with her crew in November 1866 and in the same storm the Runcorn flat *Mineral* was swamped off New Brighton with no survivors.[4] *Margaret and Elizabeth* of Runcorn laden with china clay was a total wreck on Hoyle Bank in September of the same year. Her crew were rescued by the lifeboat. On September 12th 1867 the local schooner *St. George* was overwhelmed off Llandudno when the storm tore away her tarpaulin hatch covers and the water filled her hold.[5] The sole survivor of the crew clung to the wreck for ten hours before being rescued by the men of the tug boat *Merry Andrew.* He had seen his shipmates become exhausted to be swept off the rigging by the storm. Another Runcorn schooner *Mary Elizabeth* bound for Pwllheli with coal capsized when she was struck by a heavy gust of wind off Holyhead in December 1867.[6] Two of the crew held onto spars and the tug *Speedwell* was sent to their rescue. The sea was rough and the tug master feared that the survivors would be killed if they were dashed against his vessel. Two of his crew volunteered to attempt the rescue by using the tug's small boat and the steamer was positioned to windward to afford them some protection. The manoeuvre was successful and the two exhausted men were hauled with the boat and conveyed safely to the *Speedwell.*

111

In February 1868 the Runcorn schooner *Electric* ladden with salt foundered off the Point of Ayr and three of her five men crew perished. *Amelia Hannah* schooner, was lost with her crew in September and also in 1868[7] *Annie Jane,* schooner of Runcorn bound for Courtown in Ireland from Ardrossan and laden with coal, hoisted distress signals during a storm in the roadstead off Courtown. The lifeboat *Alfred and Ernest* was launched to her assistance but because of the heavy seas the lifeboat could not reach the schooner and it was driven back on to the beach. In the meantime the schooner drifted towards the shore. Then the coastguard succeeded in firing a line to her by rocket and a hawser was pulled across to the ship and made fast. By means of the hawser the lifeboat was pulled across to the ship and at the request of the schooner's master, six of the lifeboat's crew went on board and pumped her dry. As night approached the master of the schooner feared that she would sink in spite of all their efforts and he decided to beach the vessel. Accordingly he ran her ashore and the crew were brought off by means of ropes.[8]

There were very many heroic attempts to rescue the crews of stricken ships but the following excerpt from the *Warrington Guardian* in 1882 appears to be exceptional - perhaps it is the only exception in the history of the lifeboat service.

Wreck of Runcorn Flat. Severe Censure of a Lifeboat Crew

During a heavy gale a few weeks ago the flat "Hecla" of Runcorn laden with iron ore ran ashore at Llandulas, North Wales and two of the crew, named James Williams and Robert Hughes were drowned, the captain alone, saving his life by swimming ashore. There is a lifeboat station in the neighbourhood but although the vessel was seen drifting towards the shore in broad daylight, no assistance was rendered by the crew of the lifeboat to the imperilled seamen and the unfortunate men perished within fifty yards of land.

The coroner, Dr. Evan Pierce, who held the inquest on the bodies, said he wished he had the power to commit the crew of the lifeboat for manslaughter. He characterised them as a "very brave fair weather gang who went out to practice as they called it when the sun shone brightly, but would not come out of their holes when called upon to rescue the lives of their fellow beings in a storm". He considered their conduct unmanly, unworthy, cowardly and careless and it was owing to their failing to render assistance that the lives of the two unfortunate men have been sacrificed.[9]

The jury returned a verdict of "accidentally drowned" but the coroner had used strong words to condemn lifeboat men whose courage has always been beyond question. The loss of the *Hecla* was typical of the losses among small Runcorn craft. She was a Mersey flat engaged in coastal trade for which she was not designed and she was at sea with a heavy cargo in winter weather.

Although most of the casualties occurred among the smaller craft coasting around the shores of Britain some perished a long way from home. The three masted schooner *Janie* which was the largest vessel to be built in Widnes was wrecked off Rio Grande do Sul on the 26th September 1884. The schooner *A.M. Brundrit* was wrecked off Black Island, Labrador in 1885 and *Janet and Margaret,* schooner, at Rio Grande four years later. Runcorn based ships were wrecked with loss of life almost within sight of home. The year 1885 was a dreadful one for local shipping for besides *A.M. Brundrit* lost in that year the schooners *Emily* and *Princess Marie* were both wrecked on the Isle of Man, the *Floriana* went down off Hoyle Bank and *Brodick Castle* sank near Milford Haven.

The shipping registers of the Port of Runcorn contain full particulars of all the vessels that were registered at the town. When ships were scrapped, sold abroad or lost at sea the registration was scored across and the facts were recorded in red ink at the bottom of the page. The uncertainty of life at sea is evident in many of the brief entries in the records and they make sad reading Many Runcorn ships were lost with all hands. *Blanche* schooner, was reported missing off Lundy Island in 1881. The schooner *Lancashire Lass* is recorded as having "talked to" a passing ship off West Hartlepool on December 22nd 1893. She was never seen again. The Swedish built ketch, *Dido* of Runcorn sank off the North Wales coast in 1886. Another local vessel, *Eversfield* 114 tons, sank in Liverpool Bay in January 1888. The *Three Brothers* schooner, built at Northwich in 1867 was wrecked in Bantry Bay in 1884. *William Henry* flat was sunk at Rhyl in 1884 and the flat *Lizzie* was run down by an unidentified schooner off New Brighton in the November of that year. The catalogue of disasters includes *Petrel* sunk in Whitby Bay in 1884. *Rose* yawl, sank off the Welsh coast in 1897 and *Sovereign,* schooner was lost in 1889. The *Harwarden Castle,* schooner of Runcorn, owner William Rowland was lost with all hands in 1892 and the tiny *Lydia,* which was launched in Frodsham in 1847, sank near Mostyn in September 1898. The schooner *Chase* foundered off the French coast in 1895. *Fay,* schooner 103 tons, owner Peter Sinnott of Runcorn and carrying a cargo of tar from Hamburg to Brest, caught fire thirty-five miles SW by W. of Terschelling light and burned to the waterline in May 1888. *Eva* was wrecked near Margate in December 1894 and *Bat* 62 tons, flat, foundered off Rhyl in April 1893. *Widnes* flat, was wrecked at Llandulas in 1888.

Foggy weather was a particular menace to the sailing vessels which were becalmed in busy shipping lanes where they were in danger of being run down by steamers. Collisions in fog were common occurences. The Runcorn schooner *Volunteer* laden with pig iron and bound from Ardrossan to Newry was run down by the steamer *Demetrious* in February 1871 and the schooner's master Thomas Deakin lost his life.[10] The *Cheshire Lass,* schooner, managing owner Samuel Ravenscroft of Runcorn and under the command of Captain Ellis with a load of timber from Dublin to Runcorn was in collision with the Spanish steamer *Calliengo* off the Skerries in April 1881. The schooner sank immediately but her crew managed to get clear and they were rescued by the crew of the steamer.[11] At Runcorn there was a period of acute anxiety as relatives awaited news of the missing seamen. There was great relief when Mr. Ravenscroft received a telegram informing him that all the men were safe. Other local vessels lost through collision were *Little Reaper,* schooner, abandoned in 1891 and the flat *Major* which was run down in 1895. The local schooner *Countess of Carrick* was sunk in collision in May 1901 and only her master, Tom Williams, survived.

Collisions involving two sailing vessels were so common that they were only briefly reported in the newspapers. Two Runcorn schooners collided off New Brighton in 1877, the *Louisa Ann Jane* from Poole to Runcorn and the *Jane Sophia*. The former had her main mast and bulwarks carried away.[12] The schooner *Abstainer* of Runcorn was seriously damaged in a complicated accident in the Mersey in November 1881. She was lying at anchor off Liverpool when the schooner *Thomas Ayling* ran into her. The *Abstainer* suffered yet more damage when she broke from her moorings and fell across the bows of the training ship *Indefatigable*. The *Abstainer* lost her main mast and her bowsprit and her bulwarks were carried away. She had to be towed to Runcorn for repairs.[13] In 1880 the schooner *Faraway* dragged her anchor and she was swept into the path of a large steamer to suffer a broken bowsprit and foremast. Accidents such as these and the repair of lesser injuries kept Runcorn shipyards busy in times when there were few orders for new ships.

Some newspaper accounts record a happy ending. When wooden ships were driven ashore by storms or when they were beached in a leaky condition it did not necessarily mean the end of the ship for they were sturdily constructed and they often survived being pounded ashore. The Runcorn schooner *John,* coal laden from Liverpool to Peel in the Isle of Man went ashore two miles south of the Point of Ayr in January 1885. She was abandoned by her crew but later it was found that she had escaped serious damage and after her cargo had been removed the vessel was refloated.[14]

Wooden ships were notorious for the frequency with which they developed leaks and it was often necessary for them to make hastily for the nearest port when the pumps could not control the water rising in the hold. Reports of leaky Runcorn vessels were frequent. For instance on 4th December 1886 the *Warrington Guardian* reported three Runcorn vessels in difficulties, all of them in a leaky condition. The barquentine *Ethiopian* and the schooner *Unicorn* were forced to put into Holyhead and the schooner *Cohort* had to run for Milford Haven. When experienced seamen were seeking a ship they would make enquiries in the public houses. "Does she take water?" If so, then they were not interested in signing on because pumping at sea in order to prevent salt water from spoiling a cargo of china clay could be a prolonged and arduous task.

Leaking ships were often the result of constant touching or awkward grounding which caused strain on the frames when severe pressures exerted by bulk cargoes tested the seams. The unsatisfactory approaches to Runcorn and also those at many other small creek ports meant that a vessel often had to take ground while awaiting a berth and it was under these circumstances that unsupported craft were liable to strain damage. But, some sailing ships were not water tight because they were in advanced old age. Wooden vessels of fifty or sixty years old were quite common but the Whitehaven-built *Kitty* had the most remarkable life of all for she was 118 years old when she was lost on a run from Dieppe to Runcorn in December 1883[15].

On occasion ship owners certainly contributed towards the loss of a vessel. At Runcorn in 1875 Mr. Septimus Howell of Bagillt, North Wales was prosecuted by the Board of Trade after an official enquiry had exonerated the master of the schooner *Leader* for the loss of the vessel but which had censured the owners for sending the vessel to sea in an unseaworthy condition.[16]

Without doubt incorrect stowage which resulted in the shifting of bulk cargo in heavy weather could cause a ship to founder. A local newspaper hints at this being the reason for the loss of a ship in 1908. The headline was: "Sequel to the wreck of Runcorn laden ship, Brigantine *Crossover,* 192 tons, unexpectedly founders. One survivor". The disappearance of a ship was often the subject of rumours of shifting cargo.

The dangers of life at sea in the last century were dramatically illustrated by an appeal made in 1861 by Canon John Barclay, the vicar of Runcorn, on behalf of the Shipwrecked Mariners' Association.[17] Canon Barclay said that because of the numerous demands made on the Association's funds due to the many shipwrecks in 1860 he had agreed to preach on its behalf. He was so moved by the distress among the dependants of seamen that he approached the clergy of all denominations in Runcorn and asked them to make a simultaneous appeal from their pulpits. He wrote that his suggestion "was cheerfully adopted" and thirty pounds was collected for the charity.

Courage was a prerequisite before embarking on a life at sea in the days of sail and Runcorn seamen were as brave as any afloat. The menace of winter gales must have always been in the minds of the men of the little schooners. Few acts of individual heroism have come down to us but on 29th December 1869 the Prussian brig *Konisberg,* Buenos Aires to Le Havre with hides, was wrecked on the north coast of Cornwall. Her crew were saved by a line which was swum ashore by Thomas Horton of Runcorn.[18]

Conditions and Cargoes

Besides the usual hazards to be encountered at sea, life aboard the small sailing vessel could be made more difficult by the inadequate diet and by insanitary conditions. Sailing vessels when under way were a delight to the eye but conditions aboard were often not so attractive. Many of the schooners were infested with vermin.[19] House bugs thrived in the straw mattrasses and hammocks and they even swarmed in the stuffing of the life belts. One tormented crew took desperate measures to be rid of the nuisance - they scorched the timbers of their quarters with a blow lamp! Hammocks were laid on deck and their seams were pounded with mallets in order to destroy the pests. The rotten timbers of old ships were sometimes seen to bleed as they were being sawn. When one local schooner went into dock at Birkenhead the shipwrights refused to work in her until she had been fumigated. Runcorn vessels were no worse than any others but some of the flats on the Bridgewater

Canal in 1877 were reputed to have been the very worst, being "filthy to a degree, and in many cases utterly unfit for human habitation".[20]

Insanitary ships were the rule rather than the exception during the nineteenth century and in 1888 the Runcorn Improvement Commissioners were concerned about the possibility of cholera infected ships arriving at the docks. They no doubt reflected on the fact that cholera had visited Runcorn once before. From its principal breeding grounds in Asia the disease had advanced across Europe to appear in Britain for the first time in 1831. Cholera came to England through the port of Sunderland and it arrived at Runcorn a year later and it was almost certainly carried by a member of a ship's crew. Sixteen local people died of the disease and many more were infected in Runcorn township in the summer of 1832. The emergency caused the establishment of the Runcorn Board of Health and when the disease was identified public subscription was raised in order to fit out a hospital which was granted to the Board rent free by the Bridgewater Trustees. Local authorities were always anxious about the possibility of further cholera epidemics for, in another outbreak of the disease in 1853, twenty thousand people in Britain died. The ideal conditions for the spread of cholera are overcrowding, dirt, dampness, the lack of efficient drainage and an unwholesome water supply. Runcorn had all these things in plenty in 1832 and conditions in parts of the town had not greatly improved by 1888 when the authorities considered again the precautions to be taken in case of another outbreak. The Improvement Commissioners were disturbed by the absence of a quarantine station for there was no suitable deep water mooring place near the port where infected ships could be isolated. They resolved to approach the Port of Liverpool Sanitary Authority requesting them to carry out the supervision of the cholera regulations by inspecting any suspect vessels bound for Runcorn.[21] After the visitations of cholera in 1832 a quarantine station had been established opposite Garston "where vessels lie that are put under quarantine regulations and where old men-of-war are moored that are employed in that service". The Sloyne anchorage off Tranmere was again suggested as a possible mooring place for ships found to have disease on board. Fortunately the precautions were never applied as Runcorn was spared a second cholera visitation.

The food on board a coasting schooner could be uninteresting to say the least.[22] After the fresh provisions had been consumed at the beginning of a long voyage the diet became monotonous with porridge and salt-fish or bacon and salt beef or "junk" and potatoes and butter beans being a typical main meal. The pickled beef was kept in salt water in a barrel cheerfully called "the harness cask". Seamen often acquired a fondness for junk and those who had retired from the sea would sometimes meet Runcorn vessels in harbour in Cornwall or Devon and trade a dozen eggs or tobacco for a pound or two of salt beef. Hard ship's biscuits, corned beef and cheese formed principal items of ship's fare with onions and cabbage to provide some variety. Bread, butter

116

and jam became a memory if the voyage was protracted. The expertise of the cook was frequently challenged. He was usually the youngest member of the crew and he had a thankless task for his £3 a month wage.[23]

If a vessel was destined to sail to foreign ports her master could obtain rum through the customs authorities at ten shillings a gallon. It was usually reduced to grog by adding an equal volume of water and it was issued sparingly by the master to a single tot on winter's nights. Customs concessions allowed crew members a pound of tobacco for about two shillings if the vessel was leaving British waters. Attempts to avoid paying duty on tobacco and spirits were not unknown. In 1889 for instance the master of the barquentine *Jehu* failed to convince the Runcorn magistrates that the five pounds of cigars and tobacco found hidden under his ship's poop deck were for his own use and he was given the option of paying treble duty or of going to prison for a month.[24]

It was,usual for the master of a schooner to take one third of the profits made by the vessel he commanded and the owner or owners took the remainder. In the last decade of the nineteenth century the mate would earn about £4 a month when at sea and the seamen about two pounds fifteen shillings a month. The pay was poor but food was plentiful if plain. The crew was not paid until the voyage was ended and all the cargo had been discharged. If a vessel was storm bound in harbour it was not usual for the master to make an advance payment of wages but occasionally he would let members of the crew have a quarter of a pound of tobacco the cost of which he would deduct from their wages. Some schooners were often multi-national in that masters recruited crew members from many European ports. The mate aboard the Runcorn vessel *Fox* in 1883 was from Gothenburg and two of the seamen came from Hamburg and from Holland.

Disputes over wages were not unknown. Two cases were considered in the Runcorn police court on 2nd June 1868.[25] In one a ship's captain refused to pay a seaman his full wage of two pounds four shillings for his forty days at sea. The magistrates ordered the captain to pay the full wage and also costs amounting to twelve shillings and six pence. The second case concerned Frederick Vince, the master of the schooner *Republican* who withheld eleven shillings of a seaman's wage because the man had left the vessel before she was unloaded. The court pointed out that the man had signed articles and therefore he should not have left the vessel. Nevertheless the captain was ordered to pay the man two shillings but the complainant had to pay six shillings in costs.

Sailing ship voyages could be made frustrating by persistent head winds. On some occasions a passage which under usual weather conditions would last a week could be extended into months by adverse weather. The voyage of the schooner *Florence* was an example of a prolonged passage. After being released by her tug at the Sloyne anchorage she was forced to remain in the Mersey estuary for another week because of foul weather and when she did eventually make the open sea *Florence* was beaten back by a storm. Eventually she reached Holyhead where she was storm bound for weeks. When the gales had abated *Florence* sailed south in the company of a great fleet of sailing vessels which had been held in harbour but half way across Caernarvon Bay the schooner was lashed by another storm and she was forced to return to Holyhead where she collided with another ship which had dragged her anchor and which carried away *Florence's* bowsprit. A new bowsprit was fitted and *Florence* reached her destination in Cornwall after a voyage which had lasted twenty-three and a half weeks. Such delayed voyages were common in the twentieth century as in the case of *Mary Watkinson* which met contrary winds to take one hundred and forty two days to sail from Runcorn to Padstow.

Even getting out of the Mersey estuary could be an exasperating experience. The *Warrington Guardian* for July 9th 1864 reported many local vessels crowded in the river waiting for favourable winds:

Runcorn Laden Vessels Windbound at Liverpool

> In consequence of the recent bad weather and the quarter from which the wind has, for the greater part of three weeks has been blowing, there are upwards of 300 coasting and other laden vessels, principally from Runcorn, windbound in the Sloyne at Liverpool. Some of the vessels have been detained there for four weeks and the river from the powder magazines to Tranmere Ferry slip presents a scene seldom surpassed there, even in the worst parts of the winter months.

The uncertainty of a sailing ship's date of arrival contrasted with the voyages of the steam coasters which ran to a timetable and which could be relied upon to arrive at a destination on a specific date. Yet Runcorn was to remain a sailing ship port even into the 1930s. Without doubt the inevitable change to steam among local owners was delayed because of the free towage in the Mersey estuary provided first by the Duke of Bridgewater's Trustees and by the Mersey and Irwell Company and later by the Bridgewater Navigation Company and at the end of the century, by the Manchester Ship Canal Company. The towing service was only provided from the Runcorn docks to the Sloyne and vice versa. But outgoing vessels often could not take advantage of the tow if they met head winds when they were released and they were forced to remain in the river until the wind changed. However a bribe of a couple of pounds was usually enough to persuade the tug master to go at full speed for a few more miles so as to release the schooner in open water and fair winds off New Brighton.[26]

In the 1880s and 1890s the little schooners went far afield carrying salt to Newfoundland and returning to Europe with cargoes of salt-fish to the Mediterranean countries where the fish was considered a delicacy. Runcorn vessels were to be found discharging salt-fish at Genoa, Lisbon, Naples, Gibraltar and in numerous small ports in Greece and Turkey. A ship's master would often commission an Italian artist for a few pounds to make a painting of his ship and there are still to be seen in Runcorn homes, fanciful paintings of schooners flying over the waves at break neck speed.

A 'Duker' river tug tows a schooner to the Bridgewater Docks from Weston Mersey Lock in 1900.

The first of the 'Duker' tugs, the *Earl of Ellesmere* which was built for the Bridgewater Trustees in 1857.

One or two of the larger vessels were known locally as *Rio Granders* because they brought cargoes of hides, animal bones and horns from Rio Grande do Sul in Brazil. After a voyage through tropical waters lasting some weeks such cargoes were decidedly unpleasant and when *Dashwood, Ezel, Bertha* and *Orkney* unloaded bones at the Bridgewater Docks the smell was distinctly evident in the town centre more than a mile away. Below decks the carrion reek of a Rio Grander was all pervading and her crew needed to have strong stomachs to suffer the long passage from South America.

Most schooner voyages were not to distant and romantic places. Typical passages would be from Runcorn to Plymouth with coal, then from Plymouth to Shotton steel works with moulding sand; from Shotton to Belfast with steel and Ruabon tiles and chimney pots and then back to Shotton with scrap from the Belfast shipyards. The coasting schooners carried cargoes of all descriptions such as firewood, fertilizer, potatoes, railway lines, road setts, alabaster, box wood, ochre, lead ore and limestone.

Often a schooner captain would be unlucky in that he was unable to find a return cargo. He would require ballast material for the voyage to Runcorn and river sand was ideal for that purpose. It was a saleable commodity - provided that the schooner's own crew were prepared to load it into the builder's merchant's carts on arrival at its destination. The meagre payment for fifty tons of sand hardly justified the efforts expended in loading and unloading but they were penny pinching times and the economics of the sailing ship often resulted in unscrupulous masters and owners limiting the number of crew members and also cutting the ship's provisions in order to reduce costs.[27]

The visiting schooners were built and registered at scores of ports great and small all round the coasts of Britain. They came to Runcorn and Weston Point from Appledore, Bridgewater, Brixham, Lynmouth, Padstow, Caernarvon, Bristol, Barrow, Glasgow and Liverpool and practically all the vessels were engaged in the slate, coal, salt or china trades.

Sometimes schooners were rerigged to become ketches and a number of two masted vessels acquired another mast. Some had two sets of sails white for summer and tan coloured sails for winter voyages. The traditional livery was a black hull with the metal work of winches, pumps and the bollards painted a dark green colour. Masts and spars were usually cream or light brown in colour. The figureheads were very handsome. They were gilded and brightly painted each presenting a striking feature which instantly identified a vessel. It was alleged that more than one master "thought more of his ship's figurehead than he did of his wife". Most figureheads were female but there were mythical sea creatures, Neptunes, mermaids and dolphins. *Gauntlet* had by way of a figurehead, a mailed fist, *Heir Apparent* had a carving of a boy - the future king Edward VII. In a small maritime museum in Stanley in the Falkland Islands there is a ship's figurehead which was fashioned in a Runcorn shipyard 125 years ago. The carving, blackened and smoothed by a century of gales is the only fragment left of the tiny full-rigged *Dennis Brundrit* which was wrecked in 1892. The ship remained wedged on rocks on the inaccessible Centre Island until she was swept away in a storm in 1942. The figurehead was recovered and it can still be recognised as that of a mid-Victorian gentleman dressed in a frock coat - Dennis Brundrit, J.P.[28]

The names of the schooners make interesting reading. First there were the names of the owners and those of their wives and children. Mary was most popular and among the vessels to be found in Runcorn and Weston Point docks in this century were *Mary Watkinson, Mary Ashburner, Mary Rowlands, Mary Seymour, Emily Mary, Mary Ann* and *Rhoda Mary*. Other family names included *Janet Worthington, Emily Warbrick, Margaret Hobley, Fanny Crossfield, William Ashburner, M.B. Mitchell, J. and M. Garratt* and *J.H. Barrow*. There were simple homely names such as *Mildred, Fanny, Lily, Betsy, Ada, Doris, Ethel, Nina, Bessie, Lottie, Dora, Eliza* and *Gerda*. Then there were *Hetty, Florence, Nellie May, Susie May, Katie* and *Kate*. There were dignified, aristocratic ships with *Countess of Carrick, Sir Hubert Maxwell* and *Lady Neave*. Some schooners built at Runcorn in the first half of the last century had royal titles, *Heir Apparent, Royal Adelaide, British Queen, Princess Royal, Emperor* and *Empress*. The schooners were maids of all work and *Saxon Maid, Liffey Maid, Daisy Maid, Island Maid* and *Gipsy Maid* arrived at Runcorn together with *John Milton, Tom Roper, David Owen, Richard Fisher, Arthur Wyat* and *John Clarke*. Some names suggested the quiet rural creek ports frequented by the schooners. There was *Harvest Home, Harvest King, Harvest Queen, Little Reaper* and *Gleaner*. Other visitors included *Rareplant, Royalist, Spark, Faithful, Blue Grit, Welcome, Orion, Baltic, Forest Deer, Isallt, Happy Harry, J.T. and S., Volant* and *Invermore*. The schooners had delightful names *Snowflake, Sunbeam, Woodbine, Harmony, Flower Girl, Fairy Flower, Topaz, Guiding Star, Pearl, Irish Minstrel, Wanderer*. Some names were duplicated and there were half a dozen vessels called *Guiding Star* and *Pearl* at sea at any one time. One or two names suggested speed with *Electric, Velocity, Dart, Flying Foam, Ariel* and *Speed*. The visiting craft included *Star, Evening Star, North Star* and *Bright Star*. There were unusual names too, *Touch Not, Copious, Minga, New Parliament, Hark Away* and *Clown*. From the 1860s there were many foreign vessels to be seen tied up alongside the well known ships and the record of shipping movements shows *La Naiade, Napoleon, Athalaska, Konigsberg, Augustus Zuenaker, Guillaume Tell, Viscata, Maria Sinnigs* and very many others as being regular visitors to the local docks. The list of the names of the sailing ships is legion and it is a matter of regret that space does not allow a more comprehensive consideration.

The Owners

The vast majority of the sailing ships were held by groups of local shareholders; very few were in the possession of a single owner. Every vessel had sixty-four shares as required by law. It is not known why the number of

Sailing flats and schooners in West Bank Dock, Widnes, in 1904.

Bridgewater Docks showing the china clay sheds and the pottery crate
warehouse at the beginning of the century.

A three masted barque at the Bridgewater docks at the beginning of the
century.

sixty-four shares was adopted in 1823 but Maude and Pollock in their *Law and Merchant Shipping* of 1881 put forward a rather obscure explanation: "It seems to have been selected on the supposition that the binary system of halving the ship and each of the resulting shares until the whole is reduced to sixty-four parts is practically convenient. But this does not explain why the sub-division stopped at sixty-four". In 1854 the Merchant Shipping Act settled the sixty-fourth as the invariable unit of ownership of British ships and this is still the case today.

The schooners were owned by local groups which included inn-keepers, clergymen, grocers, quarrymen, farmers and widows. Some possessed a couple of shares, others ten, twenty or more and it was usual to find that the ship's master was part owner of the vessel. During the life of a schooner the shares would change hands many times and every transaction would be recorded in the shipping register. Even the smallest sailing vessel had the details of ownership and subsequent changes noted in full.

The following entry of 1882 shows the financial investment of a group of Runcorn men in the schooner *Chase* 107 tons.[30]

Thomas Carter Cooper	Book keeper	4
Richard Shaw	Master mariner	19
George Parkinson of Kingsley	Farmer	19
Jonathan Horsefield	Coal dealer	4
James Littler	Clerk	8
John Swainson Davies	Carpenter	6
Michael Nixon	Stone foreman	4
		64

Many local men of quite modest means were prepared to invest in a number of ships. Thomas Carter Cooper, the book keeper who had four shares in *Chase* also had 56 shares in the schooner *Fox.* Jonathan Horsefield, coal dealer and his brother George, who was the licensee of the *Anchor Inn,* shared the remaining eight shares in the *Fox.* Jonathan Horsefield also had thirteen shares in the schooner *Eclipse.* The owners of the great fleets of flats and schooners were thrifty tradesmen, shop keepers, farmers and clerks. They provided the capital from their hard earned wages and sometimes they lost their investments. One shareholder in the schooner *A.M. Brundrit* was dismayed to learn that the vessel was not insured for deep water voyages when she was lost on the coast of Labrador in 1885. Her insurance cover was limited to voyages in the coastal trade only. As John Brundrit was the managing owner with the majority shareholding in the vessel he was sued by the aggrieved shareholder. The jury found for the plaintiff who was awarded £125.[31]

Free Towage and its Effect on Commerce

The steam tug boat was largely responsible for the successful development of the port of Runcorn. From the 1830s they had towed ships and trains of barges to the docks and by 1855 the first generation of Bridgewater steamers were becoming troublesome. The boats which the Trustees had inherited from the Mersey and Irwell Company were quite obsolete and in 1857 the *Pilot* and the *Hercules* were broken up to provide fencing for the company's estates. The Trustees spent perhaps £15,000 on repairs to the remaining vessels and in the purchase of a new steamer, the *Earl of Ellesmere*. The *Rival* was fitted with a new engine and "her drunken master who was, from some cause or other knocking the boat to pieces" received a warning to be more careful in the future.[32]

The *Earl of Ellesmere* was the first of a fleet of highly efficient paddle steamers. She was acquired by the Bridgewater Trustees in 1857 and she was followed by *Brackley* (1859), *Dagmar* (1863) and *St. Winifred* (1870).[33] The new steamers were to become known as "Dukers" or "Dukies" and they were unique in that they were double ended with bows fore and aft with a rudder at each end. They could lock one rudder to steam with equal efficiency forwards or backwards and thus they were ideal for operating in the difficult river channels. The "Duker" tugs were much appreciated by the barge crews who preferred to be towed by paddle boats rather than by the later screw tug boats. When the paddle tugs had sixteen or twenty barges in tow in two lines astern the wash from the paddles kept the two lines of barges separated from each other and so made easy the work of the barge men. They could attend to other duties and even relax. The later screw tug boats, on the other hand, did not create this convenient wash and it needed the utmost vigilance by the barge crews to ensure that the two columns of barges were kept a safe distance apart.

Even during the sooty Victorian age the river steamers were notorious for their smoke emission and in 1875 the Directors of the Bridgewater Navigation Company instructed their engineers that they were not to make unnecessary smoke. Each fireman and engineer on the tugs received a bonus of a shilling a month as an incentive to avoid smoke. In a case of excessive smoke the bonus was stopped for the month in which the offence occurred. For a second offence both the engineer and his fireman would be fined two shillings and sixpence. The Company regarded smoke pollution to be a serious nuisance and the directors warned that a third offence would result in the dismissal or suspension of the men responsible.[34] Without doubt the fire risk involved in towing wooden vessels with tarred rigging was an added consideration especially when the docks were full of wooden schooners and sailing flats.

The steamers consumed fuel in some quantity. The average rate of consumption in the case *Brackley, Dagmar, St. Winifred* and the *Earl of Ellesmere* was three tons of coal per tide. The later, more powerful screw tugs were even more expensive. At the turn of the century the *Bridgewater* devoured an average of four tons of coal per tide.[35]

There were unpredictable hazards to be encountered aboard the tug boats as illustrated by a local newspaper report in 1866:

Melancholy Death of a Man at Runcorn[36]

On Saturday last John Billington, second engineer of the steam tug "Iron King" was caught by part of the engine (it is said a side lever) and received injuries which caused immediate death.

The tug at the time was lying alongside the "Robert Seddon", outward bound, and the action of the tide on the paddle wheels caused the engine unexpectedly to move. The body of the unfortunate was landed at Princess landing stage and conveyed to the dead house.

Some irresponsible tug masters were prepared to take fool hardy risks to ensure that they could make the best use of tides and as late as 1875 the Bridgewater Navigation Company found it necessary to warn tug boat engineers that they

must not carry more than eighty pounds of pressure on the boiler, and should see that the safety valve blows off at that pressure. Any engineer guilty of pressing the boiler beyond the limited pressure of eighty pounds by fastening down the safety valve, or by any unlawful means whatever, will be liable to instant dismissal.[37]

It was during the 1850s that the first narrow beam tug boat appeared on the Bridgewater system. A correspondent wrote to a Warrington newspaper in July 1859 describing the work of the *Result*, a small steamer which operated on the canal from Runcorn to Preston Brook.[38] The *Result* was fifty feet long with a beam of ten feet and a draught of four feet. She was fitted with a high pressure engine of 16 horse power and she could haul trains of up to five barges along the canal at a speed of just less than three miles an hour. The little tug was also used on the Mersey between Runcorn and Weston Point and Liverpool and she often towed seven loaded salt flats which contained a total of 800 tons covering the distance from Weston Point to Liverpool in just under three hours.

The introduction of tug boats on to the inland waterways meant that the canals had to be strengthened. Because the banks could be undermined by the wash from the steam boats and their barges they needed to be protected with retaining walls and the Runcorn and Weston sandstone quarries supplied much of the stone which was used in the work of reinforcement.

In 1876 the first of a new class of twenty-six miniature narrow-beam tugs began to operate on the Bridgewater Canal. These were named after the towns and villages which were situated on the inland waterways of the region and they were each capable of towing four loaded barges to save up to half the previous cost of towing by horses. The saving thus made was not passed on to the users of the canal by way of reduced charges but it was used by the Bridgewater Navigation Company to finance the walling of the canal banks, a task which was to last until 1890.[39]

The red sandstone of the Runcorn and Weston quarries was used over a wide area of the region. As early as 1734 it had been despatched to Grappenhall where it was used for paving - the stone being transported up the Mersey to be unloaded at Wilderspool. According to Bagshaw's Directory of Cheshire for 1850 as many as 700 workmen were employed in the Weston quarry of Mr. Tomlinson alone and a footnote in the abstract for the 1831 census records "The quarries at Runcorn which afford stone for the docks and other public works at Liverpool have caused a great increase in population". The stone appears to have been taken much further afield than Liverpool but it is difficult to find firm evidence to support the claim that dressed stone was exported to New York and San Francisco although the Runcorn Official Handbook which was published in the 1930s asserts that this was so. However it does appear that quarry waste was used to ballast Liverpool sailing ships when they left for the cotton ports in the southern states of the United States. The late Mr. Harry Sandbach, ship's engineer of Runcorn, possessed a photograph of a rubble breakwater of red stone which was built to protect the sea wall at Galveston, Texas, from hurricane damage. Mr. Sandbach visited Galveston and he maintained the irregular stones of the breakwater were from Runcorn and Weston quarries and they had been jettisoned when ships discharged their ballast at Galveston in the last century. Very large blocks of Runcorn stone were transported over some distance in the last century. The four great columns at Tabley House are each more than twenty-three feet in height and each is fashioned from a single block of local stone.

The dressed stone required for the walling of the canals and for dock construction in Liverpool was delivered from the Weston quarries by means of tramways down the steep hillside to the stone dock on the Weston Canal at Weston Point. There were extensive quarries at Mill Brow in Runcorn and here the stone was conveyed by means of a tramway which ran down Sutton Street and across Heath Road to the Bridgewater Company's stone wharf on the canal at Runcorn Big Pool.[40]

When the experimental tug *Result* was being tried on the canal a number of steam vessels were being constructed in local yards. These were either tugs or "steam flats", none of which was intended for service beyond the Mersey or Weaver rivers and all were shallow draught vessels of less than 110 tons displacement. After the completion of the paddle steamer *Duke* in 1839 the Runcorn shipyards were occupied with the building and repair of sailing vessels and it was to be nearly twenty-five years before the launch of the next paddle-steamer, the 107 ton *Alice*, which was built in 1864 for the Bridgewater Trustees. *Alice* was a "composite" vessel in that although of wooden construction, she had iron frames. She was fitted with a 60 horse power engine and she may have been the last of the locally built paddle steamers for although another five steamers were to be launched at Runcorn they were all screw driven. These were *Preston* 1867, *Speculator* 1869, *Traffic* 1873, *John* 1875 and *Reginald* 1881. With the exception of *John* all were wooden craft. *Traffic* was designed as a steam lighter for the White Star Line at Liverpool and she was employed to lighten vessels arriving at Liverpool with heavy cargoes during neap tides. *Traffic* and *John* were built by Philip Speakman who took over the Albion and Castlerock shipyards in 1869. The small steamer *Reginald* which was built by Brundrit's in 1881 was sold a few years later to J. Jorgensen of Bergen, Norway and her name was changed to *Bremnaes*. The flat *Percy* also built by Brundrit's was converted into a steamer in 1887. Little steamers were also constructed at Sankey Bridges. These were *Sankey* 1872 and *Harold*, 1875 and among the few craft to be built at Widnes there was one steamer, the 74 ton *Hettie* which was launched by William Jamieson in 1879 and which lasted until 1949.

In an attempt to speed trade on the river Weaver small screw steamers were built at Northwich in the 1860s. The narrow Weaver and the Weaver canal were not easy waterways for the navigation of sailing vessels and it was hoped that steam flats would hasten traffic to and from the Cheshire saltfield. The first of the Northwich steamers was the iron screw vessel *Ariel*[41] of 1864 which was capable of carrying 200 tons of salt and which could, at the same time, tow three loaded flats. *Ariel* was followed by two wooden screw vessels *Iris* of 1866 and *Peerless* of 1867.[42] The steamers presented problems when they were launched in the shallow river and *Ariel* suffered "bruises and scratches" as she took to the water.

As the Northwich yards could not compete with the major companies which were engaged in building iron steamers they limited their ambitions to the building of small wooden vessels. But further down the Weaver shipbuilding at Frodsham was in decline. In 1856 there was a sale of shipbuilding timber and tools at Frodsham Bridge[43] and four years later, Edward Jones, the last shipbuilder, advertised that he was "declining ship building" and he offered for sale, oak trees, ash and deal planks, steam tank and boiler, lathes, drilling machines, a crane and the smithy bellows.[44] With the launch of the 40 ton flat *Fanny* in 1862 shipbuilding at Frodsham came to an end.

On the Mersey too, the building of small wooden ships was soon to end. After the closure of the Warrington Bank Quay yard in the 1850s very few iron vessels were built locally and composite craft made of wood but with iron frames were rare. When Samuel Mason died in 1857 his Belvedere yard and its equipment were advertised for sale[45] and a partnership of John Mason and George Craggs operated the yard until December 1859.[46] A new partnership of Blundell and Mason lasted until about 1879 when the yard closed. By 1880 the Brundrit Company was the only yard still building sea going craft and by then the launching channel had improved sufficiently to permit vessels of about 160 tons to take to the water.

One of the last vessels to be built by Brundrit's was the Mersey Docks and Harbour Board's "Upper Mersey" lightship *Mars* which was launched in 1886. She was an iron vessel and she was stationed off Otterspool until the

Upper Mersey Station was abolished. *Mars* was then converted into a barge and saw much useful employment until she was scrapped in 1927.

The Launchings

Although few craft were built at Runcorn between 1869 and 1875 the subsequent improvement of the river did permit the local yards to build more and larger vessels during the last years of their existence and every launch was a time for celebration. The local newspaper accounts often include a full report of the launching ceremony. Sometimes ships were launched broadside into the river and this method caused a considerable wave and it was more spectacular than an orthodox launch. The spectators waited for the mystic command "Knock down dagger!" and as the ship moved towards the water they prepared to make a hasty retreat as the return wave surged ashore. At the sideways launch of the coaster *Widders* at Brundrit and Whiteways shipyard in July 1858 the crowd scattered and the only casualty was the dog from the Royal Hotel which escaped with a thorough soaking. After the launch the newspaper report noted that "The workmen proved the liberality of their masters at Mr. Brewer's and Mr. Thomas James'" (public houses).[48] The launchings attracted large crowds and there was at least one serious accident when in June 1882 young Michael Hushin of King Street received serious injuries when large balks of timber fell on him.

It was the tradition for the builders to provide a dinner for their workmen and a typical Runcorn launch is described in a local newspaper of 3rd April 1858 when Mr. James Raynes of Messrs. Raynes, Upton and Company of Liverpool christened the sloop *James* in Anderton's yard. The report states:

> The "James" having been previously rigged and provisioned proceeded at once to sea. The workmen to the number of upwards of a hundred afterwards proceeded to the Royal Hotel where they sat down to an excellent dinner provided by the hostess, Mrs. Huxley. The cloth having been drawn, Mr. James Anderton took the chair. The usual loyal toasts were given, after which, "Success to the James" was given and responded to by Mr. James Anderton. The health of the owners was proposed by Mr. Rigby. Mr. Davies of Widnes responded. Numerous other toasts were given and a pleasant afternoon was passed the company retiring about six o'clock.[49]

Sometimes the celebration could be a more solemn affair as that when the carpenters in the employment of Philip Speakman were given a treat on 6th December 1862 to celebrate the launch of three narrow boats. The account of the occasion reported that the proceedings commenced with prayers and a hymn. The hymn was "Come let us join our cheerful songs with angels round the throne". At the end of the evening the Doxology was sung and the minister terminated the celebration with a prayer.[50]

Not all launching ceremonies appear to have been so dignified. Occasionally the workmen rejoiced to extremes and there were complaints. An unnamed correspondent writing to a local newspaper in October 1858 thought that a "launching ceremony was a beautiful scene" but he regretted

the system that accompanies such occasions as these when it is customary to adjourn to the public house, there to have dinner (good of itself) but after which a course of drinking that too often ends in excess; and when the apprentices or younger hands of the yard are introduced to a custom that has been the ruin of so many. We hope 'ere long that the masters of the yards and of the vessels will introduce a new and better system of treating the hands employed on these occasions. We cannot but think if such was the case they might hope for better success to the vessel thus introduced to the water for the first time.[51]

A vain hope when even the modest coastal schooner *Hilda* launched in Widnes in 1867 was sent on her way by dashing a bottle of champagne against her bows.

It became, the custom to provide an outing for the guests after the launch. After seeing the flat *Try* enter the water from Mr. Samuel Stock's yard at Widnes in September 1870, Miss Tryphosee Stock and her guests were towed in the vessel across the river to Runcorn from where they were conveyed in carriages to the Halton Castle Hotel where "they partook of a sumptuous lunch". They afterwards inspected the old ruins and the church and, after a pleasant stroll in Norton Park they returned to Runcorn and thence by the 7.40 train to Widnes.[52]

Mr. Stock's workmen in the meantime were entertained to a dinner at Mr. John Gerrard's West Bank Hotel in Widnes. On Saturday 23rd February 1867 the first launch took place from the yard of Thomas Wilkinson at Fiddlers Ferry and the local newspaper reporter described the celebrations which followed:

The proceedings were enlivened by the singing of some capital songs, amongst them was one composed by Mr. W. Pickton of Warrington who sang it in first rate style and was loudly applauded.[53]

When conditions for ship launches became difficult at Runcorn the river became favourable at Widnes and for a brief period there was a flurry of ship building activity at West Bank. The pride of the Widnes-built ships was the *Janie* a large three masted schooner which was built by Samuel Stock in 1875. She displaced 172 tons a surprisingly large vessel to be built at Widnes which was a young town with no tradition for shipbuilding. It is reasonable to assume that Runcorn craftsmen were engaged for her construction. Edward Gandy was also building small craft at Widnes in the 1880s and one sturdy Widnes vessel, *Maud* of 1869 survived to be converted into a houseboat in 1947. The details of the Widnes craft are to be found in the Appendix.

The building of wooden barges continued at Runcorn up to fairly recent years but shipbuilding received its death blow when the Manchester Ship Canal was being constructed. The *Runcorn Guardian* noted that as a consequence of the building of the canal "shipbuilding has become an industry of the past and this has proved prejudicial to the interests of the district".[54] Efforts had been made "to prevail upon the directors (of the

130

Manchester Ship Canal Company) to grant concessions to Runcorn but with comparatively little success and since the completion of the undertaking considerable depression in trade has been experienced".

The last large coaster built at Runcorn was the schooner *Despatch* which was launched from Brundrit and Heyes' yard in 1886. She was described as being

of exceptionally strong build and was constructed under special survey and classed thirteen years A1 at Lloyd's. The "Despatch" has been built to the order of several local gentlemen and Mr. Davies will act as ship's husband. Instead of giving the men the customary dinner Messrs. Brundrit will treat them to a day at the Liverpool International Exhibition.[55]

For many years Brundrit's arranged annual cruises on the river for their employees and their families when they hired the steamer *Preston* from the Upper Mersey Navigation Commissioners. The Bridgewater Company also provided an annual outing for their work people and the trips were big occasions. In 1880 about 450 workmen and their families were ferried to Liverpool aboard the company's tug boats.[56]

Although ship repair and barge building continued at Runcorn even after the great sea wall between the Manchester Ship Canal and the Mersey was completed, the coming of the canal brought about the end of ship construction. In any case the day of the wooden sailing vessel was coming to an end and in 1886 Runcorn was the last of half a dozen places on the Upper Mersey where the old techniques were still practised. The yards had not adopted modern methods, they had remained primitive - sufficient to provide, for the regional demand for small river and coastal craft but with few facilities to enable them to construct the iron steam coasters which were required by the end of the century. Yet strange to relate, thirty-five years after the launch of the last coaster from Runcorn slipways shipbuilding revived for a brief period at Fiddlers Ferry. Here experimental craft were built by a firm called Concrete Seacraft Limited. These ferro-concrete vessels were listed A1 at Lloyd's but they were subject to annual survey and they were restricted as to the range of voyages that they were permitted to undertake. The concrete ships were limited to coasting in British and Irish waters but they were not allowed insurance cover off the west coast of Ireland. They could be used for continental voyages from April to October but were insured only for voyages along the north coast of Europe from the port of Brest to Hamburg and in the Baltic during these months. The largest of these concrete vessels was *Cretecamp* of 753 tons built in 1919 and the *Cretecove* 747 tons launched in 1920. Although the vessels were essentially experimental ships it is interesting to note that *Cretecamp* lasted ten years. Similar vessels to a standardised design were constructed in many shipyards in Britain at this time and concrete barges were built for the Manchester Ship Canal Company during the second world war. They proved to be durable and remained in service for many years.

Notes

1. Details of individual vessels have been taken from the Shipping Registers of the Port of Liverpool or from those of the Port of Runcorn unless otherwise stated.

2. *Liverpool Mercury,* 11th January, 1865.

3. *Warrington Guardian,* 1st December, 1860.

4. Ibid., 17th November, 1866.

5. Ibid., 18th January, 1867.

6. Ibid., 7th December, 1867.

7. Ibid., 17th September, 1868.

8. Ibid., 22nd August, 1868.

9. Ibid., 11th February, 1882.

10. Ibid., 18th February, 1871.

11. Ibid., 3rd April, 1881.

12. Ibid., 10th October, 1877.

13. Ibid., 26th November, 1881.

14. Ibid., 10th January, 1885.

15. Daniel Hay, "Whitehaven's Colourful Days of Shipping", *Preview of Lakeland,* 1973.

16. *Warrington Guardian*, 23rd October, 1875.

17. Barclay, Reverend John, Annual Letters to the Parish and Parishioners of Runcorn,1861. Local History Collection, Runcorn Library.

18. Carter, C., *Cornish Shipwrecks, The North Coast,* David and Charles, Newton Abbot, 1976, p.76.

19. Messrs. Stubbs, F., Evans, A. and Broady, J., *Runcorn,* Cook, A., Eastham.

20. Hanson, H., *Canal People,* David and Charles, Newton Abbot, 1978, p.124.

21. Transactions of the Runcorn Improvement Commissioners, Vol.1889, April 5th and October 6th 1888.

22. Fowler, G., op cit.

23. Details of pay from the Crew Lists of Runcorn registered vessels. 1862-1913, County Record Office, Chester.

24. *Warrington Guardian,* 13th July, 1889.

25. Ibid., 6th June, 1868.

26. Mr. W. Dutton, Manchester Ship Canal Tug Control, Eastham.

27. Stubbs, F., Evans, E. Broady, J., Runcorn.

28. Starkey, H.F., "From Runcorn to the Falkland Isles", *Port of Manchester Review,* 1979.

29. From shipping movements reported in local press.

30. Shipping Register, Customs and Excise, Runcorn.

31.*Warrington Examiner,* 19th February, 1887.

32. Mather, F.C., *After the Canal Duke.,* pp. 272-273.

33. Superintendents' List of River Steamers, M.S.C. 1908. Port of Manchester Tugs, M.S.C. 1968.

34. Notices and Regulations Relating to Steamers. The Bridgewater Navigation Company 1875.

35. Engineer's Note book (1902). Bridgewater Department, Dock Office, Runcorn M.S.C.

36. *Warrington Guardian,* 20th October, 1866.

37. Notices and Regulations Relating to Steamers. The Bridgewater Navigation Company, 1875.

38. *Warrington Guardian,* 16th July, 1859.

39. Hadfield, C. and Biddle, G., *Canals of North West England,* Vol. 2, p.365.

40. Ordnance Survey, 1874.

41. *Warrington Guardian,* 16th July, 1864.

42. Ibid.,16th June, 1866 and 13th April, 1867.

43. Ibid., 3rd May, 1856.

44. Ibid., 21st April, 1860.

45. Ibid., 5th September 1857.

46. Ibid., 3rd December, 1859.

47. Holden, C.J., Historical Record, *Liverpool Bay Lightships,* Mersey Dock and Harbour Board, 1973.

48. *Warrington Guardian,* 25th July, 1858.

49. Ibid., 3rd April, 1858.

50. Ibid., 12th December, 1862.

51. Ibid., 14th October, 1858.

52. Ibid., 3rd September 1870.

53. Ibid ., 27th February, 1867.

54. *Runcorn Guardian,* Diamond Jubilee Supplement, 26th June 1897.

55. *Warrington and Mid Cheshire Examiner;* 3rd August, 1878.

56. Ibid.,7th August, 1880.

10
Urban and Industrial Growth after 1860

From 1869 Runcorn was situated on the main railway line to London and the Midlands but the town remained essentially a canal port. The following figures for 1873 show the tonnage of foreign and coastwise trade at the Bridgewater Docks.[1]

Imports		Exports		
Coastwise	Foreign	Coastwise	Foreign	Total
256,251	59,481	199,394	27,843	542,969

It can be seen that the coastal import trades were the most important two thirds of which consisted of pottery material. The staples of traffic never varied. Half the coastal export consisted of salt cargoes with most of the remainder being coal. Much of the foreign trade was salt exported to northern European fishing ports.

Urban development at Runcorn and Weston reflected trade and industrial expansion and after a period of no new industrial growth between 1851 and 1860 Wigg's soap, alkali and copper works was built close to the entrance of the Old Quay Canal. The new factory was a major manufacturing concern and the first plant to be built since the Bridgewater Trustees had followed a policy of curbing the building of new chemical works on their properties. The new Wigg works displeased Sir Richard Brooke who now had a factory little more than a mile from his house at Norton Priory and his estate lay in the path of the prevailing wind from Wiggs.[2]

After 1860 Runcorn began to regain some of its pre-1850 growth rate. The advance of chemical science had greatly increased the output from the two soapworks and in the next few years pottery, brickmaking and caustic soda manufacturies were established. As practically all the industry in the region was sited on the waterways it depended upon a ready supply of small craft for the transport of materials to the works and in consequence there was much employment in the shipyards.

The new housing of the 1860s was not confined to the strip of land between the river and the Bridgewater Canal for development now took place along the southern side of the canal with linear growth extending towards Halton Village. Another, larger area of small dwellings to be known as Newtown, was built on the fields to the south of Runcorn Town Bridge. A number of chapels were built. The entire costs of building Camden, St. Paul's and Halton Road Methodist churches were borne by Thomas Hazlehurst, the soap manufacturer, whose generosity also extended over a wide area of the region.[3] (He contributed towards the building of so many Methodist churches that he was invited to lay no less than ninety-nine foundation stones. He regretted that he had just failed to acquire the extra silver ceremonial trowel which would have made his impressive display cabinet complete). The Runcorn Improvement Commissioners had governed the town since 1852 and by 1860 a market hall, a court house, a theatre and a public hall had been built, a municipal cemetery had been opened and a subscription library had been established. Weston village also expanded after mid century with the establishment of the Runcorn Soap and Alkali works on the Weston Canal. One of the new plants required 500 workers and this was largely responsible for an eighty per cent increase in the population in Weston and Weston Point in the thirty years from 1851 to 1881.[4]

The industrialisation of the area blighted the attractive landscape. Ormerod, the Cheshire historian, lamented the passing of picturesque Runcorn, a process which he maintained had begun with dock extensions. He voiced his distaste for the changes in 1882 when he declared

> Nor have these mercantile improvements been effected without a considerable sacrifice of the tastes and feelings of the admirers of the picturesque in a part of the country which for rural beauty of a more varied description could scarcely have been surpassed.[5]

Runcorn had become cramped, smokey and bustling but the devastation of the rural scene on the north bank of the Mersey proceeded at remarkable pace. Within thirty years of the establishment of John Hutchinson's No. 1 works at Widnes, factories and waste tips had spread over farmland and marsh and by 1860 the town was already notorious for its ugliness.

> "Houses and streets spread themselves over open spaces around the works and in very few years Widnes was transformed from a pretty, sunny, riverside hamlet with quiet sleepy ways, into a settlement of thousands of labouring men, mostly Irish, with dingy unfinished streets of hastily constructed houses with works that were belching forth volumes of the most deleterious gases and clouds of black smoke from chimneys of inadequate height, with trees that stood leafless in June, hedgerows that were shrivelled in May. The air reeked with gas, offensive to the sight and smell and large heaps of stinking refuse began to accumulate.[6]

The name *Woodend* had fallen out of use. It was hardly an appropriate description for a district which was devoid of vegetation and woodland.

The Bridgewater Navigation Company

When the Duke of Bridgewater died in 1803 he left his canal and coal mines to be run by a Trust of three individuals with a Superintendent who possessed dictatorial powers. The Trust was to last for

> as long as the lives of all the Peers of the House of Lords and of their sons who were living at the time of the Duke's death and for a further twenty-one years as allowed by law.[7]

In fact the Trust did last exactly a hundred years until 1903 although the navigation part of the Trusteeship was sold to the Bridgewater Navigation

Company in 1872 with a completion of the transfer occurring in 1874.[8] The Duke's canal and the old Mersey and Irwell Navigation with their docks and warehouses passed into the hands of the Bridgewater Navigation Company for a purchase price of £1,115,000 on July 3rd 1872. Although the Trustees had sold their undertakings to the railway companies, namely the Midland, the Manchester, Sheffield and Lincolnshire Company, the railway chairmen, Sir Edward William Watkin and William Philip Price, acted as individuals during the transactions and the railways were not to control the waterways even though many of their shareholders were also shareholders of the new Company.

From the start the Bridgewater Company was selective in its Runcorn trade and improvements were inaugurated at the Bridgewater Docks in order that the Company would be in a better position to compete with its rivals. In 1875 a new dock, the Fenton, which was named after the chairman of the company, was completed at a cost of £50,000.[9] The new dock was equipped with the latest in hydraulic cranes and tips. Railway sidings were added and three large sheds were built for the storage of china clay. The dock area was also equipped with the latest high level tramways. The Fenton Dock was the last of the major dock works to be undertaken at the Bridgewater and Old Quay systems for, even as it was nearing completion, the whole concept of trade on the upper river was being challenged by the persuasive propaganda being disseminated by the promoters of the Manchester Ship Canal and within seven years the first Manchester Ship Canal Bill would be deposited for the 1883 Parliamentary session.

But in the meantime the Bridgewater Company was experiencing difficulties from its inception. The rationalisation of trading activities was regarded with suspicion by the dock porters whose strike in 1874 severely disrupted traffic. The Company was also unfortunate in the timing of its foundation for it came into being just as the sailing channel to Runcorn was deteriorating rapidly. Maintaining and marking the route had become more demanding and many more buoys were required to plot the safe route above Garston. Sixty buoys had been sufficient in 1860 but fifteen years later over a hundred were necessary[10] by which time there had been a considerable loss in business with trade departing to Liverpool docks.[11] The new company must have viewed with concern the competition which was growing at Weston Point. The Weaver Trustees had introduced towage services for vessels between their navigation and Liverpool in 1863 and trade on the Weaver promised to soar when steam coasters and steam flats were able to proceed up river. The Delamere Dock was opened by 1870 and it could take large coasters and, with the dynamic Edward Leader Williams as the engineer in charge, the Weaver was improved to make it navigable for sea going vessels.[12]

Major developments were also taking place across the river at West Bank Dock at Widnes where a large industrial complex was being created in the same way as the factories had been attracted to group around Widnes Dock on the St. Helens Canal twenty years earlier. At West Bank Thomas Fleetwood built his Phoenix Chemical Works on reclaimed marsh land in 1865 and five years later his factory was using large quantities of salt in order to produce four thousand tons of salt cake annually beside 750 tons of bleaching powder and some superphosphate.[13] Other industry soon followed with the Hall brothers of St. Helens and Robert Shaw of Runcorn building their works next to Fleetwoods. In 1867 yet another alkali factory, that of Richard Powell and Richard Penny was started at West Bank Dock.[14] The new works and the dock were served by a system of private railway lines which connected with those of the railway company and the vast growth of the Widnes alkali industry in the 1865 to 1875 decade took place on this large open site which extended from the river to Ditton Road.

Among the cargoes discharged at West Bank there were considerable quantities of salt and limestone and cargoes of burnt ore from Silloth and Dublin, copper ore from St. Tudswal's Roads and pig iron from Scotland.[15] The outgoing commodities included coal for various small ports in North Wales, St. Helens bricks for Northern Ireland, fertilizer for Whitehaven and for Scottish ports and chemicals carried in river craft to the Port of Liverpool. As noted previously the ascendancy of Widnes as the more important centre of chemical manufacture was helped by the Bridgewater Trustees' curbs on industrial building in Runcorn. The alkali manufacturers turned to West Bank where land was cheap and rail transport facilities were good.

Even after the sale of the Bridgewater undertaking to the railway controlled Bridgewater Navigation Company the system continued to hold more than its own against railway competition. The new company's modern facilities at the Fenton and Arnold Docks enabled them to compete profitably with the railway ports even though the Mersey was extremely perverse. Indeed there was a rise in the number of locally registered ships but these were small craft. In fact in 1872 there was only one vessel of more than one hundred tons displacement. There were seventy-six sailing vessels of between fifty and a hundred tons and forty sailing craft and three steam boats of less than fifty tons. In all a total of one hundred and seventeen sailing craft and three steamers totalling 6,427 tons.[16]

The peak year for the registration of ships at Runcorn was 1881 and the following table shows the number of vessels registered at the port from its designation as an independent port in 1862. It can be seen that among the few craft registered in the early years there were no steamers. From less than a thousand tons of shipping in 1862 the total rose to 9,200 tons with 157 vessels in 1881. After that date registered tonnage declined until Runcorn was incorporated in the Port of Manchester in 1894.

	Sailing Vessels (under 50 tons)		Sailing Vessels (over 50 tons)		Steam		Totals	
	No.	Tons	No.	Tons	No.	Tons	No.	Tons
1862	3	90	11	819	—	—	14	909
1863	5	149	16	1141	—	—	21	1290
1864	12	438	26	1765	—	—	38	2203
1867	23	901	54	3648	—	—	77	4544
1872	40	1484	76	4909	3	44	119	6437
1881	43	1695	110	7455	4	125	157	9275
1893	31	1281	93	6576	9	545	133	8402

Vessels Registered at the Port of Runcorn, 1862 to 1893[17]

Table 10:1

Old photographs of the Bridgewater Docks show a crowded scene with small coastal craft filling every available berth. It is noticeable that there are no steam vessels to be seen. This is almost certainly a precaution against the risk of fire with so many wooden vessels moored closely together in the limited dock area.

The slow improvement in the navigable channel from about 1877 encouraged a recovery in business bringing an appreciable rise in the number of craft entering the port. The decline of the early years of the decade was arrested and between 1877 and 1880 an additional 441 vessels entered from foreign, colonial and from United Kingdom ports. The following table indicates the progressive revival of trade.[18]

	Cleared		Entered	
	Vessels	Tons	Vessels	Tons
1877	2316	195,276	2420	190,465
1878	2489	208,797	2598	220,453
1879	2685	223,000	2928	241,572
1880	2754	234,049	2861	237,073

Vessels (Steam and Sail) to and from Foreign Countries and British Possessions and Coastwise at the Port of Runcorn, 1877-1880.[19]

Table 10:2

While the Mersey showed marked improvement near to Runcorn there were problems persisting further down river and in 1877 it became obvious that the route along the south shore near Stanlow was fast closing. By the end of the year it was impassable and on Christmas Eve the oil lamp in the lighthouse at Ince was extinguished. The lighthouse was closed and additional lights were erected at Dungeon, Hale, for traffic now using the northern passage.[20] It was to be another six years before the lamp in Ince lighthouse was relit when the meandering channel had once more moved across to the Cheshire shore.

Coastal shipping was showing a substantial recuperation by 1879 with 2695 sailing and steam vessels entering the docks. West Bank dock was busy and in addition to the many flats carrying the products of the chemical industry to Liverpool docks, a dozen schooners left for coastal ports each week. But West Bank was to remain a primitive dock and throughout its hundred year existence there were to be no improvements and the quayside facilities remained basic. The entrance always presented difficulties for the unpowered vessel and the dock could accommodate only the smaller schooners and steamers.

At Runcorn there was one aspect of the coastal trade which began to lose ground in the face of railway competition when the trade in roofing slates which was the oldest business of the port, began to experience a definite falling off.[21] Slate had been shipped to Runcorn and Frodsham in pre-Tudor times and Welsh slate was found in quantity in fifteenth century layers at Norton Priory when excavations were being carried out between 1971 and 1977. By 1875 the Welsh slate area had been linked to the main railway system of northern and central Wales and as a result there were fewer cargoes for the schooners. The decline in the coastal traffic in slates can be seen in the fate of the small Welsh ports. Whereas Caernarvon had forty-one coasters registered at the port in 1851 there remained only two vessels by 1900.[22] But Runcorn was to remain a major outlet for the North Wales quarries. The slate wharf at the Bridgewater Docks was covered with neat ranks of roofing slates, arranged according to size, stacked on edge and packed with straw awaiting transhipment via the canal. There were twenty-four standard sizes and slates were a cruel cargo to unload for they had to be discharged by hand being thrown up from the hold of the coaster to be caught by men on deck who then passed them to others on the quay. Every slate in an eighty or ninety ton cargo was landed in this way.[23]

The staples of the import trade remained constant throughout the years with pottery material being the principal item. Sixty-two per cent of imports from foreign sources in 1873 came in French ships and most of the cargoes were flints. A further sixteen per cent of the 'foreign' shipping brought china stone from the Channel Isles. From the peak year of 1872 when foreign imports were worth £200,000 the trend in business was a downward one and by 1883 the value of foreign goods had fallen to £118,000. In 1873 cargo was carried from the Port of Runcorn to twelve countries, cargoes being mainly salt or coal. The value of foreign exports never approached that of imports. From a mere £7,259 in 1859 exports grew in value to reach £51,000 by 1868 and from 1871 to 1874 they were worth over £40,000 per annum on average but after 1874 they declined to average £24,000 over the following years. About a quarter of the tonnage landed at Runcorn in 1873 was from foreign sources or from the Channel Isles and about one seventh of the cargo tonnage leaving the port was destined for foreign ports or ports in British possessions overseas.

The table below indicates the foreign and colonial trade at Runcorn from 1869 to 1873.

	Cleared		Entered	
	Vessles	Tons	Vessels	Tons
1869	214	25,251	225	24,898
1870	267	30,404	380	40,605
1871	387	45,320	304	32,546
1872	210	28,510	240	29,307
1873	190	25,905	257	27,564

Number and Tonnage of Vessels that Entered and Cleared from and to Foreign and British Possessions at Runcorn from 1869 to 1873.[24]

Table 10:3

The patterns of Runcorn's foreign trade in 1873 can be seen in the following table. Although most of the overseas voyages were short passages to northern Europe with the bulk of the traffic coming from ports in northern France and the Channel Isles there was a lively trade developing in bones from South America. The export trade in salt to Russian Baltic ports was a healthy one but here again it is noticeable that most outgoing voyages were of short duration to France, Holland and Belgium. In the figures for 1873 the beginnings of the Newfoundland salt trade can be ascertained with two ships carrying cargo to North America.

	Entered		Cleared	
	Vessels	Tons	Vessels	Tons
Russia (Baltic)	—	—	22	3389
Sweden	—	—	—	—
Norway	4	298	—	—
Denmark	2	193	10	1099
Germany	19	2067	12	1676
Holland	—	—	46	5510
Belgium	2	278	22	2492
France	159	16463	57	8693
Spain, Portugal	8	1100	3	376

140

	Entered		Cleared	
	Vessels	Tons	Vessels	Tons
Italy	—	—	3	411
Mexico, West Indies	—	—	3	581
Central and South America	17	2817	—	—
Channel Isles	43	4003	5	620
British North America	—	—	2	318
Other Countries	3	345	5	890

Number and Tonnage of British and Foreign Vessels that Entered and Cleared to and from Various Foreign Countries and British Possessions at Runcorn in 1873.[25]

Table 10:4

The period of Runcorn's expansion came to an end in the 1870s. The failure of the local chemical industry to develop after 1850 because of the Bridgewater Trustees' refusal to sell or lease land for factory sites coupled with the wretched conditions at the approaches to both canals were the main reasons for the decline in urban and industrial growth. Between 1852 and 1881 Runcorn's population and its buildings increased by 70.5 per cent and 76.3 per cent respectively but during the next thirty year period the growth was 17.1 per cent for population and 24.4 per cent in buildings.[26] The development of the docks also ceased in the mid 1870s with the construction of the Fenton Dock which was completed by the Bridgewater Navigation Company in 1876. After this date no further large scale developments were to be undertaken at the port until the Tollemache Dock at Weston Point was opened in 1885. The optimism which had been generated by the boom of the 1850s and 1860s was quickly dispersed by the almost catastrophic silting of the 1870s.

For more than twenty years from 1850 the Old Quay Docks of the Mersey and Irwell system had been in slow decline.[27] Here physical expansion was impossible because of the nature of the site. Hemmed into a small area by the housing of Runcorn township there was little space to extend dockside facilities and except for the transfer of the Company's boat building and repair facilities from Manchester to Old Quay in 1837 there had been no expansion since the major works carried out in 1829. Warehouse accommodation remained minimal, facilities for loading and discharging vessels were basic and the difficult sailing channel to the dock gates often barred the entrance to all craft above the size of a river flat. Further problems for Old Quay occurred between 1863 and 1868 when the railway bridge works often closed the channels to up river traffic and the railway company had to provide steamers to tow vessels through the maze of scaffolding. But the greatest handicap to the Old Quay system was the fact that the docks were never served by a railway link and although the canal carried traffic to and from the Manchester conurbation, the waterway did not have the Bridgewater Canal's lucrative business with the Midlands.

There were yet more difficulties on the Mersey and Irwell undertaking between Warrington and Salford where the nine sets of ancient locks had degenerated since the mid 1840s and the neglect of the waterway had reduced to less than 50 tons the size of vessels able to reach Manchester. Furthermore as proposals for a ship canal on the Navigation's route were being seriously considered in the 1870s little had been done to improve the waterway. In fact the Mersey and Irwell had assumed a minor role from 1845 when it was purchased by the Trustees of the Bridgewater Canal.

From about 1877 the problems of the Port of Runcorn began to ease when the Mersey channels started to improve and the timing of this development proved most fortunate in that it coincided with the period of greatest expansion in the Widnes alkali industry. As the production of chemicals increased so did the demand for raw materials and the resulting barge traffic to the river and canal side factories became heavy. At the same time the pottery industry's need for supplies appeared to be insatiable and the need for china clay, china stone, flints and whitening grew as the potteries in the Five Towns increased production. Even in the face of railway competition the amount of crated pottery sent to Runcorn by the canals did not lessen and by the end of the century as much pottery was being despatched to Liverpool from the Bridgewater Docks as had been the case before the coming of the railways. The fortuitous change in the upper Mersey enabled the coasting schooners to discharge potters' materials at Runcorn with little difficulty and from 1877 the canal boat registers show a healthy trade at the Bridgewater Docks.

Foreign exports also showed some recovery after the sudden fall from 1874 but they were never again to attain even half the value that they had been at the beginning of the 1870s. A similar situation occurred in the case of foreign imports which fell steadily from a peak in 1872 to make a brief recovery in 1878 but which continued in decline thereafter. The poor state of the river had a lasting adverse effect upon Runcorn's foreign trade and the port was never able to recover the foreign business which was lost during the difficult years.

From 1877 public health authorities were required to inspect the living conditions on board canal craft and the Runcorn registry of canal boats is complete from the first year of registration until 1949.[28] The register books are of particular interest as they tell us something of trade routes and the variety of cargoes as well as giving a glimpse of the industrial activity of the district with the growth or decline of the commercial enterprises of the local business community. Between December 6th 1878 and December 1st 1879 there were 705 canal boats recorded at Runcorn. Of these, 352 were wide boats, that is craft which besides operating on the wide Bridgewater and Mersey and Irwell Canals could also use the rivers being propelled either by sail or by being towed. There were 329 narrow boats, 23 narrow beam tugs and one wide steam tug. These statistics do not give the complete picture of the volume of canal traffic to the docks because other craft were registered at Nantwich, Northwich and at Stoke-on-Trent and many of these were employed in carrying to and from Runcorn.

The Bridgewater Company was the largest carrier on the inland waterways with 274 boats - the majority of which were flats. All were registered for "general cargo" but an additional thirteen were registered specifically for the transportation of timber "on the Bridgewater Canal and adjacent" that is on the river and also the Mersey and Irwell Navigation Canal. Of the independent carriers in 1878 the Anderton Company of Stoke-on-Trent was the largest operator with 62 narrow boats and this number was to treble during the following thirty years. The Anderton craft were registered for the transportation of pottery material and five of the boats were listed as fly boats - that is narrow boats which were worked by shifts. Other locally based fleets of canal craft were of considerable size. Simpson, Davies and Company, coal and salt carriers and ship brokers of Bank House, Runcorn and also of Winsford and Wigan owned 64 craft registered for the carriage of general cargo five of which were wide boats for river use. Samuel Taylor had 20 canal boats, four being sailing flats whilst William Bate of Lowlands Road, Runcorn, coal merchant, flat and boat builder and dealer in building and moulding sand owned nineteen flats and twelve narrow boats in 1879. Fred J. Abbott who appears in the 1874 directory as a foreman boat builder, owned eight craft most of which were registered for the carriage of "grain flour and wheat on the Bridgewater Canal and adjacent". By 1891 Abbott and Walton, his partner, had twenty-two canal and river craft operating to Old Quay Mills. Jonathan Horsefield of Canal Street had twelve boats working to Manchester, Leigh and the Potteries whilst Philip Speakman had ten wide boats on the canals.

The first year of registration of canal craft records a number of minor independent carriers working to and from Runcorn. Typical of these was Henry Urmson of Bridge Street who owned five sailing flats which were used between Widnes, Runcorn, St. Helens and Manchester. Another small firm was that of Robert Evans with seven narrow boats which were mainly employed in the carriage of stone and coal. Some local men gained a livelihood by operating a single boat and many owners from Warrington, Middlewich, Liverpool and Manchester registered their craft at Runcorn. By the end of 1879 there were twenty-two owners of single boats in the local register.

A number of chemical firms owned sailing flats for use on the river and canals. In addition to Hazlehurst's, the Runcorn Soap and Alkali Company of Weston had seven craft employed to carry ores and chemicals between Weston Point and Runcorn and Liverpool and the Union Acid Company of High Street had five boats for transporting acid and soda on the Bridgewater Canal. Charles Wigg and Co. (Wigg, Steel and Company) of Old Quay had three sailing flats and a little steamer all of which carried iron and sulphur ore and chemicals between Widnes, Runcorn and Liverpool.

Narrow boat families at the Bridgewater Docks at the beginning of the century.

It appears that the initial work of inspection and registration of canal boats took longer than a year and by 1880 possibly 850 boats were registered at the Port of Runcorn. With the coastal trades continuing to prosper the number of canal craft needed for the transhipment of cargoes showed a steady increase. The following table gives the initial canal boat registrations with the yearly additions to the register. The figures do not show the number of boats which were withdrawn as unserviceable during the period.

		Boats		Boats
Registered in	**1879**	709	**1883**	10
	1880	32	**1884**	10
	1881	20	**1885**	20
	1882	17	**1886**	15

Numbers of Canal Craft Registered at Runcorn from 1879-1886

Table 10:5

So by December 1886 a total of 823 canal craft had been registered by the local authority. It is not possible to estimate with any degree of certainty the total number of men and women who worked the boats but the narrow craft were usually licensed to allow living accommodation for three whilst the wide boats had a complement of four, five, six and in one or two cases even seven boatmen and family members. Life on board could have been difficult for many of the boats carried unpleasant cargoes of manure, night soil, animal bones and chemicals. It has been calculated that by 1875 the Bridgewater Navigation Company employed 3260 men and 445 horses on their waterways and of the tonnage carried, fifty per cent had been brought on the Mersey estuary.[29]

Labour Relations at the Docks

By the standards of his time the Duke of Bridgewater was an enlightened employer. He paid good wages, built houses which he let at reasonable rents and he kept a close watch on those tradesmen and shopkeepers who might have been inclined to exploit his people. The Duke met doctor's bills, encouraged thrift and generally made every effort to care for the well being of those in his employment. He took particular care of former employees who were aged or who had been injured in his service and as a consequence the Duke was held in high regard. He was able to maintain excellent labour relations and in this respect he set a pattern for others to imitate so that generally the canal companies of the eighteenth century were looked upon as good employers. But labour disputes were not unknown and productivity and cost of living bonuses are not twentieth century phenomena. In 1796 the Mersey and Irwell Company received a letter from the *Seven Stars* in Warrington from flatmen who required an increase in wages and they threatened to withdraw their labour if they were refused. In the negotiations which followed the men secured not only a rise in wages but also productivity and cost of living bonuses as well as the guarantee of one week's notice of termination of employment.[30] Flatmen were essential workers and they knew it. On them depended the economic success of the region. The employers saw that they were well looked after and the men's demands were often met in full. When trade was slack in 1832 the Mersey and Irwell Company found the flatmen temporary jobs as dock porters. This necessitated some of the regular dock porters losing their jobs but the Company argued that the porters were in a better position to find new work, whereas skilled flatmen would be hard to find when business picked up again.[31] The Mersey and Irwell also found employment ashore for old flatmen who were no longer fit to continue their arduous task on the flats. This same altruistic attitude was also to be found in the Weaver Navigation Company's dealings with its employees.

During the era of the Bridgewater Navigation Company however, labour relations at the docks do not appear to have been harmonious and the local newspaper reports suggest an unrest which persisted among the flatmen and dock workers throughout much of the Company's existence. A couple of years before the Company was formed there had been trouble at the docks. In 1871 the dock porters had been on strike for better wages and they again withdrew their labour in 1874 in an attempt to obtain an increase.[31] When in 1879 the Bridgewater Company proposed to reduce the dock workers' wages by seven and a half per cent in order to bring them in line with the pay of unskilled workers in the factories there was an instant walk out.[32] A serious disruption of trade occurred in February and March 1884 when the Bridgewater flatmen received notice that their wages were to be cut by a shilling a week and it was widely believed that the reduction was a prelude to a lowering of the wages of the dock labourers and other employees of the Company.[33] The strikers were informed by the Company that unless there was an immediate return to work their earnings would be reduced by another shilling a week when they did resume work. In Runcorn there was much sympathy for the men because their demands were just and because their conduct during the strike was exemplary. One procession of local flatmen was impressive in its orderliness - "the men preserving admirable order and singing hymns marched through the town their appearance evoking much astonishment among the townspeople". Led by the Salvation Army band, a hundred and twenty flatmen marched from Delph Bridge, via Shaw Street and Lowlands Road to Devonshire Square where a meeting was held in the Forester's Hall. Large assemblies of flatmen also gathered in Warrington and here too, the meetings exhibited excellent order. The men "sang songs of sacred character with many of them sporting blue ribbons as an indication of adherence to the abstinence principles". The men claimed that a wage of £1. 13. 7d. for eighty hours work was typical and they pointed out that the working time of a flat was seven days a week. They claimed that they were striking to safeguard the earnings of many others engaged in

146

maritime occupations and public feeling was aroused sufficiently to cause subscriptions be raised for the strike fund.[34]

Throughout the stoppage the *Warrington Guardian* showed undisguised sympathy for the flatmen but on March 1st when announcing the end of the strike there was a definite change in the paper's attitude. It is not clear why the report then emphasised the case for the company but the account favours the Bridgewater Company as being enlightened employers:

> A fact which should have been mentioned earlier is that each flat is provided by the Company with five tons of coal per year, besides being furnished with beds, bolsters and blankets, cooking utensils, brushes and oil for cabin use. Each flatman also receives an overcoat every year and, so far as this goes we understand that no carrying company treats employees with such generosity. When the men are incapacitated through old age from following their employment on board the flats they are found some light occupation on shore.

The report goes on to conclude that after the "idleness, big processions and loquacity they had to accept the inevitable with the best grace they could muster".[34]

The Company's threat was duly carried out and their reprisals were severe. The striker's wages were reduced by two shillings a week and as some jobs had been taken by other men during the stoppage a number of flatmen were thrown out of work.[35]

Trade Fluctuations

The recovery in maritime trade at the Port of Runcorn continued to rise until 1889 when the construction of the Manchester Ship Canal created difficulties in the upper river and trade declined from then until 1894 when the Customs Port of Runcorn was abolished to become part of the new port of Manchester. The Board of Trade's Annual Statements of the Shipping and Navigation of the United Kingdom do not include Runcorn as a separate entity after 1893 by which time it had become foremost in coastal trade among the small ports of the north west. Twenty years previously shipping entering and clearing Runcorn had been two-thirds that of Whitehaven and there had been twice as many vessels entering the Dee but by 1893 Preston, Whitehaven and Chester had been eclipsed by Runcorn which had more coastal craft entering and leaving with greater tonnages being handled than any of the other small ports. Of course, Liverpool was pre-eminent with four times Runcorn's share of coastwise shipping movements. Furthermore, coastal cargoes handled at the Liverpool docks were ten times the tonnages loaded and discharged at Runcorn. The coastal traffic at the five ports for 1893 is tabulated below and an analysis of the figures shows that the average coasting vessel at Liverpool was about 230 tons, at Whitehaven vessels were about 120 tons, whilst river conditions in the upper Mersey and in the Dee limited craft at Runcorn to about 85 or 90 tons and at Chester from 65 to 70 tons displacement.

	Entered		Cleared	
	Vessels	**Tons**	**Vessels**	**Tons**
Runcorn	3,083	264,542	3,065	281,793
Preston	773	77,886	791	88,257
Chester	1,994	125,382	1,899	135,426
Whitehaven	2,239	264,556	2,189	255,633
Liverpool	12,583	2,640,920	13,210	3,311,749

Sailing and Steam Vessels Entered and Cleared at Each Port in the Coastal Trade in 1893.[36]

Table 10:6

The figures above include traffic to Ireland. Presented separately the Irish trade at the five ports is as follows:

	Entered		Cleared	
	Vessels	**Tons**	**Vessels**	**Tons**
Runcorn	145	12,070	217	17,289
Preston	87	7,191	88	7,044
Chester	188	14,776	312	24,084
Whitehaven	848	115,252	589	74,807
Liverpool	4,392	1,120,011	4,460	1,167,632

Sailing and Steam Vessels Entered and Cleared from and to Ireland from Each Port in 1893.[37]

Table 10:7

From the above tables it can be seen that less than five percent of Runcorn's coastal import trade and seven per cent of the export trade was with Ireland and this traffic was a much smaller proportion than at any of the other north-west ports. The figures for 1893 indicate that Whitehaven's coal trade to Ireland made up twenty-seven per cent of that port's coastal shipping and thirty-eight per cent of the coastal imports came from Ireland. Chester too had a larger share of the Irish trade with ten per cent of its ships engaged in carrying Irish goods into the port and with fifteen per cent of its coastal vessels carrying to Ireland. Put into context, however, the coastal traffic of the north-west was completely dominated by Liverpool whose Irish shipping tonnage was nine times that of the combined trade of Runcorn, Preston, Chester and Whitehaven.

The table overleaf gives the coastal trade at Runcorn from 1879 to 1892 and it is interesting to note that there was a ten fold increase in the number of small steamers using the port over the fourteen year period.

	Entered	Tonnage	Cleared	Tonnage
1879	2,570	204,466	2,391	189,907
1880	2,462	196,908	2,449	199,249
1881	2,393	199,223	2,271	183,396
1882	2,293	188,627	2,219	183,741
1883	2,337	201,263	2,210	190,981
1884	2,605	214,243	2,409	203,304
1885	2,606	211,367	2,612	212,634
1886	2,800	224,410	2,829	228,027
1887	3,269	260,668	3,235	259,606
1888	3,145	243,733	3,144	246,078
1889	3,398	262,599	3,321	258,978
1890	3,088	242,819	3,132	248,787
1891	2,873	219,113	2,851	218,016
1892	2,376	188,487	2,316	188,403

Steam Vessels Entered and Cleared Coastwise

	Entered	Tonnage	Cleared	Tonnage
1879	125	9,481	100	6,853
1880	127	10,693	121	8,516
1881	154	10,196	163	10,921
1882	126	10,293	137	10,539
1883	150	11,595	151	11,615
1884	358	34,677	334	31,732
1885	418	41,814	423	40,571
1886	491	47,757	485	45,661
1887	592	51,252	594	51,750
1888	819	70,116	798	68,038
1889	1,008	76,249	972	75,410
1890	1,096	82,338	1,108	88,366
1891	1,199	85,238	1,193	87,924
1892	1,169	90,972	1,163	100,541

Sailing Vessels Entered and Cleared Coastwise
Coastal Traffic at the Port of Runcorn, 1879-92[38]
Table 10:8

The table below shows the annual returns for all foreign and coastwise shipping at Runcorn for the last nine years of its existence as a separate customs port.

	Cleared		Entered	
	Vessels	**Tons**	**Vessels**	**Tons**
1886	3,434	294,436	3,485	298,402
1887	3,954	331,805	4,041	335,897
1888	4,049	331,479	4,128	335,983
1889	4,350	343,161	4,529	355,380
1890	4,301	347,880	4,341	348,996
1891	4,093	313,738	4,196	320,889
1892	3,530	299,716	3,697	314,003
1893	3,174	319,289	3,243	317,186
1894	3,243	313,801	3,236	311,791

Vessels (Steam and Sail) to and from Foreign Countries and British Possessions and Coastwise at the Port of Runcorn, 1886 to 1894[39]

Table 10:9

Foreign Trade

Whilst the coastal trade recovered in the late 1870s the foreign trade declined. J.D. Porteous, quoting Board of Trade figures for 1872 and 1884 shows the considerable decline in foreign exports and imports at the Bridgewater docks at illustrated in the table below.[40]

Year	Coastwise	Foreign	Coastwise	Foreign	Total
1873	256,251	59,481	199,394	27,843	542,969
1884	251,541	22,246	196,200	12,411	446,398

Trade of the Bridgewater Docks, Runcorn, 1873-84 (Tons)

Table 10:10

In 1881 there were seventeen countries trading to Runcorn and in 1883 cargoes were despatched to ports in twenty-five foreign countries as well as to the West Indies and Canada.[41] For incoming cargoes the French trade predominated with flints being the principal commodity. By 1881 there was also the brisk trade developing with Brazil with the importing of animal bones and in 1883 business had become considerable with thirty-five vessels from Rio Grande discharging at the Bridgewater docks.

As far as exports were concerned the traditional salt trade was still the most important as it had been since the 1860s and cargoes were shipped to Russian ports on the Baltic and to Germany, Holland, Belgium and Scandinavia. The shipment of salt to the Newfoundland and Canadian fisheries also increased throughout the 1880s and from this time local schooners were specifically built for the Atlantic crossing. There were three main trade routes: to ports in northern Europe, to Newfoundland and to Brazil. Traffic to and from the Mediterranean was slight and there was no trade to north African ports. During the 1880s the long established business with the Channel Islands flourished and imports of china stone amounted to forty-one cargoes in 1881 and thirty in 1883. Next to salt, coal remained the chief item to be exported.

The sources of foreign cargoes and the destinations of foreign exports for the years 1881 and 1883 are tabulated below.

| | 1881 | | | | 1883 | | | |
| | Entered | | Cleared | | Entered | | Cleared | |
	Vessels	Tons	Vessels	Tons	Vessels	Tons	Vessels	Tons
Russia (Baltic)	-	-	34	6448	-	-	40	8069
Norway	9	1529	9	1649	2	195	4	677
Denmark	-	-	19	3065	2	194	22	3059
Sweden	-	-	-	-	1	99	1	152
Germany	25	2610	8	1449	11	1257	3	604
Holland	6	715	58	6962	5	618	57	6901
Belgium	1	56	14	1343	-	-	13	1294
France	101	10,678	19	2692	138	14,320	7	870
Spain/Canaries	12	1752	4	655	2	249	2	406
Italy	1	99	-	-	1	96	-	-
Greece	1	185	1	126	-	-	1	144
Turkey	1	186	-	-	-	-	1	122
Mexico	2	467	-	-	-	-	1	255
Brazil	11	1890	2	305	35	5341	7	1224
Channel Isles	41	3793	8	469	30	3244	9	591
Brit. N. America	-	-	6	1245	-	-	10	1268
Argentine	-	-	-	-	2	647	-	-
Portugal/Azores	-	-	-	-	6	991	1	155
West Indies	-	-	-	-	2	657	-	-

	1881				1883			
	Entered		Cleared		Entered		Cleared	
	Vessels	Tons	Vessels	Tons	Vessels	Tons	Vessels	Tons
Other countries	3	296	-	-	10	2286	7	818
Other British Possessions	-	-	-	-	-	-	2	326

Number and Tonnage of British and Foreign Vessels that Entered and Cleared to and from Various Foreign Countries and British Possessions at Runcorn in 1881 and 1883[42]

Table 10:11

The greater part of the foreign trade was carried in British vessels and it is interesting to note that although small steamers were engaged in the coastal trade there were no steamers operating to Runcorn from foreign ports in 1881.[43] Free towage to and from the mouth of the estuary resulted in Runcorn remaining a sailing ship port until the third decade of the twentieth century. An analysis of British and foreign ship movements in 1881 is given in the following table.

Entered							
British		Foreign		Total		Tons	
Sailing	Steam	Sailing	Steam	Sailing		Steam	
191(20,376 tons)	-	21(3503 tons)	-	212	-	23,879	

Cleared							
British		Foreign		Total		Tons	
107(12,779 tons)	-	75 (13,649 tons)	-	182 ·	-	26,428	

Vessels Entered and Cleared from and to Foreign Countries and British Possessions from Runcorn in 1881. Number and Tonnage of Sailing and Steam Vessels with Cargo and in Ballast[44]

Table 10:12

During the year 1881 the flags of ten nations could be seen at the docks. Of the foreign shipping the most prominent were Norwegian, German and Dutch vessels which were loading salt for their fishing industries. The table gives the number of foreign vessels trading to Runcorn in that year.

152

	Entered		Cleared	
	Vessels	Tons	Vessels	Tons
British	192	20,505	107	12,779
Russian	-	-	1	173
Swedish	-	-	1	319
Norwegian	7	1,464	38	8,127
Danish	3	358	10	1,223
German	4	779	11	1,856
Dutch	4	495	4	515
French	3	470	6	913
Spanish	-	-	1	185
Greek	1	185	1	185

Vessels of Each Nation using the Port of Runcorn in 1881.[45]

Table 10:13

From the figures which were presented by the Bridgewater Navigation Company when they opposed the Manchester Ship Canal Bill in 1885 (Appendix, p.228) it can be seen that Runcorn's foreign trade never recovered from the difficult years in the mid-1870s. There was a temporary increase in foreign trade in 1878 when the river channels had improved but trade could not be maintained and after that peak year traffic to foreign ports declined until the port of Runcorn became part of the port of Manchester in 1894.

Professor Porteous has made an analysis of foreign shipping movements at Runcorn for 1894 in order to discover the orientation of trade.[46] He found that 30% of traffic was to ports on the near continent of Europe, nearly 18% of foreign trade was with Scandinavia, 3% to Iberia and nearly a half, 48.5%, was to North America.

Servicing and Supply

The Golden Jubilee of Queen Victoria's reign in 1887 coincided with the twenty-fifth anniversary of Runcorn's establishment as a bonded port and it was also the year in which the Manchester Ship Canal construction was started. This might be an appropriate date at which to consider the ship owners of Runcorn and also the various trades and industries of the town which were necessary for the maintenance of maritime commerce.[47] There were no large fleets of vessels in the ownership of one firm but often one man had the controlling interest in three or four vessels. Typical of the pattern of ownership was Mr. J. Foulkes who had the schooners *Alert, Snowflake* and *Sunbeam* and Mr. Thomas C. Cooper who was managing owner of *Chase, Fox* and *Guiding Star*. The schooners *Emily, Harvest King, Harvest Queen* and *Janet Worthington* were in the ownership of Thomas Rayner whilst Mr. R. Clark of Weaver Villa, Weston Point had three schooners, one of which, *The Saint,* was registered at Runcorn whilst *Ballinbreich Castle* and *Ann Clark* were registered at Bideford and Liverpool respectively. Mr. Clark also owned the barquentine *Ethiopian* which he registered at Runcorn. *Sovereign* was owned by Mrs. A.M. Howard, James Pritchard of Duke's Fields owned *Gleaner* and *Little Reaper* whilst Mr. G. Millington of Waterloo Road had *Emily Millington* and *Sarah McDonald.* Generally most of the registered owners had one vessel. *Blanche* was owned by her master, Mr. J. Owen and for many years *Four Brothers* provided a living for her master and owner, Thomas Anderson. Other single ship owners were John Heath of Widnes with *Truth Seeker,* Mr. R.B. Toft with *Countess of Carrick,* Samuel Ravenscroft had *Helen McGregor* whilst Mr. J.S. Davies was the principal shareholder and manager of *Despatch.* The picture is one of small enterprises based upon modest capital with all the vessels engaged in coal, salt and china clay trades.

The ownership of the ships changed frequently and the rise and fall of family interests is clearly discernable as the century progressed. There is a noticeable reduction in the size of 'family' fleets. A case in point is Samuel Ravenscroft who owned several vessels in the 1840s but by 1881 the fleet had been reduced to four and by 1887 only one ship remained. By this date other local names which were prominent in the 1840s had gone from the list of owners and by 1887 one does not find S. Wylde and Company, Hazlehurst and Company or Ellis and Company. Very few steamers were owned by local men and these were small vessels being either tugs or steam barges. John Beckett of Leinster Street had the small screw steamer *Hannah Beckett,* Mr. Finlay of Farrington Buildings, Percival Lane had the iron screw vessel *Confidence* and Mr. W. Rowland had two small steamers *Hebe* and *Lady Kate* both of which were registered at Liverpool. The little steam flat *Reginald* built by Brundrit's in 1881 was owned by Mr. A. Green in 1887. A similar pattern of ownership was the case with the flats some of which had been dismasted to become towing barges. Hill and Grundy, Salt Union, Settle Speakman, Richard Abel and William Cooper were the principal local owners by the turn of the century.

Inshore fishing had been of some significance. From 1868 all fishing boats had to be registered under the Sea Fisheries Act and by 1872 there were fifty-three boats at Runcorn. Three of them were listed as first class boats each being over fifteen tons displacement. Another thirty-five boats totalling 169 tons, were listed as second class boats. In addition a further seventeen small craft are entered in the records as being boats "navigated by oars alone".[48] By 1883 the number of fishing boats had been much reduced and there were then only thirteen boats of all classes manned by thirty men and boys of whom only four men were regularly employed in inshore fishing. The rewards were hard earned for the sailing smacks had to seek catches off the Lancashire coast and off the mouth of the Dee as the Mersey had become polluted. It now appears an absurdity to record the fact that on 4th August 1728 "30,000 herrings and upwards were caught in the River Mersey at Hale".[49] Some local families had been engaged in fishing and shrimping for generations. The White family of Ince and Elton had been fishing in the early years of the eighteenth century and when some of the men came to Runcorn in the 1840s they continued the family tradition and some of their descendants were still engaged in fishing up to recent times. The Albiston's of Rock Mount, the Lomax, Woods, Hambleton, Shaw and Ankers families were amongst those who kept fishing smacks over many years.

It seems that the number of smacks registered at one time reflected the prevailing social conditions. When times were hard and there was little employment ashore the number of boats increased. Sometimes there would be as many as forty with owners from Widnes, Warrington and Runcorn. At the beginning of this century the little boats were sometimes described as sailing sloops. They averaged about eight tons and they were of strong construction. Some lasted to be fitted with motors in the 1930s. Although the ownership of the boats changed frequently they usually remained in the hands of families who had long been involved in fishing and shrimping. The names of the little boats were as varied as those of the schooners *Edie, Polly, Lena, Emily, Ploughboy, Etna, Harlequin, May Baxter* and *Lady Lathom.*

To keep the sailing vessels equipped and provisioned there were numerous repair and supply facilities ashore. The schooners and sailing flats required a constant supply of rope, sails, paint, lamp oil and groceries. Blacksmiths, riggers and carpenters were always in demand as were the ships chandlers who supplied the needs of the ships and the narrow boats. Among the ship brokers advertising in 1887 were R. Clark and Company of Top Locks, ship owners, and Howard and Company, brokers, and salt and coal merchants of Waterloo Road. Other brokerage firms were those of Thomas Toft of Top Locks and Potter and Sons of Duke's Dock who also advertised that they were carriers by canal.

Runcorn had a number of sail making establishments. William Cooper, rigger, sail and tent maker also made flags and sold ropes at his premises at Waterloo Bridge. Richard Abel sailmaker, canvas merchant and general ship chandler had his workshop at Washington Buildings, Top Locks and Samuel Ravenscroft described himself as a "sail, stack cover and cart sheet maker". Fred Hayes of Waterloo Road combined two businesses, those of grocer and sailmaker. In Percival Lane and Rutland Street there were rope walks, one of which was operated by steam power. Other nautical trades included Joseph Pegg, river Mersey pilot of Loch Street who advertised his hull cleaning and painting services to the owners of iron ships with "Pegg's Prepared Composition" being specially recommended for an excellent finish. Mr. R. Hampson, copper, iron and tin plate worker, advertised that he was a "brass and other fog horn maker" whilst Mr. Pickens of the Portrait Rooms in Bridge Street guaranteed photographic work of "unsurpassed truthfulness, brilliancy and high finish". His speciality was the instantaneous picture of moving objects such as animals and ships. In High Street Mr. J.B. Bankes sold and offered for hire, ships' chronometers, mariner's compasses and nautical instruments.

Many of the local shopkeepers relied upon the patronage of ships' crews and the butchers in particular stressed their connections with shipping. They often advertised themselves as "family and shipping butchers" and they declared that they could supply ships at the shortest notice.

There was an astonishing number of public houses in Runcorn, Halton and Weston at the end of the last century. The returns of fully licensed houses and beer houses for the County of Cheshire in 1891 show that Runcorn had eighty-seven public houses and there were seven more in Halton and another seven in Weston. This represented a licensed house per 230 of the population of Runcorn and one for every 191 of Halton's inhabitants. The names of the public houses have a nautical flavour suggesting the sea and ships. For instance in Church Street there was the "Man at the Wheel", in High Street there was the "Holyhead Harbour", the "Waterman's Arms" in Queen Street and the "Anchor" in Brunswick Street. There was yet another "Anchor" in Halton Road. In addition there was the "Rope Inn", the "Navigation", the "Sloop Inn" and, at various times three establishments called the "Ship Inn". The local press reports often suggested that a turbulent atmosphere prevailed in the dock area. It was alleged that there were so many public houses in Percival Lane that if a thirsty seaman took a thimble of beer in the first one near to the docks and he then doubled the quantity at every pub as he went up the lane he would become incapably drunk before he reached Top Locks. An exaggeration perhaps but shipbuilder, Mr. Philip Whiteway JP, was renowned for his severity when passing judgement for drunkness. In his obituary in the *Warrington Guardian* of 23rd February 1873 it was suggested that this strict attitude was necessary because drunkeness had become a serious social problem in the town. The obituary concludes:

If in his capacity as a magistrate he was more inclined to do justice than to love mercy every excuse is to be made in the consideration that the severe sentences for which of late he had become proverbial were chiefly passed on drunkeness - the vulgar vice which is the base and blot of this place and parish.

There is no doubt that Police Inspector Millington and sergeants Cooper, Blair and Woolley and their constables were kept busy in Runcorn's dock area in 1887. The *Runcorn and Widnes Chronicle* of the turn of the century gives some idea of the restless atmosphere which often existed and the reports of the petty sessions make interesting reading. "Murderous Assault at Runcorn Docks". "Struggle with Gigantic Sailor". "Runcorn Boatman Charged With Stabbing". "Violent Sailor Gets Three Months". "Ship's Captain Charged With Wounding". It is probable that the high incidence of death by drowning in Runcorn in the early years of this century can be correlated with excessive drinking. Death from drowning was a remarkably frequent occurrence. A local newspaper report of 1905 gives an account of the work of the Runcorn District Life Saving and Grappling Corps. In the first four years of its existence this voluntary organisation recovered fifty-two bodies from the docks and canals.[50]

In the tiny public houses the distinctive accents of Cornwall, Devon, Gloucester and North Wales were heard. Seamen from foreign ships mixed with the strangely attired narrow boat folk and the pubs were hazy with pipe tobacco smoke. The favourite brands of hard tobacco were "Irish Roll", "Nailrod", "Cavendish" and "Pigtail". The larger houses advertised well seasoned Manilla cigars and the licensee of the London and North Western Hotel advised that he was the sole agent for "GB Whiskey" which he claimed "was recommended by the medical faculty for rheumatism etc". When the docks were crowded with shipping or when icy conditions slowed traffic on the canals, seamen and boatmen often had time on their hands. It was then that trouble and rowdy behaviour occurred and the Salvation Army and Missioner Shaw and his volunteers were hard pressed in their efforts to defuse the situation.

By 1885 the Bridgewater dock system at Runcorn had sixteen acres of water area with about two and a half miles of quay berths adjacent to which were some thirty seven acres of quayside space. A total of 438 men were employed at the Old Quay and Bridgewater docks with another 379 being engaged in barge and boat building and repair or as tug or flat crews. The docks were equipped with eleven hydraulic cranes, three hydraulic lifts, eleven steam cranes and at the Fenton Dock there were three hydraulic tips. Over the twelve years from 1873 to 1884 a yearly average of 3,872 vessels entered and left the Runcorn docks. The Bridgewater Company's figures for the movement of canal craft through the locks in 1883 is quite staggering for no less than 60,303 boats passed up and down the locks in that year.[51] Tonnages carried on the canal were impressive enough but the carriage of goods by road was not an easy matter. From their eighteenth century origins the docks had evolved as an integral part of a canal port where cargoes were transhipped to and from narrow boats. Over the years little attention had been given to improving the road entrance to the docks and this was a situation which was to continue until the age of the motorway.

The depth of water at the Bridgewater entrance was approximately seventeen feet at spring tides and this enabled a vessel with a cargo of about 700 tons to have easy access. At neap tides the depth of water was about eight feet whilst at the Old Quay entrance it was six feet. Over the river at West Bank the dock entrance had only four feet of water at neap tide.[52]

For the twelve year period the average trade at Runcorn docks was nearly 490,000 tons a year of which 281,514 tons were imports.[53] In addition about a million tons of goods were carried between Liverpool and the Bridgewater Company's inland waterways. This traffic consisted of trains of barges pulled by the river paddle tugs and the towage operations were precisely arranged to suit the tides. The efficient organisation of the barge traffic is described in *The Canals of North West England* by Charles Hadfield and Gordon Biddle:[54]

> Within five hours the Liverpool dock gates would be opened, tugs would collect their trains of barges, deliver them to Runcorn about high water, collect others, take them back to Liverpool and distribute them, and return to their moorings at the Duke's dock before the gates closed.

The assembling and despatch of the barge trains at Runcorn was an operation demanding speed and precise timing -

> At tide time the craft leaving the docks were brought to the tidal basin (which was also used as an ordinary ship dock) and the gates closed; the vessels then moved out, ships and barges together through the one entrance. Barge trains were then made up along the wall running from the tidal entrance to the old line of locks.[55]

Craft using the Bridgewater Canal down to the river used the old line of locks and the new line was used for traffic going to Manchester. Barge transport was of central importance to Runcorn's own industries which had all been sited to receive supplies via the waterways. From Liverpool docks hides from South America, Africa and Europe arrived at the tanneries together with consignments of materials from which tanning extracts were obtained such as mimosa bark, chestnut wood, sumac and Columbian divi divi. By 1900 tanning was all important with Runcorn soon to become the nation's leading centre for leather production. Of the four tanneries, Highfield tannery alone increased its capacity for hides from 50 hides in 1888 to 8,000 a week in 1932.[56]

The fast and efficient handling of traffic on the upper river was carried out with the precision of a well rehearsed parade. Speed was essential. Viewed from Runcorn Hill, the Mersey at high tide took on the appearance of a regatta with scores of small craft moving to Runcorn, Weston Point and Widnes. A few hours later at low water, they had all disappeared.

At Liverpool in 1885 there was the Duke's barge dock in the centre of the dock area. This was one of the few docks not controlled by the Mersey Dock and Harbour Board but the Bridgewater Trustees' Egerton Dock at Liverpool had been transferred to the Harbour Board at the formation of the Bridgewater Navigation Company.

The volume of barge traffic posed problems for the Upper Mersey Navigation Commissioners whose Superintendent of lights and buoys reported in 1883 that the route between Runcorn and Garston was "winding, unsettled and intricate". Fearful weather in January 1881 had interrupted shipping when ice formed on the river and Superintendent Davies reported briefly:

> The river is literally filled with ice which is creating sad havoc among the buoys and it is a great impediment to navigation.

Twenty hollow buoys broke adrift and several were never recovered and a number of the solid wooden buoys were swept away and lost. Four perches which were positioned on the shoreline were also carried away by the ice and

Davies reported that he had the greatest difficulty in keeping the course of the channel marked. His reports also indicate that working conditions for the crew of the buoy boat *Preston* were severe in the extreme. Conditions aboard the lightvessels were very unpleasant in heavy weather and storms on the river could put them in real peril. On 14th October 1881 the lightship *Rival* parted her moorings and drifted up the river. The anchor was released and it held the vessel until the gale had abated but fifteen fathoms of chain and the mooring stone were lost.[57]

Six years after the lamp in Ince lighthouse had been extinguished the great migration of the sailing channels once again brought the navigable passage to the Cheshire shore and on 31st October 1883 the light was relit. By 1894 the Upper Mersey Navigation Commissioners had three lightships stationed in the river between Runcorn and Garston. The old *Rival* was in a poor condition and Davies reported that "the hull is far decayed although it will last some time yet". *Rival* was stationed off Speke, *Miner* was below Ditton Brook and the *Shamrock* was off Dungeon Point. The light vessels were strange looking craft. They were barge-like in appearance with a tall steel tower amidships to carry a ball as a day mark and an oil lantern by night. Each had a distinctive red hull bearing in white, the large letters UMC.[58] The light vessels were frequently involved in collisions and had to be withdrawn from service to be replaced by old river flats which had been improvised as temporary light vessels. These old wooden craft were not entirely satisfactory replacements for even the slightest collision was enough to damage the timbers to result in them being removed from station for recaulking. The Upper Mersey Commissioners never assigned a light vessel to serve a specific navigation system or dock. At their monthly meeting in July 1878 the Commissioners had decided that their light vessels would not be used exclusively for the benefit of a particular port unless that port requested a lightship and the port authority was prepared to meet the costs of providing the vessel and maintaining it on permanent station.[59]

By the end of the century over a hundred buoys were needed to indicate the safe channels within the Commissioner's boundaries and there were perhaps another hundred miniature buoys on the stretch from Runcorn to Warrington. It is doubtful whether the channel to Warrington was ever lighted by the Upper Mersey Commissioners.

Notes

1. Porteous, J.D., *Canal Ports,* Academic Press, London, 1977, p.162.

2. Brooke of Norton Collection D24/B1, Cheshire C.R.O.

3. St. Paul's Wesleyan Church, Runcorn, Centenary Publication 1917.

4. Porteous, J.D., op. cit., p.162.

5. Ormerod, G., *History of the County Palatinate and City of Chester,* Vol. 11.

6. Allen J.F., *Some Founders of the Chemical Industry,* Sherrat and Hughes, Manchester, 1906, p.141.

7. The Bridgewater Department Handbook, M.S.C. Co. 1968, p.40.

8. Ibid. p.41.

9. *Runcorn Guardian,* 3rd June 1876.

10. Superintendent of Lights and Buoys, Bridgewater Navigation Co. 1875.

11. *Warrington Guardian,* 19th Feb. 1876.

12. Hadfield, C. and Biddle, G., *Canals of North West England,* Vol.11, p.381.

13. Hardie, D., *A History of the Chemical Industry of Widnes,* ICI, 1950, p.75.

14. Ibid., p.76.

15. "The Shipping Movements," *Warrington Guardian,* 1870-1875.

16. Annual Statement of Navigation and Shipping of the U.K. Board of Trade, 1872, p.204.

17. Ibid. For 1862 p.411; 1863 p.426; 1864 p.445; 1867 p.485; 1872 p.421; 1881 p.170; 1893 p.221.

18. Ibid. 1877-1880.

19. Ibid.

20. U.M.N.C. Superintendent of Lights and Buoys, Report December 1877.

Lindsay, J., *A History of the North Wales Slate Industry,* David and Charles, Newton Abbot, 1974, p. 180.

22. Ibid., p. 180.

23. Mr. G. Weedall, Bridgewater Docks, Runcorn 1970.

24. Annual Statements, Board of Trade, 1873, p.256.

25. Ibid., 1873, p. 177

26. Porteous, J.D., op. cit., p.163.

27. Mather, F.C., *After the Canal Duke,* Clarendon Press, Oxford, 1970. p.289.

28. Runcorn Canal Craft Registers, 1877-1949, Cheshire C.R.O.

29. Wheat, G., *On the Duke's Cut,* Transport Publishing Company, Glossop, 1977, p.25.

30. Norton P., *Waterways and Railways to Warrington,* Railway and Canal Historic Society,1974, p.15.

31. Hanson, H., *Canal People,* David and Charles, Newton Abbot, 1978, p.147.

32. *Warrington Examiner,* 11th and 18th January 1879

33. *Warrington Guardian,* 20th February 1884.

34. Ibid., 23rd February 1884.

35. Ibid., 1st March 1884.

36. Annual Statements, Board of Trade 1893, p.183.

37. Ibid., p. l 83.

38. Ibid., 1879 to 1880, Vol.1880,p.126; 1881 Vol.1881,p.127; 1882 to 1886,Vol.1886, p.129; 1886 to 1890, Vol. 1890, p.131; 1891 to 1892, Vol. 1892, p.183;

39. Ibid., 1886- 1894.

40. Porteous, J.D., op. cit. p.162.

41. Annual Statement Board of Trade, 1881, p.101.

42. Ibid., for 1881 p.101 and for 1883 p. 125.

43. Ibid., 1881 p.79.

44. Ibid., 1881 p.79.

45. Ibid., 1881 p.117.

46. Porteous, J.D., op. cit., p.186.

47. Details of ownership, Lloyds Register, 1887.

48. Annual Statement of the Navigation and Shipping of the United Kingdom, Board of Trade 1872, p.178.

49. Poole, C., *A History of Widnes,* Swale Press, Widnes, 1906, p.147.

50. Undated newspaper cutting from *Runcorn and Widnes Chronicle.*

51. Minutes of evidence. Opposition by the Bridgewater Navigation Company and the Mersey and Irwell Navigation Company to the Manchester Ship Canal Bill, 1885.

52. *Ship Canal News,* 21 April, 1888.

53. Ibid.

54. Hadfield, C. and Biddle, G., *Canals of North West England,* Vol. 11, pp.367-368.

55. Ibid., Vol. II, p.368.

56. *Runcorn. The Official Guide,* 1933, p.26.

57. Upper Mersey Navigation Commission, Superintendent of Lights and Buoys, Report October 1881.

58. McRoberts, J., "The Mersey Lighthouses", *Sea Breezes,* Vol. 47, No. 336, 1973, p.47.

59. Upper Mersey Navigation Commission Minute Book, 29 July, 1878.

11
The Port of Runcorn and the Manchester Ship Canal

The expansion of trade between the Liverpool and Manchester regions in the nineteenth century inevitably encouraged schemes for a more efficient transport system between the two towns. The railways which linked the two cities were a natural response to pressures from merchants and industrialists who found that communications by water were unsatisfactory. By 1830 the eighteenth century concept of slow transit and small tonnages in canal barges was outdated and from about 1877 the business men and shippers of Manchester began to explore the feasibility of schemes for bringing a seaway to the city.

The story of the promotion and construction of the Manchester Ship Canal has been well documented and recorded by contemporary writers and photographers and the history of the last great feat of Victorian civil engineering and municipal enterprise is outside the scope of this present work. However, it is appropriate that reference should be made to the effects the building of the Canal had on Runcorn before it was finally completed throughout its length to Manchester.

As noted previously ship canal projects were not new in the 1880s. After the 1825 proposals for a canal from the Dee via Frodsham, Lymm and Didsbury to Manchester had been rejected by Parliament and Sir John Rennie's plans for a deep canal had failed to get the support of the public in the 1840s there was still a considerable correspondence in the Liverpool and Manchester newspapers which showed that the idea of a ship canal had not been totally rejected. But interest in the railways with the prospect of rapid transport attracted the attention of Victorian society in the first half of the century. The psychological impact of railways was tremendous and the ship canal movement was eclipsed. However, interest in seaway projects began to revive in the 1870s and 1880s at a time when there was serious recession in trade in Manchester which was particularly acute in the Greater Manchester districts. There was much anxiety in all sections of the community when it became known that some major manufacturing concerns were considering moving their premises from Manchester to the Clyde in order to benefit from the cheaper carriage of raw materials. In brief it was contended by the textile manufacturers:

> that to turn out goods at a low figure from the spindles and looms of Lancashire was of little account unless you could also carry them at a low figure to the place where they were wanted.[1]

The disastrous effects of the existing railway rates on Manchester's trade was crippling and they prompted local entrepreneurs to consider again the possibility of creating a deep canal which would bring ocean going vessels to the city and from 1877 influential members of the business community and the city's Chamber of Commerce began to disseminate their views in the local newspapers. By 1882 a provisional committee had been appointed with powers to obtain a detailed survey of the rivers Irwell and Mersey and two eminent engineers, Messrs. E. Leader Williams and Hamilton H. Fulton were asked to report on the feasibility of a ship canal project. The report was favourable and Leader Williams' scheme was adopted by the committee.

On 9th November 1882 a conference was held with representatives of the various businesses of Manchester and Salford and the plans were enthusiastically endorsed. A week later a general meeting of the Manchester Chamber of Commerce passed a resolution approving the scheme and a mass meeting of working men adopted a resolution in favour of the proposed Parliamentary Bill in the Free Trade Hall in Manchester on the same day.[2]

There then followed a tedious two year struggle to get the Bill through Parliament. The first Bill was passed by the House of Commons on 6th July 1883 but it was rejected by the Committee of the House of Lords. The plans for the canal were amended but the second Manchester Ship Canal Bill was rejected by the Committee of the House of Commons on August 1st 1884. After further alteration the third Bill was presented and it received the Royal Assent on 6th August 1885.

Two years later on 3rd August 1887 the Bridgewater Navigation Company was purchased by the Manchester Ship Canal Company for £1,710,000 and the new company acquired the whole of the Bridgewater properties consisting of the Bridgewater Canal and its docks and the Mersey and Irwell system. On 8th June 1887 the contract for the whole of the ship canal works was let to Mr. T.A. Walker and on 11th November the first sod was cut at Eastham by Lord Egerton of Tatton.

Inevitably the plans to bring a seaway through Merseyside aroused concern in Widnes and Runcorn. The Ship Canal project was viewed with apprehension by the Widnes Local Board which opposed the Bill in 1885. The Board pointed out that a large trade was carried on between Liverpool and Widnes and that sometimes as many as sixty vessels a day left Widnes for Liverpool and beyond. The Widnes Local Board believed that the canal works would have a detrimental effect on the channels of the river which would make the navigation of craft to the town more difficult.[3] The Upper Mersey Navigation Commissioners were quick to voice their disapproval for as early as December 1882 they declared their opposition to the Ship Canal proposals.[4]

There was similar anxiety among the ship owners of Runcorn and in March 1885 the Improvement Commissioners conducted a poll among the rate payers upon a resolution to empower the Commissioners to oppose the Manchester Ship Canal Bill.[5] The result of the poll showed that 1415 votes were cast in favour of the resolution with 381 against, a majority of 1034. Some indication of the indifference with which the poll was regarded can be seen by the fact that of the papers handed into the returning officer 687 were blank and a further 84 were spoiled. Later that month a meeting of Runcorn ship owners which included Messrs. R. Toft, J. Pritchard, R. Clark, J.W. Shore, J. Anderson, E. Marwood, G. Millington, O. Thomas, S. Ravenscroft, J. Howard, T. Rayner and S. Beckett agreed to leave their interests in the hands of the local authority but they insisted that the Ship Canal Company should concede their demands for free towage to and from Runcorn for vessels of up to 500 tons. They were optimistically looking into the future because in 1885 there were no local men who owned vessels of more than 150 tons displacement. In fact laden craft of 500 tons could not reach Runcorn. According to a report in the *Warrington Examiner* of 13th September 1884 the largest vessel ever to dock in the Upper Mersey was the barque *Lido,* 475 tons, which had arrived at Weston Point with a cargo of bones from South America during the previous week.

Of Runcorn's 157 vessels only six sailing craft were more than 100 tons with another 104 between 50 and 100 tons and there were only four small steamers each less than 60 tons displacement registered at the port.

The first large ocean going ships came to Runcorn while the Manchester Ship Canal was being built. The Canal Company commenced to use the completed section from Eastham to Weston Mersey Lock in 1892 and on 22nd July a temporary port called Saltport was established at the mouth of the river Weaver at Weston Point. It was to be another eighteen months before the waterway was complete to enable vessels to reach Manchester and in the meantime Saltport prospered. As the name suggests, salt cargoes shipped down the Weaver formed the chief export commodity. Contemporary photographs show that Saltport was a busy place with both sides of the canal equipped with steam cranes for unloading salt from barges or for discharging timber onto the wharfs from the large sailing ships.

The four masted ship, *Fort Stuart* of Liverpool, 2313 tons, with a draught of twenty-four feet was the first large sailing ship to enter the Ship Canal. She was towed by the tug *Wrestler* to Saltport where she loaded 3,750 tons of salt which was destined for Calcutta. On August 11th 1893 it was reported that there were eleven ships with a cargo carrying capacity of 20,000 tons at Saltport and five sailing ships with cargoes of resin, another five with timber and two steamers were also on passage to the new port. The first foreign vessel to arrive at Saltport was the Norwegian timber ship *Deodata* from Shediac, New Brunswick. The directors of the Manchester Ship Canal Company presented her owners with a handsome clock and barometer bearing an inscription stating that she was the first foreign ship to load and unload in the canal. *Deodata* left Saltport with a cargo of salt.°

Some Liverpool merchants regarded the new port with apprehension. A report in the *Lancashire General Advertiser* of December 9th 1892 described the scene which occurred when the first cargo of timber was unloaded at Saltport:

We understand that the Pitch Pine and Export Timber Company have found that the charges of the Ship Canal Company as compared with Liverpool gave them a saving upon the stored portion of the cargo upwards of five shillings a ton. Their ordinary business as importers is to sell the cargo as a whole or, occasionally in two portions to the Liverpool dealers who in turn sell the cargo in comparatively small quantities to merchants and consumers inland. The Pitch Pine and Export Timber Company did all they could to get the Liverpool merchants to purchase their first Saltport cargo in the ordinary way but co-operation amongst the Liverpool people was so complete that they refused to have anything to do with the cargo although the saving as compared with Liverpool is acknowledged.

The Liverpool timber merchants adopted a sullen, suspicious attitude. There were no buyers and the sale was abandoned. The newspaper account goes on to state:

The latter (the Liverpool timber merchants) evidently with a view to exerting their influence against a continuance of imports upon the Manchester Ship Canal, collected together about fifty yards from where the timber was lying for sale and would go no nearer to the broker and consequently the sale was an absolute fiasco as intended by the Liverpool people it should be. As an example of its effect, it may be mentioned that the cargo imported by another firm is at Saltport in the timber pond without one stick being sold.

In spite of the early opposition, timber cargoes arrived regularly and trade at the temporary port became brisk. Three ships arrived in June 1893. The *Avon,* 1590 tons, of Liverpool, arrived from Pensacola, USA, to discharge 1,817 loads of sawn pitch pine. The Norwegian barque *Golden Horn* 1,028 tons, unloaded 550 standards of spruce deals, and the barque *Birnam Wood* 1,305 tons from West Bay, Nova Scotia discharged 630 standards of spruce to be distributed inland via the Shropshire Union and Bridgewater Canals. After a voyage of five months by way of Cape Horn the barque *Agnes* arrived at Saltport from Port Blakeley, British Columbia with a cargo of Oregon pine and the barque *Ceres* discharged 1,500 tons of pitch pine from Mobile, USA. Another sailing vessel, the *Paul* from La Union unloaded a cargo of fustic - a wood yielding a yellow dye which was destined for the dyers of east Lancashire. Most of the ships using Saltport were much larger than any previously seen on the upper river and Marshall Stevens, the Ship Canal manager stated that besides the Runcorn traffic of 12,000 tons a month, 90,000 tons of new business came to Saltport in 1892.[7]

On 2nd June 1892 the Manchester Ship Canal Company gave notice of their intention to close temporarily all entrances between the tideway and the dock and navigation systems at Runcorn and Weston Point with the exception of the Delamere Dock.[8] These arrangements came into operation on the first of July and the Company made provision for the efficient clearance of cargoes at Runcorn at no extra cost to the importers and shippers. They continued to tow incoming vessels via the Mersey to Weston Point docks or through Eastham locks then via the completed section of the Ship Canal to Saltport. At both places barges were available to convey cargoes at the Company's expense to Runcorn by way of the Runcorn and

Weston Canal. Canal craft passing between Runcorn docks and the Bridgewater Canal and destined for Widnes or Warrington were also routed via the Runcorn and Weston Canal. These arrangements satisfied John Brundrit, quarry owner of Runcorn who appears to have been the spokesman for the local ship owners and traders. In a letter to W.H. Collier, the Manager of the Bridgewater Department of the Manchester Ship Canal, a Mr. Meadowcroft had reported in March that Mr. Brundrit had been prepared to call a public meeting if the arrangements appeared to be detrimental to the interests of the town's ship owners.[9]

The task of keeping trade moving during the excavations in front of the docks was a formidable one. Some idea of the size of the problem can be seen when one considers the volume of coastal traffic immediately prior to the closure of the entrance. In the china clay trade alone in the four months from November 1891 to April 1892 sixty-five schooners arrived from Fowey, forty-seven from Par, thirty-three from Charlestown, seventeen came from Pentewan and thirty-two from Teignmouth. During the same period seventeen schooners came from Bideford, forty-six from Plymouth, twenty-seven from Falmouth, twenty-one from Poole and five from Newquay.[10] The Ship Canal Company's efforts to provide an efficient service were largely successful in spite of the year long closure of the dock entrance and on 12th July 1893 the manager of the Bridgewater Docks was able to announce that the river entrance was once again open for traffic.

When the water was admitted into the Ship Canal to Runcorn the uncertainty of entry for large vessels was a thing of the past. Previous to this event ships' masters were unable to get vessels into Runcorn unless there was sufficient water in the upper estuary but the Ship Canal enabled ships to reach the docks regardless of the slate of the tide. Before the coming of the canal it was not unusual for a large vessel to have to wait eight or twelve days in the estuary before getting to Runcorn.[11]

At the end of 1893 the first large consignments of timber arrived at Runcorn's new lay-by when *Katahdin* from Parrsboro, Canada, arrived with 1,857 loads of deal and the barque *Bessie Markham* discharged 450 standards of spruce deals, the whole of which was sent to Manchester importers by Bridgewater canal flats.[12] The first steamers to use the lay-by were those of Fisher, Renwick and Company who began a weekly service from London bringing cargoes of skins, sugar and tea for transhipment via the Bridgewater Canal.[13]

To enable craft to enter the ship canal from the river the Ship Canal Company built four locks in the vicinity of Runcorn. Weston Marsh lock at the Weaver mouth became the entrance to the Weaver Navigation whilst Weston Mersey lock enabled shipping to enter the Weaver docks from the estuary. The Bridgewater Docks were served by Bridgewater lock and Runcorn Old Quay lock entrance was built near to the site of the docks of the old Mersey and Irwell which, together with the Runcorn end of the Runcorn to Latchford canal was swept away in the building of the Ship Canal.

As the Ship Canal neared completion there was rivalry to determine which should be the first ship to reach Manchester. On 7th December 1893 *The Examiner and Times* reported:

> At present the "Sophie Wilhelmine" from West Bay, Nova Scotia laden with deals is in the locks at Eastham being unrigged so that she can pass under Runcorn Bridge so that she may be the first ship to pass along the length of the Canal.

The question of whether large sailing vessels could pass under Runcorn railway bridge caused some controversy and there was a lively debate on the subject in the *Manchester City News* in the middle of 1893.[14] It was argued by some that the newer sailing vessels of the time were built with their steel lower and top masts in one piece and that it was becoming the fashion for most large vessels to have at least the fourth jigger mast in one length. Some sailing ships then in the Liverpool docks such as *Garfield* and *La France* were cited as being too lofty to pass under the bridge and it was thought that twenty per cent of the full rigged ships of 1893 could not be towed to Manchester because they could not unship their top masts. In the plans which had been laid before Parliament it was specified that there was to be a clear headway of seventy-five feet at the state of the tide when most vessels would pass under Runcorn Bridge. When the task of housing a ship's top mast ceased to be possible because of changes in design in the later tall ships, cargoes for Manchester and Warrington had to be discharged at Runcorn lay-by and then lightered up to their destinations. The lay-by could accommodate the largest vessels of the day being 1,500 feet long with a depth of water of twenty-six feet alongside.

When the Manchester Ship Canal was opened throughout its length in 1894 Saltport was bypassed by the Weaver traffic and although the wharfs remained until 1905 they were little used and the jetties were finally dismantled to leave no trace of the temporary port.[15] Saltport was the scene of a spectacular fire in 1893 when two large sheds used as fitting shops and stores were totally destroyed. The large warehouse which contained eight thousand casks of resin also caught fire but the efforts of a large gang of workmen resulted in the building being saved.[16] The mushroom port was never recognised by the postal authorities even though ships from America, Europe and the major ports of the United Kingdom acknowledged "Saltport" as their destination.

Even though Runcorn lay-by began to receive the largest square rigged vessels, none were ever registered locally and their crews were mainly recruited at their home ports. Runcorn remained essentially a canal port for the hundred ton coastal sailing vessels. Of course there were many local seamen who signed for ocean voyages in larger craft and there are memorials in the parish church bearing testimony to those who died on distant voyages.

The Manchester Ship Canal was finished at the end of 1893 and it was ceremonially opened on January 1st 1894 - the day after Runcorn had lost its independence as a customs port to become part of the Port of Manchester. In

A Mersey flat heavily laden in the early years of this century.

Runcorn Ferry had been in existence in the twelfth century. The photograph
shows the last ferryman when the service ended in 1905.

1894 Runcorn achieved Urban District status and the council adopted a coat of arms for the town which had, as its central motif, a full rigged sailing ship.

The widely held prediction that the Ship Canal would attract many new industries to line its banks did not materialise in the Runcorn area but the canal now situated Wigg works on deep water and a few years later, Salt Union developed a new plant which enabled large steamers to come alongside the works. There was also an instant and lasting impact on the Runcorn waterfront. After playing a vital role in supplying building materials for the Ship Canal works and for Salford dock construction the Old Quay system disappeared. Old Quay mills were demolished and Brundrit's Mersey Street graving slip was modernised and it became the public slipway in order to compensate the town for the loss of its ship repair facilities. The yard was leased to Messrs. Stubbs who specialised in schooner and barge repair and who continued to service wooden vessels until the last days of sail. The old Castle Rock yard, the site of Ethelfleda's early tenth century Saxon fortress, escaped the attentions of the canal builders and by the end of the century it was in the ownership of Richard Abel and Sons who continued to build and repair wooden barges until the 1960s.

The Ship Canal Company did make some concessions to Runcorn. They sited their tug boat depot at Old Quay. In addition a new yard for the building and repair of barges was built at Runcorn Big Pool. This Sprinch Yard, as it became known, had the latest equipment and it was claimed to have been the finest boat building yard of its time. There were four dry docks which could accommodate six craft at one time and the yard was responsible for the maintenance of over two hundred canal craft.

Whilst it is true that from 1894 Runcorn's docks were adversely effected by the Manchester Ship Canal and by the general decline of trade on the old waterways with which they were linked, there still remained a considerable coastal trade and a vast barge traffic on the upper Mersey. It has been estimated that the coastal trade supplied about eighty per cent of Runcorn's trade in the first year that the canal was open and of the total traffic to Manchester, barges transported twenty-six per cent of the tonnage carried.[17] The Ship Canal now provided an easy route from the estuary but it was not the usual practice for the small sailing vessel to be towed from Eastham via the canal to Weston Point or Runcorn. However, sailing ships with a cargo carrying capacity not exceeding four hundred tons and laden exclusively with pottery materials which arrived in the Mersey on tides which did not permit them to reach Runcorn or Weston Point by the tideway would be towed up the canal free of charge but the Ship Canal Company was prepared to grant this concession only to those vessels which carried cargoes from traditional sources. When adverse tidal conditions prevailed on the river free towage on the canal was available for those craft bringing china clay, blue clay, chert stone and china stone from the south coast of England and also for ships with bones or bone ash from South America and those laden with felspar from

169

Norway and Sweden.[18] The normal entry to Runcorn and Weston Point for small craft was via the river to Weston Mersey lock for entry to the Weaver docks, to the Bridgewater lock for the Bridgewater docks and the Bridgewater Canal with another lock into the Ship Canal at Old Quay for craft passing between Widnes and Runcorn. At Warrington, Walton lock formed the connection between the canal and the Mersey. The river steamers of the Bridgewater Department of the Ship Canal Company continued to provide free towage between the Sloyne anchorage and the estuary locks at Runcorn.

Salt continued to be a main export commodity from Runcorn but trade fluctuated considerably. The *Liverpool Mercury* of 10th July 1896 reported a scene of unexampled shipping activity due to very large salt shipments at Runcorn and Weston Point. In eleven days fifty-three sailing and steam ships were loaded by the Salt Union and its various distributors with over 15,000 tons of salt. The report stated that in 1895 the two ports had shipped 138,000 tons of salt and it predicted that if the boom continued at its extraordinary pace shipments could reach 400,000 tons in 1896. The demand for Cheshire salt came from many quarters. Salt was required in quantity on Merseyside for curing hides, for soap making, for glassworks and for the chemical industry. Besides its universal use as a condiment, it was needed for preserving fish and meat for use on dairy farms and for glazing pottery. Salt was carried in Liverpool ships to India, to the West Indies, to the Baltic countries and to the Mediterranean. The Weaver carried over one and a quarter million tons of salt in 1881 but after that date traffic lessened considerably in face of competition from the railways and from brine delivery pipe lines.

The Manchester Ship Canal works no doubt played an important part in altering the channels of the upper river, whether for better or worse cannot be determined for nature continued to reshape the navigable routes and to present constant challenges to the Upper Mersey Navigation Commissioners. By 1895 the old light ship *Rival* was in poor condition and, in arctic-like conditions in February, floating ice coming down river severely buckled the iron plating on her bows. Weather conditions were extraordinary and the superintendent of lights and buoys decided that *Miner* was also in danger from the ice and he moved her from her station. The Commissioners' other light vessel, *Shamrock,* had been driven ashore on Ince Bank during a gale in the previous month and while she was undergoing repairs the flat *Yankee* was equipped as a temporary replacement and towed to *Shamrock's* station. *Rival's* misfortunes continued into 1896. She needed repairs in February and later suffered considerable damage when a flat towed by the steamer *Queen of the Mersey* rammed her. The lightship's mooring chain was slipped to save her from foundering and she was towed to Runcorn for repairs and the flat *Garnet* was used as a replacement. The storm which had caused the collision also resulted in *Shamrock* parting her cable to be driven ashore at the river Weaver tidal opening. She received little damage but an inspection of *Rival's* hull decided the Commissioners against returning the old vessel to her station and she was replaced by a new light vessel, the *Vencedora*.[19]

In the decade ending in 1890 there were thirty sinkings in the river channels, about the same number in the next ten years and no less than forty-two recorded sinkings between 1900 and 1910.[20] Some sinkings were unusual or spectacular. In March 1889 the flat *Ernest*, owner Settle Speakman, hit the piers of the railway bridge and sank but was removed by her owner next day. The narrow boat *Sarah Alice* suffered the same accident a couple of weeks later. She too was successfully salvaged.

The flat *Ouse* was also fortunate after hitting the bridge in August 1890. She sank but was refloated by her owners two days later. The flat *Fanny Ann* was not so lucky. She sank under the bridge in 1877 and blasting operations could not be undertaken because of the possibility of injuring the bridge but the rip tides soon solved the problem and *Fanny Ann* broke into pieces and the wreckage quickly disappeared below the sand. The *Llanfair* met an unusual end when she grounded off the Bridgewater Docks in September 1888. The vessel sprang a leak causing her cargo of lime to slake and *Llanfair* caught fire. A few days later her remains were blown up to clear the channel. Swift action had to be taken to remove the wreck of the mast flat *Star* which sank in a gale off Weston Point in 1899 and the explosion and the tides scattered her cargo of bones far over the sands. *Sea Spray* of Glasgow went aground on a sandbank off Delamere Dock laden with 627 tons of salt in July 1897. She broke in two and the wreck was quickly removed by the East Coast Salvage Association of Leith. Some of the flats had many lives. The *Victory* belonging to Coopers of Widnes was sunk three times before finally being blown up in 1913. *Annie* a flat belonging to Abel's of Runcorn was also sunk and salvaged on three occasions.

There were sinkings all along the route from Garston to Warrington. The steamer *Tudor* grounded and broke up off Otterspool in July 1889 and between September 1879 and October 1886 the flats *Joseph, Greenland, Elk, Lilac, Willie, Samuel, Eliza, Diamond, Supplement* and *Spider* had been sunk off Oglet or off Hale. *Albion* and *Henry* came to grief off Woodend in 1889. *Bertie* (Abel's) was driven ashore at Hale with a cargo of phosphate rock in July 1891 and she was refloated a couple of days later. The flat *Hannah* (T. Robinson) was sunk off the Bridgewater entrance in October 1891 in a collision with *S.S. Gower* but survived to be refloated to see further service. The flats *Hugh* and *Mersey* did not survive a collision with *S.S. Cygnus* in February 1892 off Weston Point and they were destroyed. The tug *Walton* sank at Walton Arches in October 1889 but was removed next day. *Ann Marie*, flat, owner Abels, with a cargo of gravel sank near Bank Quay and was salvaged in August 1893.

The sailing flats and the steam barges carried weighty cargoes of river sand, gravel, coal, sugar and road stone and as their wide hatches were often uncovered they could easily be swamped by sudden squalls: The sand flats were particularly susceptible to danger in rough weather and as often as not they were overloaded. Some of the sand was obtained from the shore at New Brighton or Eastham and loading a flat was a back breaking task. When the flat settled on the shore the crew would throw the sand up on to the deck where it would be thrown down into the hold. A team of men might be employed in working round the vessel shovelling in sand until it seemed that the flat was grossly overloaded. When the loading was finished the hatch boards and their canvas sheets were secured over the hold, the ventilation and deadlights were firmly shut and even the galley flue was closed off. The incoming tide would creep up the vessel and across the deck but she was held tight to the bottom by the weight of her heavy cargo and by the grip of suction below her keel. The crew would climb up the mast and the stays and commence a rhythmic rocking of the flat. When the water was up to the hatches and it appeared that the vessel would never float, she would suddenly jump off the bottom to bob like a cork on the tide.[21]

The sand flats carried builders' sand and glass making sand to Coopers at West Bank, Widnes. The fine silver glass sand was loaded into railway waggons which were carefully sheeted to prevent the sand blowing away on its journey to Pilkington's glass works in St. Helens.

Wrecks and obstacles and the shifting channels made arduous the work of the Upper Mersey Navigation Commissioners' Superintendent of Lights and Buoys and from about 1897 he began to keep a close watch upon another activity which at times threatened to obstruct the sailing channels. This new development was the establishment of a shipbreaking industry at Hale.[22] One tends to associate the area with rural peace and agriculture and the shore atmosphere is one of light, space and tranquility and yet by 1900 the site of the old salt refinery at Dungeon, about a mile to the west of the lighthouse had become the scene of considerable industrial energy. There was sufficient depth of water at high tide at Old Dungeon pier to enable large iron ships to be taken alongside for scrapping. A couple of steam cranes on a short length of makeshift track and a scrap yard enclosed by a corrugated iron fence comprised the breaker's premises and vessels of surprisingly large dimensions towered over the fields awaiting the attentions of the breakers. The ships were, in the main, the first generation iron barques, schooners and pleasure paddle steamers. Tugs, coastal steamers and larger vessels were dissected not by the use of oxy-acetylene cutting apparatus but, by the crude but effective method of using chisels to sever the heads of the rivets which fastened the plating together.[23]

The salvaged iron and steel was loaded on the little steamer *Progress* which regularly towed three loaded flats up river to Monks Hall iron works at Atherton's Quay at Warrington. The valuable copper and bronze was bought by Liverpool dealers who removed it from the shore by horse and cart. Often complete deck cabins were lifted ashore to be sold as office buildings. The cabins also served as living accommodation for the breaker's men. Ships' furniture, carpets, lifeboats, ropes and lamps were sold off before the work of demolition began. On one occasion a sizeable mid-Victorian warship arrived. The guns had been removed in the naval dockyard but the vessel's massive construction meant the provision of much needed employment for the men of the neighbourhood. This ship was the antiquated 3,500 tons ironclad *H.M.S. Resistance,* a barque-rigged sail and steam warship which was laid down in 1859. *Resistance* had finished her useful life as a target ship before being beached off Oglet in order to be lightened prior to her being scrapped at Dungeon Pier in 1900.

The Superintendent of Lights and Buoys noted the arrival of the old vessels. They could represent a considerable hazard to the stream of shipping which was using the river to Runcorn and Widnes and he watched their progress with interest and anxiety and his reports often reflect growing concern when the large hulks were towed up river. His fears were justified for one very large vessel did run aground. This was the ancient coastal defence ironclad *H.M.S. Glatton,* a turret ship of 5,000 tons and drawing eighteen feet nine inches of water, which became struck on the Black Rocks just outside the breaker's yard of Messrs. J.J. King at Garston in 1903. This yard lay within the boundaries of the Upper Mersey Commission and for a month in the autumn their Superintendent watched the situation carefully as the derelict was lightened and eventually towed off the rocks to be tied up at the breaker's wall. The Superintendent's relief was short lived for the old Ellerman Line steamer *Plantain* beached awkwardly off Oglet at this same time and she presented problems until she was lightened and towed to the pier at Dungeon. Although the arrival of the worn out old ships meant much needed employment, they could bring unforeseen nuisance. A present day resident of Hale village recounts how one night his grandparents took refuge on a farm gate when a regiment of rats which had been driven out of a hulk by the rising tide abandoned the vessel and scuttled across the fields in search of new homes.

The breaker's yard at Hale had been established by a Scottish firm but it was later acquired by Richard White and Sons, Engineers, of Ditton Road, Widnes. White's ceased their shipbreaking business in 1912 when the channel at Hale became too intricate to permit large ships to berth at Old Dungeon wharf.

The Tall Ships

The advent of the Manchester Ship Canal changed the maritime character of Runcorn. With the arrival of the massive square rigged ships at the lay-by the docks assumed the appearance of a genuine deep water port. For thirty years the magnificent tall ships were frequent visitors to the lay-by where they discharged cargoes of timber or grain which was lightered up the Ship Canal to timber merchants and millers in Warrington and Manchester.[25] Among the best remembered are the four masted steel barque *Lawhill* 2,816

173

A narrow beam canal tug towing barges onto the tideway from the Bridgewater Canal about 1886.

American timber ships at Saltport in 1893.

tons built in Dundee in 1892 but registered in Finland from where she brought cargoes of timber. Other ships included *Hougomont,* a steel barque of 2,428 tons, *Garthwray* 1,937 tons and *Garthpool.* In 1907 *Garthwray* distinguished herself by beating the French barque *Duquesne* by four days on a passage from San Francisco to Runcorn. During the first three decades of this century *Hiawatha* 1,562 tons and *Monkbarns* 1,911 tons were often to be seen at the lay-by. Perhaps the best known was the iron *Macquarie* a full-rigged ship of 1,965 tons. She was the last square rigged sailing ship built on London river and it was claimed that she was the strongest sailing vessel ever built. In August 1904 *Macquarie* arrived at Runcorn on her last voyage under the red ensign. She was sold to Norwegian owners and lasted for many years before finishing her days as a coal hulk in Sydney, Australia. She was scrapped in 1953.

The arrival of a grain ship was a source of satisfaction for the local dockers for it meant nearly three weeks of highly paid work with wages rising to £4 a week. The grain had to be bagged and the bags stitched before they were loaded into barges. Whale oil was unloaded at the lay-by. The oil was pumped from the sailing ship's tanks into special barges each of which contained three small tanks. The cargo was then taken to Hazlehurst's soap works or to Crosfield's at Warrington. Sometimes the oil would arrive in barrels and these often found their way into dockers' homes where they were cut down to make handy wash day tubs. It was widely believed that the evil smelling whale oil when used as a liniment could give relief to sufferers from rheumatism. Samples were brought ashore for those who were prepared to suffer the reek in an attempt to alleviate the complaint. One enterprising dock worker bought whale bones which he fashioned into attractive walking sticks and then sold for a handsome profit.

After their long voyages the members of the crew of a tall ship needed to replace their worn out clothing before they could go ashore. As the ship tied up she would be met by local outfitters who cried their wares. Mr. Pat Collins had his well known patter:

> I've got your going aloft trousers and your going ashore kit.
> I've got everything you need lads.
> My Green River knives will shave a mouse to sleep,
> I've got your hard weather oilskins.
> And your London feather beds.

Mr. Collins would then pass out his handbills which gave details of his bargains.

At Runcorn two chandlers in Percival Lane remained to serve the sailing ships in their latter days. Hewitt's or Carter's provided for all their needs. Oil, rope, canvas sea boots and oilskins, biscuits and groceries were obtainable until late at night. The ships' masters would sit on coils of rope discussing nautical affairs whilst victualling their vessels and the stores were delivered to the ship by the chandler's boy with a handcart. It was claimed that Hewitt's could supply everything a captain needed except the vessel itself.

The Mersey Mission to Seamen at Runcorn continued to be a tranquil haven for seamen and the indomitable Missioner, William Shaw, was tireless in his relief work among the destitute families of boatmen and flatmen. He had built a Mission Church in Station Road in 1891 and his influence was felt beyond Runcorn for in 1880 he had helped to establish a Mersey Mission at Ellesmere Port. His wife provided him with active support in this charitable work and for thirty-seven years she gave practical help to many needy individuals among the boat people. She died in 1913 and a stained glass window in the Mission Church was dedicated to her memory. After forty-six years work of incomparable altruism Mr. Shaw retired in 1921 and it seemed hardly possible that a man of similar standing could be found to replace him. However, his successor, Samuel Towers, proved to be a Missioner of equal ability and generosity and he soon won a reputation for unselfishness that equalled that of "Captain" Shaw. Although Mr. Towers was to serve the Mission for many years the Station Road Church was universally referred to as "Shaw's Mission". Few ships came to Runcorn after the war and in 1946 the Mersey Mission to Seamen was closed and its work was taken over by St. Michael's Church in Greenway Road, the parish church in which the Mission was situated. The building in Station Road was sold to the Cheshire Education Committee in 1956 and it was demolished in the early 1970s to make way for a new road.

The tall ships were impressive but Runcorn and Weston Point continued to remain principally schooner ports. What might be described as the golden years of the schooners was the period from about 1885 to 1910 and their story has been magnificently told by Basil Greenhill in his comprehensive work *The Merchant Schooners*. In his two volume work the author records the history of British schooners with detailed account of their voyages, cargoes, owners and builders as well as recalling much of the nautical tradition and flavour of the times. This present volume would not be complete without similar consideration of the last years of the sailing vessel at Runcorn with some reference to the all important supportive trades and nautical facilities ashore.

The last schooner to be built at Runcorn was the 145 ton three masted *Despatch* which left the slipway at Brundrit and Hayes' yard in 1886. She was one of the Newfoundland salt carriers and she lasted twenty-seven years before becoming a total loss off Holyhead in 1913. But most of the local vessels were engaged in coastal waters in the china clay, coal, salt and slate trades and their adventures were many and varied. *John Henry* and *Julia* were lost off the North Wales coast in 1903, *Mary Elizabeth* came to grief on Bardsay Island in July 1910, *Fox* was smashed to pieces near Fishguard in 1911 and the ketch *Sarah* was wrecked at Nefyn in March 1910. There were further casualties. *Harvest Queen* disappeared in the Irish Sea on Christmas Eve 1912. *Gleaner* was last seen on November 5th 1918, *Truth Seeker* foundered with all hands in 1923 and *Red Tail* left St. Valerie on 13th June 1917 never to be seen again. In a single week in 1904 three Runcorn owned vessels were sunk with heavy loss of life. The little steamer, *Percy* owned by Brundrit and Company and laden with road setts from Penmaenmawr collided with *S.S. Plover* in the Mersey and *Percy's* master and her fireman were drowned. The local steamer *Blanche* was sunk in collision off Fleetwood and seven of her nine man crew were drowned and in that same week came the news that the schooner *Emily Mary* had been lost with all hands. In August 1902 and 118 ton schooner *Janet Worthington* was sunk in collision with *S.S. Roddam*. There were losses among Runcorn steamers. *Nautilus* was driven ashore at Formby in 1893 and *S.S. William Rowland* of Runcorn, 363 tons, was sunk in collision with a dredger at Liverpool in 1909. The steamer's master was the only man drowned of her crew of ten. The local steamer *Cecil* was wrecked at Le Croton on the French coast in 1917. When the German advance overran much of the Belgian and French coalfields in the first world war Runcorn schooners were used to carry Lancashire coal to French ports and *Emily Millington* was sunk off Bishop's Rock by a submarine three weeks before the Armistice in 1918. Also in 1918 *Sunbeam* was driven ashore at Southport and in October attempts to salvage her were abandoned.[26]

Without the benefit of radio communications some schooners simply vanished without trace. Other crews were more fortunate but suffered fearful experiences before being rescued. A case in point was *Eva Lena* bound for Port Dinorwic from Widnes with coal in August 1900. The little schooner was hit by a severe storm off Llandudno. The ship's boat was lost, the main gaff was broken and the mizzen sail was torn away. *Eva Lena* sprang a leak and began to drift towards the shore. By midnight the schooner was helpless, and lit by lightning which the crew admitted was a terrifying experience in itself, the men took to the rigging expecting to be washed away and drowned at any moment. After clinging to the rigging for four hours, daylight found them drifting into Llandudno Bay and by this time the three man crew was in an exhausted condition. Fortunately they were seen from the shore and John Williams and John Hughes of Llandudno put off in a small boat. They managed to pull the men off the schooner and found one man to be in a semi-conscious condition. The *Eva Lena* continued to drift and sank after striking a rock near to the Little Orme. When the tide went out her cargo was recovered.[27]

Of course shipping disasters were not restricted to vessels on the Runcorn register for many vessels of other ports were lost on passages to and from the Mersey. In the four weeks from mid February to the middle of March 1908 for instance, the *Richard Fisher,* a three masted schooner from Barrow, turned over in a gale off New Ferry and sank with all hands. A few days later *Rareplant,* 128 tons, and bound from Runcorn to Par was cut down in fog off the north coast of Cornwall by the steamer *Hartland* and *Hodbarrow*

Miner left Runcorn for Truro on the 2nd March and was wrecked on the north Cornish coast with one survivor.

The dubious Mersey channels continued to present problems for the sailing flats. In February 1895 the Upper Mersey Navigation Commissioners' Superintendent reported that the approaches to Weston Mersey lock were very good but in March 1903 his successor, William Yates, reported that there was no navigable channel to the lock and he described the passage to the Bridgewater dock as being "long, narrow and difficult for large vessels". A year later he reported that there was no way through to the Bridgewater lock.

Winter weather on the treacherous Mersey was a source of danger and anxiety for the flatmen. The era of the sailing flats is not well documented and the occasional paragraph at the foot of a column in an old newspaper which reports the death of a flatman does not convey any impression of the river's sudden storms and rushing tides. The Constable's accounts for the township of Runcorn at the end of the eighteenth century contain items of expense incurred for the funerals of seamen and flatmen (often unknown) whose bodies were recovered from the river. Among the tombstones in the Parish churchyard are some recording tragedies of long ago. One is inscribed: "Here resteth the body of John Tuckfield of Runcorn who was called for in a storm, October 26th 1824, aged 29 years", and in the quiet churchyard at Hale is the grave of John Maddock who was drowned in the river on February 27th 1819 aged 35. His stone has the following verse:

> Though stormy blasts on Mersey's waves
> Have tossed me to and fro
> In calm repose by God's decrees
> I harbour here below.
> My body now at anchor lies,
> My soul no more oppresst
> Has steered its course
> By love divine
> And gained the port of rest

The flats sank with amazing frequency.[28] Most of the casualties were amongst those owned by Cooper's of Widnes and Abel's of Runcorn whose vessels carried sand and gravel from the mouth of the estuary. Between 1900 and 1928 there are thirteen recorded sinkings of Cooper's flats and barges and Abel's had no less than seventeen. The majority were mast flats and nine of Abel's and five of the Cooper's vessels could not be raised and they were either blown up by the water bailiff or they were pulled apart by their owners. Some flats destroyed themselves in bizarre fashion. In March 1907 Cooper's mast flat *Elizabeth* let go her anchor and ran over it so that the flukes pierced the hull. She blocked the channel at Dungeon Point and had to be destroyed. On 19th February 1910 the light vessel *Shamrock* "sank at her moorings through sitting on her anchor". The *Industry* a flat belonging to William Cooper did the same thing in 1916 and a dredger belonging to Cooper's sank when the grab got under the vessel off Garston in March 1908. There were some spectacular groundings in the upper river. The screw tug *Bridgewater* of the Manchester Ship Canal Company ran aground with twenty flats in tow in May 1920 and in September of the same year, the river tugs *Dagmar, St. Winifred* and *Earl of Ellesmere* assisted by two small tugs with twenty-one flats and barges in tow grounded off Weston Mersey lock.

Whilst Yates was reporting the worsening state of the river at Weston Point and at the Bridgewater lock in 1903, the river from Old Quay to Warrington began to show remarkable improvement. The Upper Mersey Commissioners may have been failing in their duties by not marking the channel in this stretch of river and other interests began to take a hand. Yates discovered that a number of buoys not belonging to the Commissioners had been placed in the river between Penketh Bank and the lower end of Bank Quay Reach and upon enquiry he found that they belonged to Crosfields. The superintendent could not understand the necessity for the alien buoys and he observed:

> For what purpose Messrs. Crosfield and Son had placed them there I do not know insomuch as I consider the channel to be in better condition for navigation than I have known it before.

Mr. Yates did not approve of the unofficial buoys and he had them removed and he set perches to mark the channel. At Old Quay too, the approaches were most satisfactory and in December 1904 the *Runcorn and Widnes Chronicle* reported that the heavily laden *S.S. Emerald* of Glasgow, 304 tons, passed through Old Quay lock into the Manchester Ship Canal. She was the largest vessel to do so up to that time being two hundred feet long with a beam of thirty feet.

But problems persisted down river and the barge traffic, the sailing craft and the small steamers combined with the tortuous channels and the elements to make difficult the work of the crews on the light vessels. *Vencedora* suffered two collisions in 1902 and *Shamrock* was hit three times between 1900 and 1902. The old *Miner* was scrapped in 1900 and her fog bell was removed to Hale lighthouse to replace the one cracked by constant use. The *Miner's* replacement was *Arthur Sinclair* completed in 1902. *Arthur Sinclair* suffered a serious collision when she was struck by the mast flat *Eustice Carey*. The master of the light vessel, Joseph Harrison, of Bridgewater Street, Runcorn died from the injuries he received. At the inquest the coroner was informed that the deceased was seventy-six years of age! New lights were installed on the three lightships in 1911. These occulting lamps could be seen in ordinary conditions at a distance of eight miles. The last light vessel built by the Commissioners was the *G.R. Jebb* which was launched at Sankey Bridges in January 1913. During the 1920s the light vessels were sold and their lantern towers were removed and erected on shore at Hale Decoy, Pickering's Marsh and at Dungeon Point.

The old lighthouse at Ince had been demolished to make way for the Ship Canal but Hale Head lighthouse remained vital for the safe navigation on the river. By 1902 it was in need of repair and oak beams and iron stays were used to reinforce the tower. At the same time extensive repairs were made to the keeper's cottage. The repairs to the lighthouse were of a makeshift nature and in 1906 a start was made in building a new one. The new Hale lighthouse was completed in the new year and on January 28th 1907 the light shone for the first time. The modern tower was sixty three feet high and it was equipped with a fixed white light of 500 candle power.

Between the world wars a new innovation was tried. These were the bell buoys. Some had small paddle wheels inside which revolved to cause a clapper to ring the bell. They were not wholly successful as they required a swift tide to work the paddles efficiently. At high water when craft were using the channels the tide was slow and the bell buoys did not function properly. During the 1940 emergency when invasion appeared to be imminent and the ringing of bells was forbidden the clappers were chained and after the war the mechanism of the buoys was found to be fused with rust and they were scrapped.[29]

The Upper Mersey Commissioners were swift to prosecute persons who interfered with the delicate navigation in their channels. The manager of the Hutchinson's Estate at Widnes was held responsible for allowing rubbish to be tipped on Widnes marsh. He was fined in 1911 when old timbers floating in the river had been mistaken for buoys in misty weather.[30] Unmanned vessels drifting on the river were a menace. After a collision in 1901 involving the schooner *Industry* and the steamer *Hermod* the schooner was abandoned by her crew. Heavily laden with chalk stone, *Industry* drifted up river to become grounded near to Poole Hall. She was not seriously harmed and was towed to Runcorn. The mast flat *Fanny* belonging to Abel's was often involved in minor escapades, but in December 1902 she broke from her moorings and drifted through the north arch of the railway bridge tearing down the fender posts and the navigation lights on the bridge before threatening to ram vessels near to West Bank. It would also appear that even when in dock vessels were not certain of a safe berth. When the schooner *Argus* laden with iron ore was tied up in West Bank Dock in July 1865 she suffered an accident which nearly cost the lives of two of her crew who were sleeping on board. The schooner subsided on the ebb tide and embedded herself in the mud. In the evening when the tide flowed into the dock she stuck fast and would not rise with it, consequently she was soon overflowed and the mate and a seaman narrowly escaped drowning. Conditions at West Bank were alleged to have been the reason for the sinking of a steamer in 1908. The North Lancashire Steamship Company brought an action against the owners and the manager of West Bank Dock when they claimed that their steamer *Lancashire* had sustained damage on projecting masonry in the dock which so strained her seams that she sank on the Silecroft Sands. Eleven days later she was salvaged and taken to Barrow but there was not enough evidence produced in court to show where she had received her injuries.

The old river continued to claim many lives and the catalogue of fatal accidents is too long to recount. Most fatalities occurred among the flatmen and the barge crews in foul weather. Briefly reported were the loss of a man from Cooper's mast flat *Sandfly* which sank in 1900 and the death of the master's son on the flat *Emily* which, on route to Wigg's works, struck an abutment of the railway bridge in 1904 and the boy was thrown overboard and drowned. The mate's wife died in the sinking of *Hawthorne* in 1910 and the crew of three of the steam barge *Severn* died when she sank after hitting a pier of the transporter bridge in 1918. Two men died in *Weaver* in 1916 and the crew of three men drowned when the little steamer *Sandmail* sank after striking a buoy in a gale in 1923. When the barge *Ferndale* was being towed in the company of other barges in February 1928 a sudden gale sprang up and the barge master was thrown overboard and drowned. Such was the strength of the wind that the crews of the other barges could not render assistance as they were forced to lie flat on deck in order to avoid the same fate. On February 11th 1928 Cooper's grab hopper *Grinkle* sank off Oglet with the loss of her crew of six. She had loaded 400 tons of glass makers' sand from the shore at Eastham and her lights were last seen as she passed Speke at 10.30 that night. There was a full gale blowing and when it abated the next day *Grinkle* was found lying upside down in the channel. She could not be raised and was subsequently destroyed by order of the Mersey Docks and Harbour Board. The disaster to *Grinkle* brought double grief to the Rathbone family of Widnes for both Isaac Rathbone and his son were drowned in the disaster.[30] Thirteen years previously Isaac's daughter had been drowned in the sinking of the *Lusitania*. There was a final tragedy in January 1945 when the steam barge *D* owned by Cooper's, was lost off Hale with her crew. Two days later the vessel had completely disappeared below the sand.

The last schooners to be damaged in the upper river were the *Englishman* and the *Mary Ann Mandal* both of which were badly strained after grounding in 1928. *Mary Ann Mandal* never recovered and she went to the breakers. The owners of the *Englishman* brought an action against the Upper Mersey Navigation Commission alleging that the vessel grounded because the channel was not adequately marked and they were successful in their claim. By 1920 the channel to the Bridgewater Docks was unusable and in that year the lock from the tideway into the Ship Canal was closed. From this time onwards the larger craft entering the canal from the upper river passed through Weston Mersey Lock. But all was not well at Weston Mersey and within a few months of the closure of the Bridgewater entrance a long standing dispute between Brunner Mond and Company and the Manchester Ship Canal Company came before the High Court.[31] Brunner Mond and certain traders of the Cheshire salt district alleged that the Ship Canal Company had failed to fulfil its statutory obligations under the Ship Canal Act of 1885 with regard to Weston Mersey Lock and its approaches. Witnesses for Brunner Mond stated that before the canal was constructed vessels drawing fifteen feet of water could use the entrance to Weston Point docks. The channel had been straight and, it was claimed, navigable in all weather. Sailing vessels had been towed in trains of four or six and barges in trains of twelve and the channel was wide enough to allow vessels and trains to pass each other. After the canal was constructed the main navigable channel had shifted to the Lancashire shore and it had become difficult. The access channel to the lock had silted up, its length had increased and because of the many bends, the number of vessels in the train had to be reduced. Counsel for the Ship Canal Company hastened to point out that between 1903 and 1919 the number of vessels passing through the access to Weston Mersey Lock was 119, 845 of which 11,625 were sea going ships.

Brunner Mond and Company claimed that the Ship Canal Company had failed to provide a satisfactory outlet for their traffic to the Mersey and in consequence they had a right to use the Ship Canal to Eastham free of tolls and ship charges. The Ship Canal Company made counter claim against Brunner Mond in order to recover unpaid canal dues. The hearing lasted twenty-six days and judgement was given for the Manchester Ship Canal Company on all points. Brunner Mond's appeal went to the House of Lords where it was dismissed. The cost of the litigation was over £100,000.

The old "Duker" river paddle tugs of the Ship Canal Company lived to reach venerable old age. They had been built for the Bridgewater Trustees between 1857 and 1870. The *Earl of Ellesmere* was nearly seventy years old when she went to the breakers in 1926 with *Brackley, Dagmar* and *St. Winifred.* The *Helen, Queen of the Mersey* and the inefficient *Gower* had been scrapped some years previously. The Weston Point Towing Company had also provided a service for schooners and barge traffic for many years on the upper river. Their ancient *Gladiator* which was built in Northwich in 1873 was broken up together with *Emulator* in 1931. The *Liberator* also built at Northwich was comparatively young at twenty-one years of age when she went to the scrapyard in 1927. *Aviator* was used for many years by Richard Abel and Sons Ltd. to tow their barges up and down the river. With the departure of the old paddle tugs the Ship Canal Company provided screw driven vessels for towing on the upper river. These were *Agnes Seed* which was destroyed by a boiler explosion in 1932, *Runcorn, Ellesmere Port, Salford* and *Manchester.*

In 1922 the Upper Mersey Navigation Commissioners had replaced their aged buoying tender *Preston* with *Lady Windsor* which they purchased from a Cardiff salvage firm for £850. The new buoy boat was kept in constant employment even though there was now a noticeable decline in river traffic. There was still some trade by the old river to Warrington and among the small steamers on regular passage were Crosfield's steam barges *Glitto* and *George, Nonie* belonging to the Bishop's Wharf Carrying Company and *Panary, Problem* and *Pater* of Fairclough and Sons. At 117 tons with a laden draught of just over eight feet the motor vessel *Pater* was the largest of the Warrington craft. The channel to Warrington was still marked by scores of small buoys which were made for the Upper Mersey Commissioners by Mr. Walter Barr, tinsmith of Runcorn and every year the Commissioners made an annual inspection of the river aboard their buoy vessel up to their statutory boundary at Bank Quay.

Up to the first world war Brundrit's sailing vessels *Swallow* and *Swift* transported Welsh granite to Runcorn then returned empty to Penmaenmawr. The flats used red Runcorn sandstone as ballast and at Penmaenmawr the thrifty Welsh villagers retrieved the best of the jettisoned stone and used it to build their local school. In the 1890s Brundrit's delivered Penmaenmawr macadam for Runcorn's roads at nine shillings and ten pence a ton and stretches of their sett paving are still to be found in the town to this day. Brundrit's had been quick to realise the potential of the Brunner-Mond works at Winnington and during the factory's early difficult years they were prepared to supply Brunner Monds with limestone on "use now and pay later" terms.[32] There was still a demand for Runcorn stone and Messrs. W. Guest and Son of the quarries on Runcorn Hill advertised stone for use as engine beds, grindstones and for building river and dock walls. The proprietor declared that "the quarries are adapted for shipping to all parts by sea, canal or rail". Besides Brundrit and Hayes who were importing slate into Runcorn there were two other slate firms Messrs. Simpson and Davies and Bostock, Yeomans and Matthews.[33] Up until the 1930s the little steamers *Enid, Pandora* and *Velinheli* owned by the Dinorwic slate quarries were engaged in regular trade to the Bridgewater Docks.

Whereas the Runcorn docks saw many foreign flags, Weston Point docks were concerned almost solely with coastal shipping until fairly recent times. Customs regulations did not permit the landing of duitable goods at Weston Point and the few foreign vessels to be seen were those discharging flints. Large quantities of flints arrived from France and from the Cloyne Mineral Company in the Republic of Ireland. Some furnace clay for Birmingham foundries came from Ireland as well as quantities of granite blocks required for lining the Staffordshire potters' grinding mills. Carbide was also imported from Norway. One rather surprising *outgoing* cargo from Weston Point was a regular shipment of potters' materials to the Arklow Pottery Company which required a constant supply of refined material from the Staffordshire factories. Ground flints, ground stone and saggers were frequently despatched to Ireland aboard the schooner *Venturer*. The schooner brought in raw flints and took bags of refined flint as the return cargo. On one occasion during troubled times in Ireland *Venturer* was held up at Weston Point while her cargo was examined. It was unusual for crated machinery to be exported through Weston Point and loading was refused until the authorities were satisfied that the crates contained harmless merchandise. The boxes were opened to reveal an innocent consignment of machinery for the Arklow pottery.[34]

The End of an Era

In the decade before the second world war the age of the sailing ship came to its end. The big square rigged vessels had all but disappeared by 1930 and the few survivors had become objects of curiosity but the little schooners continued to come to Runcorn and Weston Point for a few more years. When they needed costly repairs they were laid up. Too slow and unreliable to compete with the fast dependable coastal steamers, the schooners had had their day. They were obsolete. Many were worn out, war time losses had been severe and as few had been built since the turn of the century their numbers dwindled rapidly. With the decline of the sailing vessel their specialist repair and supply facilities ashore became fewer. There were other factors which hastened the end of sail. The small hatches of the schooners and the obstruction caused by the rigging made it difficult for the newer cranes to load and discharge cargo quickly. There were also problems with the insurance of ageing vessels. Between 1920 and 1930, in an effort to win business some schooners were fitted with auxiliary engines and their span of useful life was increased but often the Bolinders motors were not fully appreciated by captains who had spent all their working lives under sail and consequently the engines were not used to best effect. Often they were not well maintained by the crew and as a result engine performance was frequently less than satisfactory.

Mr. George H. Grounds of *The Glen* Runcorn continued to work a sizeable fleet of merchant schooners into the 1930s. He owned *Fanny Crossfield, J.H. Barrow, Mary Miller, Mary Sinclair, Shoal Fisher, Gauntlet Bidsie and Bell* and *Mary Watkinson* most of which remained registered at their original home ports of Barrow or Lancaster but by 1939 the schooners had disappeared from the Mersey scene. Their work was being done by the steamer and the motor lorry. Some locally built vessels had lasted to the end of the sailing ship era. The *Harvest King* which was built by Brundrit's in 1879 was still trading on the Irish coast in 1949. *Snowflake* was withdrawn from service when her master, Captain Pinch died. She was bought by Jugoslavian owners for trading in the Mediterranean. They fitted her with an auxiliary motor and changed her gentle name to *Hrvat*. She was still plying the Adriatic after the war. The Runcorn built *Alert* was abandoned after losing her sails and anchor in a storm in Moelfre Bay in 1936. She was picked up next day and towed into harbour. In the following year she was sold to the Marquis of Anglesey who converted her into a motor yacht but she was not a success in her new role and during the war she was broken up. The *Pet* registered at Runcorn was wrecked in 1931 on passage from Runcorn to Fisherrow on the Forth with a cargo of salt. Her crew summoned help by setting fire to their bedding on deck. The *Shoal Fisher* owned by Mr. G.H. Grounds of Runcorn and one of the last British sailing vessels to trade in deep water, went down after a collision in the Bay of Biscay in 1932. The Runcorn owned schooner *Gauntlet,* Charlestown to Kirkaldy with china clay, sank off Flamborough

The schooners *Snowflake, M.E. Johnson, Englishman* and *Dunvegan* at Runcorn in the 1920s.

The schooner *Volant* under repairs at Stubbs' yard in the 1930s

Head in 1927 and the crew were rescued after thirty-eight hours continuous work at the pumps. *Guiding Star* 103 tons, was wrecked in April 1928.

Mary Sinclair 118 tons, remained to the very last days of sail at Runcorn. She had sailed in the china clay trade for Mr. Grounds until the early 1930s when she was sold to her elderly master Tom Williams, who had spent his entire working life in sailing ships. Captain Williams was proud of his schooner and few ships were as well kept. He searched for cargoes all round the coasts of Britain and *Mary Sinclair* was kept busy until February 1936 when she was seriously damaged in a collision with a buoy in the Mersey estuary and had to be beached. She finished her days as a towing barge and was broken up at the beginning of the last war.

It would require another book to give full account of the history of the individual sailing ships which frequented the upper Mersey ports. In the first forty years of the century hundreds of vessels came to the docks at Runcorn, Weston Point and West Bank and to attempt to record the story of them all would simply create a catalogue which, although of interest to many, might be outside the bounds of this present work. Some mention of the latter day schooner masters however, is appropriate.[35]

The best known master was Captain Kerfoot Janion who came from one of Runcorn's oldest families. One of his ancestors, a Kerfoot Janion of 1788 had held all the public offices in the township for a yearly salary of £5. Captain Janion was born in 1853 and at the age of eleven he served as ship's cook on his father's schooner. Before he was in his teens he worked the Irish Sea and had sailed round the north of Scotland. When his father died Captain Janion became the owner and master of *The Union* which was engaged in the slate trade between Port Dinorwic and Runcorn. A superb seaman with an easy going but shrewd disposition, Captain Janion never lost a ship or was involved in serious collision. He suffered tragedy however, for his youngest son was lost overboard from the schooner *Gleaner* off Anglesey. A handsome man with a pointed Imperial beard, Captain Janion was always willing to give a chance to any likely youngster who wanted to make a career at sea. He sometimes accommodated lads who had left home without parental approval and whose yearning for the sea was too strong to resist. The author's father was one such boy who, although he did not make a career of the sea, remembered Captain Janion and the *Gleaner* with affection to the end of his life. The *Gleaner* was lost with all hands shortly after Captain Janion left her to take command of another schooner.

Hans Jensen, the Danish captain of the *Alert* kept a very smart ship. The first task after coaling was to scrub and polish the schooner until she was as neat and tidy as any private yacht afloat. When it came to pride in appearance *Alert* was in a class of her own.

Captain West of the *Mary Sinclair* in the 1920s was the subject of a conundrum known to the local children of the time:

The wind was west
And West steered we.
The wind right aft
How could that be?

When a schooner master had a financial stake in the vessel he was often tempted to economise. Captain West was alleged by some of his crew to have been sparing with victuals and if the men did not go hungry, they were not over fed. In an effort to economise Captain Pinch sailed with a crew of four but Captain Cundy was more generous in his ship's complement for he believed that a crew of five was necessary for efficiency.

Captain Harry Clare, the master of the schooner *Halton* followed family tradition for his father and grandfather had been schooner masters. For generations the Dunbavand and Abram families had provided master mariners and to this day the descendants of their early nineteenth century schooner captains are still concerned with ships and the sea.

Captain William's pride, the *Mary Sinclair* appears to have been the last of the locally owned schooners. She was the end of a long tradition of Runcorn sailing ships stretching back over two centuries. Yet there was just one more nostalgic echo from the past thirty-seven years after *Mary Sinclair* had been laid up. In October 1973 the schooner *Charlotte Rhodes* motored up the Manchester Ship Canal and was moored near to Bridgewater House at Runcorn. She was widely known for her appearances in a popular television series. Her cargo was very different from those carried by the schooners of the past, for *Charlotte Rhodes* brought up-to-date freight. She was being used as a publicity venture and local businessmen were invited on board to see the latest in computer systems. Six years later the old wooden vessel was destroyed by an explosion and fire in Amsterdam harbour.[36]

The sailing flats departed the scene at the same time as the schooners. During the last years of the nineteenth century they had grown in size so that they were unable to enter the inland canals although they could still use the docks at West Bank and Runcorn. Some of the larger two masted "jigger" flats were capable of carrying 200 ton cargoes but they were limited to 175 tons when they used the Ship Canal in this century.[37] *Eustace Carey* and *Santa Rosa* were the last flats to work the coast under sail alone. The jigger flats *Winifred* and *E.K. Muspratt* were fitted with paraffin motors and continued to work the coast between Liverpool and Fleetwood. They finished their working lives plying between Castner Kellner works at Weston Point and Liverpool and Birkenhead docks.[38] Many others were demasted to become "dumb" towing barges and they were still being used by the Liverpool Lighterage Company by Richard Abel's and by Bishop's Wharf Carrying Company into the 1970's.

The establishment of Castner-Kellner works at Weston Point in 1896 saw the first large scale industry to come to the Runcorn district for some years but its arrival did not make an immediate impact upon the depression which occurred in the alkali industry of Widnes and Runcorn during the 1890s. The recession coincided with a slowing down of maritime trade. There had been a brief rise in imports which began about 1892 but this trend was over by 1896 and with the coming of the Ship Canal the coastal trade became depressed. The general recession in trade caused much hardship in the district and the Mersey Mission to Seamen's soup kitchen was busy as long as Mr. Shaw was able to find the necessary contributions from charitable sources to keep it going. In 1897, the year of Queen Victoria's Diamond Jubileee celebrations the *Runcorn Guardian* commented upon the adverse effects the Ship Canal had had upon Runcorn's prosperity.[39] Unemployment was high and the prospects for an improvement in trade and industry were bleak. Nevertheless the newspaper declared that "although labouring under somewhat adverse conditions the townspeople have decided to enter with enthusiasm into the Diamond Jubilee celebrations".

Runcorn began to suffer from increasing competition from the Weaver Navigation which began to capture some of its Potteries traffic after 1895 but from about 1897 there was a temporary improvement in both the export and coastal trades at the Bridgewater Docks but the increase in trade could not be maintained and, from the turn of the century, a gradual then accelerating decline took place at both Runcorn and Weston Point. The first world war severely disrupted long established trade patterns and the upper Mersey ports never recovered from the dislocation of traffic. The salt trade to Newfoundland was a casualty of the war and an attempt to revive business ended with the last crossing of the Atlantic by *Alert* and *Snowflake* in 1922. Recovering briefly in 1919 total trade at the Runcorn docks was down to 124,428 tons in 1925 to continue in rapid decline to become a negligible 32,881 tons in 1951. At Weston Point it was the same story with tonnages falling from 200,000 tons in 1938 to 40,000 tons in 1954.[40]

At the Bridgewater Docks an attempt had been made to arrest the decline in trade by making the docks more convenient for shipping. In August 1935 an important change was made in the method of dealing with traffic. For decades the lock gates from the Tide Dock into the Ship Canal had been opened and closed on each tide twice a day. The gates between the Tide Dock and the Alfred and Fenton Docks were also opened and closed as necessary but, to make the docks more viable and to reduce manning requirements they were dredged so as to deepen them to give a level of water the same as that of the Ship Canal itself. The barge traffic continued to muster at 1½ hours to Liverpool high water and move out to meet the tide but it was now possible for shipping entering and leaving the docks to do so at any time during the day or night. This was a boon for ships using Eastham Locks but the changes did not have the desired effect and the docks continued in decline to become virtually moribund by 1950.

On the other side of the river the traffic in sulphur and copper ore to the Widnes works on the St. Helens Canal gradually succumbed to the intense pressure of road and rail competition. Gossage's steam barges ceased to deliver tallow and oil when the works closed in 1933. After the war there was little trade but sometimes on their return from the Sankey Sugar refinery, Burton's barges would find a cargo of chemicals in drums at Widnes awaiting delivery to Liverpool docks. The canal had ceased to fulfil its original purpose for coal, once the the main staple of trade on the waterway, was no longer transported from the colleries to the Mersey.

In good times and bad the Upper Mersey Commissioners were obliged to keep the river channels safe for navigation but by 1920 they faced a loss in revenue because of lessening trade. It was obvious that if the trend continued they would find it impossible to meet the costs of their obligations. By the Upper Mersey Act of 1920 the Commissioners were empowered to increase their dues. Vessels trading between the upper Mersey and other coastal ports now paid annually sixteen pounds eleven shillings up to 150 tons, twenty-five pounds if less than 300 tons and thirty-two pounds per annum if in excess of 300 tons burden. These charges were in force until 1948 when the Comissioners were authorised by statutory instrument to increase the dues by forty percent and a further increase was allowed in 1956.

The task of plotting the river channels was just as arduous as it had been in the busy late Victorian times and in 1932 the buoying vessel *Lady Windsor* was withdrawn and replaced by *Jesse Wallwork*. This vessel was the former steam trawler *U.K.* which was modified by Yarwood's of Northwich and renamed after the serving Chairman of the Commissioners. *Jesse Wallwork* followed the tradition of her predecessors in that she worked the river for many years. In 1963 the old steamer was replaced by *Jesse Wallwork II* a Worcester grain barge, formerly *Sunrisen*. The motor vessel *Jesse Wallwork II* was the last of the sturdy little craft especially commissioned to carry out the vital job of laying and relaying buoys to mark the changing navigable channels.

During the 1930s and 1940s the navigation on the river dwindled rapidly and the remaining history of upper Mersey shipping is a story of contraction and closure. The Duke of Bridgewater's old line of locks became disused in the late 1930s and they were closed under the ship Canal Act of 1949. By another Ship Canal Act of 1966 the Canal Company was empowered to close and fill in the new line of locks, the old dock area and also the Francis and Arnold docks. The Runcorn and Weston Canal has been filled in to provide additional quay space for modern docks and the old warehouses which were built for the Potteries trade were demolished. The river tugs of the Manchester Ship Canal Bridgewater Department were withdrawn from service in 1948 and in the same year the St. Helens Canal was nationalised. For a few more years the canal was used by barges carrying sugar to the Sankey Sugar Company's refinery and the canal was closed in 1963. The West Bank dock of the Hutchinson Estate Company no longer exists. Hale Head light is extinguished and at the time of writing, Sprinch yard is being swept away by extensive new road works.

In June 1973 a winding up Bill was presented to Parliament and the Upper Mersey Navigation Commission went out of business just three years short of its centenary. The river is no longer buoyed, for today there is no commercial traffic on the upper Mersey whatsoever.

Not long before the final closure Mr. William Snelson, of Runcorn, the last Clerk to the Commissioners had the unique experience of standing upon the Seldom Seen Rocks, the only man within living memory to do so. During a period of very low neap tides following a spell of exceptionally dry weather the rocks became visible and Mr. Snelson was able to appreciate something of the importance and the difficulties of navigation on the upper river in times past. The whole area of rocks was strewn with broken propeller blades, anchors, winches, chains and fragments of sunken flats.

Postscript

The opening of the new road bridge across the Mersey in 1961 together with the new dock roads which were connected to the motorways at last solved most of the problems which had always bedevilled the port. The Bridgewater Docks became an attractive proposition for industrial south Lancashire and tonnages increased from a mere 50,000 tons in 1957 to over 773,000 tons in 1973. The dock entrance has been widened and the docks deepened to enable larger vessels to enter and the future points to continuing expansion and development.

Notes

1. Linton, W.E., *The Manchester Ship Canal.* The Movement and its Pioneers, Hind, Hoyle, Light Ltd., Manchester 1901, p.2.

2. Ibid., p.7.

3. *Widnes Weekly News,* 14th March 1885.

4. *Warrington Guardian,* 17th January 1883.

5. Ibid., 4th March 1885.

6. *Journal of Commerce,* 16th AuLancashgust and 12th September 1893.

7. *Lancashire General Advertiser*, 9th December 1892.

8. W.H. Collier, Manager the M.S.C. Company. Letter to Importers and Shippers June 2nd 1892.

9. J. Meadowcroft, Letter to W.H. Collier, March 21st 1892.

10. Shipping movements, *Warrington Guardian,* November 1891 to April 1892.

11. *Ship Canal News*, 21 st April 1888.

12. *Runcorn Guardian,* 9th December 1893.

13. *Examiner and Times,* 7th December 1893.

14. *Manchester City News,* 1st and 7th July 1893.

15. Farnie, D.A., *The Manchester Ship Canal and the Rise of the Port of Manchester 1894-1975,* Manchester University Press, 1980, p.99.

16. *Mail and Economic News,* 27th February, 1893.

17. Chaloner, W.H. and Ratcliffe, B.M., *Trade and Transport.* Essays in Economic History in Honour of T.S. Willan, Manchester University Press, 1977, p.189.

18. Manchester Ship Canal Company Regulations 1894.

19. Upper Mersey Navigation Commission, Superintendents Reports 1896.

20. Ibid. List of Wrecks and Casualties 1876-1946.

21. Information Mr. A. Cooke, M.S.C. Lockmaster, Eastham.

22. The account of the breaker's yard at Hale was compiled from conversations with the late Alderman John Ludden of Widnes who was employed at the yard in his youth and from Mr. E. Dorrian of Great Sankey whose father was in charge of operations at the yard just prior to its closure. Details of vessels from UMNC List of Wrecks and Casualties.

23. Mr. E. Dorrian, Mr. F.A. Gilbody, 1970.

24. Dr. W.N. Howell, Hale.

25. Farnie, D.A. op. cit., p.61.

26. The Shipping Registers. The Customs House, Runcorn.

27. *Llandudno Advertiser,* 10th August 1900.

28. Upper Mersey Navigation Commission. List of Wrecks and Casualties.

29. Mr. W. Snelson, Upper Mersey Navigation Commission.

30. *Widnes Weekly News,* February 14th 1928.

31. *Liverpool Daily Post,* December 3rd 1920; The Times, December 8th 1920; Liverpool Echo, February 16th 1921; Journal of Commerce, May 14th 1923.

32. Dr. Dennis Brundrit, Kelowna, Canada.

33. Kelly's Directory 1907.

34. Mr. H. Hobley, Manager, Weaver Docks, Weston Point, 1970.

35. Information from A. Evans, W. Dutton, A. Cook.

36. *Daily Telegraph* 12th October 1979.

37. Mr. W. Dutton, M.S.C. Co., Eastham.

38. Ogle F.L., Mainly About Flats, Sea Breezes, Vol. 45, No. 312. Dec. 1971, pp.887-888.

39. *Runcorn Guardian,* Supplement 26th June 1897.

40. Hadfield C. and Biddle G., *Canals of North West England,* Vol. 2. pp.374-375.

Appendix

Vessels Built at Runcorn

The lists of locally built vessels have been compiled from the Shipping Registers of HM Customs and Excise at Liverpool and Runcorn, from Lloyd's Registers and from newspaper accounts of launchings and shipwreck. The lists are certainly incomplete but they provide some record of the extent of ship building in the eighteenth and nineteenth centuries.

	Tons	Type as Built	Builder
1778 Cooper	70	Brig	
1791 Royal Charlotte	92	Flat	
1792 Manchester	139	Brigantine	
1792 Worsley	130	Schooner	
1794 Rochdale	133	Brigantine	
1798 Sampson	140	Brigantine	
1800 Ann	102	Snow	
1802 George and Ann	95	Sloop	
1802 Sarah	57	Flat	Wm. Wright, Chas. Hickson
1803 Anne	59	Flat	Wm. Wright, Chas. Hickson
1806 Friends	92	Galliot	
1806 Rhydland Trader	38	Flat	
1807 Bettys	132	Barquentine	
1808 Bradshaw	108	Galliot	
1811 John and Ann	64	Flat	
1812 Commerce	46	Flat	
1815 Jane	63	Flat	Wm. Wright
1816 Duke of Wellington	59	Wood paddle steamer	Wm. Wright
1816 Prince Regent	57	Wood paddle steamer	Wm. Rigby
1821 Holyhead Trader	76	Sloop	
1823 Sarah	52	Flat	
1824 Maria	46	Flat	John Weedall
1825 Manchester	40	Wood paddle steamer	
1825 Elizabeth	42	Smack	
1833 Ann	50	Flat	
1834 Patent	45	Flat	
1834 Rival	50	Wood paddle steamer	
1836 Tower	47	Wood paddle steamer	J. Rawlinson
1837 James and Sarah	63	Schooner	

Vessels Built at Runcorn (cont.)

		Tons	Type as Built	Builder
1838	Susan		Schooner	
1838	Thomas	97	Schooner	
1838	Thomas Mason	62	Schooner	Samuel Mason
1839	Gem	33	Smack	
1839	Duke		Wood paddle steamer	
1839	Elfleda	116	Schooner	
1839	Maria and Elizabeth			
1840	John	55	Schooner	Brundrit & Whiteway
1840	John and Henry	72	Schooner	
1840	British Queen	107	Schooner	Anderton
1841	Catherine	50	Sloop	
1841	Princess Royal	97	Schooner	Anderton
1841	Margaret	102	Schooner	
1841	Susannah	45	Flat	
1841	Doris	137	Schooner	J. Sothern
1841	Ann Widnell	36	Sloop	
1842	Alice	49	Flat	
1842	Ellen	69	Schooner	
1842	Philip	72	Schooner	Brundrit & Whiteway
1842	Mersey	92	Schooner	
1842	Heir Apparent	132	Schooner	
1842	Hugh Lupus	64	Schooner	Bridgewater
1843	Commerce	55	Flat	
1843	Mary Jane	111	Schooner	Brundrit & Whiteway
1843	Sarah and Ann	100	Schooner	Samuel Mason
1844	Martha	38	Flat	
1844	Mountain Maid	53	Sloop	
1844	Julia	73	Schooner	Brundrit & Whiteway
1844	Jane		Flat	
1845	Fanny	71	Schooner	
1846	Sarah	77	Schooner	Brundrit & Whiteway
1846	Ino	75	Schooner	
1847	Margaret and Martha	66	Schooner	
1847	The Port	65	Schooner	
1847	Rosalie	215	Brig	
1848	Empress	68	Schooner	Anderton
1848	Duke	80	Schooner	Brundrit & Whiteway
1848	Speculator	43	Flat	Smauel Mason
1849	Alice	42	Flat	
1849	William Court	56	Schooner	
1849	Edward and John	29	Sloop	
1850	Shamrock	65	Schooner	

Vessels Built at Runcorn (cont.)

		Tons	Type as Built	Builder
1850	Ann	50	Flat	
1850	Margaret	21	Smack	
1850	Ellesmere	75	Schooner	Brundrit & Whiteway
1851	Emperor	70	Schooner	Anderton
1851	Emmeline	70	Schooner	
1851	Sir Robert	68	Schooner	Brundrit & Whiteway
1851	Eliza	39	Flat	
1851	Rose and Margaret	32	Sloop	
1852	May	57	Flat	
1853	Eva	134	Brigantine	
1853	Anne Chesshyre	451	Ship	Brundrit & Whiteway
1853	Anne Walker	128	Schooner	Samuel Mason
1853	Uncle Tom	52	Flat	
1854	Brackley	88	Schooner	Brundrit & Whiteway
1855	Alma	118	Schooner	Brundrit & Whiteway
1855	Mary Houghton	71	Schooner	Brundrit & Whiteway
1855	Penmae	54	Sloop	
1855	Borland	141	Barquentine	
1856	Edward Whitley		Flat	
1856	Dennis Brundrit	462	Ship	Brundrit & Whiteway
1856	Reviresco	114	Brig	
1857	Ellen Owen	132	Brigantine	
1857	Bertha	87	Schooner	J and T Johnson
1857	Cheshire Lass	85	Schooner	
1857	Squall	7	Sloop	Brundrit & Whiteway
1857	Samuel	67	Flat	
1857	Selina	99	Schooner	
1857	Delhi	57	Flat	Anderton
1857	Llanfair	52	Sloop	Brundrit & Whiteway
1858	Widders		Sloop	
1858	Robin	43	Flat	
1858	Gipsey Queen	31	Smack	
1858	Kingfisher	35	Smack	
1858	James	67	Sloop	Anderton
1858	Gwyder	55	Smack	Brundrit & Whiteway
1858	Star	37	Flat	
1859	Lymm Gray	123	Brig	Anderton
1859	Jessie Roberts	69	Schooner	Anderton
1859	Alice	65	Schooner	Brundrit & Whiteway
1859	Elizabeth and Ann	55	Flat	
1859	Bertie	61	Smack	Brundrit & Whiteway
1860	Duck	34	Smack	
1860	Quanita	190	Brig	Anderton

Vessels Built at Runcorn (cont.)

		Tons	Type as Built	Builder
1861	Priory	88	Schooner	Brundrit & Whiteway
1861	Lancashire Lass	56	Schooner	
1861	Swan	36	Flat	
1861	Ada	36	Sloop	
1862	Rival	106	Schooner	Mason
1862	Barlochan	227	Barque	Anderton
1862	Francis	55	Schooner	
1863	Phoebe	123	Schooner	Mason
1863	Eclipse	78	Schooner	Brundrit & Whiteway
1863	Sandfly	19	Flat	
1863	Julia	40	Flat	
1863	Hannah	53	Flat	
1863	Jessie	32	Flat	
1863	Laffak	42	Flat	
1864	Alice	107	Wood Paddle Steamer	
1864	Oak	42	Flat	
1864	Listers	50	Flat	
1864	Frances Mary	44	Flat	
1865	Eliza	62	Flat	
1865	Jessie	132	Schooner	Anderton
1865	Swift	66	Flat	Brundrit & Whiteway
1866	Parker	58	Smack	
1866	William	63	Sloop	
1867	Preston	42	Wood Screw Steamer	Brundrit & Whiteway
1867	Comet	56	Flat	Joseph Clarke
1868	Red Tail	80	Schooner	Blundell and Mason
1868	Swallow	67	Smack	Brundrit & Whiteway
1869	Emily			Speakman
1869	Pride	79	Flat	Blundell & Mason
1869	William Bowden	130	Schooner	Brundrit & Whiteway
1869	Speculator	32	Wood Screw Steamer	
1872	John Ellis		Flat	
1873	Traffic	83	Wood Screw Steamer	Speakman
1874	James	34	Flat	Anderton
1875	John	65	Iron Screw Steamer	Speakman
1875	Rose	44	Flat	Speakman
1877	St. Helens	68	Flat	
1877	Florinda	71	Flat	

Vessels Built at Runcorn (cont.)

	Tons	Type as Built	Builder
1877 Clara	84	Flat	
1878 Martyn	67	Ketch	Brundrit & Co.
1878 A.M. Brundrit	112	Schooner	Brundrit & Co.
1878 Agnes	48	Flat	John Stubbs and Son
1878 Widnes	51	Flat	
1878 William and Alice	90	Flat	John Stubbs and Son
1878 Fiona	54	Flat	Speakman
1879 Harvest King	100		Brundrit & Co.
1879 Bryan	87	Flat	
1879 Garston	68	Flat	
1879 Willie	69	Flat	Brundrit & Co.
1880 Snowflake	96	Schooner	Brundrit & Co.
1881 Reginald	116	Screw Steamer	Brundrit & Co.
1882 Lilly Heaps	56	Flat	Brundrit & Co.
1883 Sunbeam	135	Schooner	Brundrit & Co.
1883 Fox	100	Schooner	Brundrit & Co.
1884 Elizabeth Bennett	154	Schooner	Brundrit & Co.
1885 Alert	147	Schooner	Brundrit & Co.
1886 Despatch	145	Schooner	Brundrit & Co.
1886 Mars		Lightship	Brundrit & Co.
1887 Percy	85	Flat	Brundrit & Co.

Vessels Built at Widnes

1861 Lilly	57	Schooner	Samuel Stock
1863 Flora	50	Flat	Samuel Stock
1867 Hilda		Schooner	Samuel Stock
1868 Excelsior	28	Flat	Wm. Cooper
1869 Maud	71	Schooner	Samuel Stock
1870 Try	75	Schooner	Samuel Stock
1875 Janie	172	Schooner	Samuel Stock
1879 Hettie	74	Wood Screw Steamer	Wm. Jamieson
1890 Annie	39	Flat	Edward Gandy

Vessels Built at Frodsham

1728 Armitage	40	Sloop	
1737 Ann	35	Brigantine	
1746 Benin	50	Brig	
1748 Vine	30	Sloop	
1760 Peggy and Mary	83	Barquentine	
1786 Mentor	71	Flat	
1786 Molly	92	Dogger	

Vessels Built at Frodsham

Year & Name	Tons	Type as Built	Builder
1787 Sutton	74	Flat	
1788 Olive	71	Flat	
1788 Swan	54	Flat	
1791 Ellens	71	Flat	
1791 Hornet	74	Flat	
1792 Frodsham Trader	42	Flat	
1793 Friends	60	Flat	
1793 John and William	74	Flat	
1793 Wilderspool	76	Flat	
1794 Mills	73	Flat	
1795 Betsey	48	Flat	Wm. Hayes
1799 Ann	75	Flat	Isaac White
1800 Nelson	73	Flat	
1801 Supply	74	Flat	
1802 Alice and Ann	59	Flat	
1802 Stag	77	Flat	
1802 Mary Ellen	80	Flat	
1802 Peggy and Mary		Flat	
1803 Merry Harrier	78	Flat	
1803 Tom	69	Flat	
1804 Young James	78	Flat	
1805 Penketh	76	Flat	
1808 May	24	Flat	
1811 Mary Ann	75	Schooner	
1812 Lydia	50	Sloop	
1815 Sparling	62	Sloop	
1815 Waterloo	61	Schooner	
1816 Kent	100	Galliot	Wm. Hayes
1816 Jane and Ann	68	Schooner	
1818 Mary	42	Flat	
1821 Isabella	74	Schooner	Hayes & Urmson
1824 Collins	39	Sloop	
1826 St. George	54	Flat	
1831 Frances	95	Schooner	
1835 James	84	Schooner	
1837 Briton	53	Flat	Wm. Hayes
1838 Sarah	68	Schooner	
1839 Kendal Castle	85	Schooner	
1839 Importer	69	Schooner	
1839 Pearl	66	Schooner	
1840 Rigby	72	Schooner	
1844 Hero	57	Flat	Wm. Hayes
1847 Lydia	48	Flat	

Vessels Built at Frodsham

	Tons	Type as Built	Builder
1851 Mary Ann		Schooner	
1856 Emily Constance	65	Schooner	
1857 Hannah	38	Flat	Edward Jones
1858 Edward	64	Flat	Edward Jones
1858 Vixen	54	Flat	Edward Jones
1858 Alice and Mary	54	Flat	
1858 Mary Bollind	100	Schooner	
1860 Mersey	50	Flat	
1862 Fanny	40	Flat	

Iron Vessels Built at Warrington

1840 Warrington	99	Paddle Steamer	Bridge Foundry
1841 John Wilson Patten		Brig	Bridge Foundry
1842 Libya	125	Schooner	Bridge Foundry
1845 Die Schoen Mainzen	108	Paddle Steamer	Bridge Foundry
1846 Enterprise	74	Schooner	Bank Quay
1846 Neptune	42	Sloop	Bank Quay
1849 Trout	58	Schooner	Bank Quay
1852 Invincible	66	Paddle Steamer	Bank Quay
1853 La Perlita	84	Screw Steamer	Bank Quay
1853 Startled Fawn	1165	Ship	Bank Quay
1853 Tayleur	1979	Ship	Bank Quay
1854 Lady Octavia	1272	Ship	Bank Quay
1854 Medora	392	Barque	Bank Quay
1854 Deerslayer	500	Barque	Bank Quay
1854 Liverpooliana	800	Ship	Bank Quay
1855 Retriever	500	Screw Steamer	Bank Quay
1855 Conference	531	Ship	Bank Quay
1855 Sarah Palmer	1301	Ship	Bank Quay
1855 Mystery	424	Barque	Bank Quay
1857 Sarah Sands	-	Ship	Bank Quay

Information from Lloyds registers and from the Liverpool and Runcorn Shipping Registers. Further details of iron vessels built at Warrington are to be found in the *Warrington Guardian* 8.10.1853; 17.10.1853; 17.9.1853; 28.10.1854; 16.12.1854; 29.4.1854; 20.5.1854; 24.4.1854.

The *Warrington Guardian* of 29.4.1854 describes the *Golden Vale* a large ship of 1440 tons which was nearing completion. This vessel does not appear in Lloyds registers or in the Liverpool Shipping Registers and it must be assumed that the ship was given another name.

Company names for the Bank Quay yard were Tayleur, Sanderson and Co. 1846; Tayleur and Co. 1853; Bank Quay Foundry Co. 1856.

Vessels Built at Sankey Bridges

	Tons	Type as Built	Builder
1807 Hannah	79	Flat	
1808 Mary	64	Flat	
1810 John	59	Flat	
1812 Royal Oak	68	Flat	
1822 John Clare	56	Flat	
1826 Wellington	33	Flat	
1826 Duke of York	75	Flat	
1828 Hugh	47	Flat	
1829 Clarence	82	Schooner	
1830 True Briton	44	Flat	
1832 Hero	43	Flat	
1834 Heart of Oak	41	Flat	
1836 Elizabeth	51	Flat	
1837 William	44	Flat	
1840 Bettys	44	Flat	
1841 Martha	36	Flat	
1842 Sarah		Flat	
1843 Margaret	43	Flat	
1844 Alfred	54	Flat	
1846 Britannia	60	Flat	
1855 Adelaide	57	Flat	
1857 Jane	53	Flat	
1860 Gilbert Greenall		Sloop	
1862 Hannah	56	Flat	
1863 Susanah Kurtz	59	Flat	
1864 Bat	62	Flat	
1868 Ellen	38	Flat	
1869 Mayfly	61	Ketch	
1871 Annie	47	Flat	
1872 Sankey	73	Screw Steamer	
1875 Harold	78	Screw Steamer	
1879 John	74	Flat	
1880 Edith	82	Flat	
1889 Harry	67	Flat	
1905 Eustace Carey	92	Ketch	
1906 Santa Rosa	94	Ketch	
1913 G.R. Jebb	69	Lightship	

Builders' names - Up to 1831 - William Clare. From 1832 to 1861 John Clare. After 1861 Executors of John Clare. At an unknown date the yard became known as Clare and Ridgeway.

Vessels Built at Fiddlers Ferry

All launched into the river Mersey. All vessels had one deck and one mast, were flat rigged and carvel built on wood frame with round stern.

1859	Bream	72	Flat	T. Wilkinson
1865	Mus	80	Flat	T. Wilkinson
1867	Vendace	68	Flat	T. Wilkinson
1868	Carp	72	Flat	T. Wilkinson
1868	Brill	105	Flat	T. Wilkinson
1869	Rudd	78	Flat	W. Wilkinson
1869	Perch	81	Flat	W. Wilkinson
1870	Dace	141	Flat	W. Wilkinson
1871	Dab	78	Flat	T. Wilkinson
1871	Chub	139	Flat	W. Wilkinson
1872	Luce	143	Flat	W. Wilkinson
1875	Roach	107	Flat	T. Wilkinson
1879	Bret	83	Flat	W. Wilkinson
1879	Rav	90	Flat	T. Wilkinson
1882	Grig	78	Flat	W. Wilkinson
1885	Sprat	81	Flat	T. Wilkinson

Vessels built at Fiddlers Ferry and launched into the Sankey Canal

1877	Rose C	82	Flat	Hill and Grundy
1879	Edith Mary	86	Flat	Hill and Grundy
1880	Ann and Martha	70	Flat	Hill and Grundy

Vessels Built at Runcorn

	Sailing Vessels	Tonnage	Steam Vessels	Tonnage
1867	7	421	1	28
1868	9	565	2	134
1869	11	734	3	45
1870	14	779	4	484
1871	2	185	-	-
1872	-	-	-	-
1873	4	309	1	45
1874				
1875				
1876				
1877	3	233	-	-
1878	10	808	-	-

	Sailing Vessels	Vessels Built at Runcorn Tonnage	Steam Vessels	Tonnage
1879	7	663	-	-
1880	7	640	1	180
1881	6	440	4	301
1882	8	600	1	86
1883	3	290	6	730
1884				
1885				
1886	4	352	1	70
1887	1	89	1	135
1888	-	-	2	225
1890	1	80	-	-
1891	3	259	-	-
1892	2	139	2	88
1893	-	-	1	77

From the "Annual Statements of the Navigation and Shipping of the United Kingdom" H.M.S.O. 1868 - 1893
1868 to 1872 Vol 1872 p.211.
1873 Vol 1873 p.91.
1877 to 1880 Vol. 1880 p.271.
1881 p.204.

Runcorn

Limits of Port and Legal Quays, 31st March 1847.

We the under signed being three of the Commissioners of Her Majesty's Treasury of the United Kingdom of Great Britain and Ireland do hereby under the authority of an Act passed in the Session of Parliament holden in the ninth and tenth years of the Reign of Her present Majesty Queen Victoria entitled "An Act to amend the Laws relating to the Customs" appoint Runcorn to be a Port in that part of the United Kingdom called England and do hereby declare that the Limits of the said Port shall commence at a certain place called Warrington Bridge following the course of the River Mersey and including both shores until a line can be drawn from Chapel Farm House on the Lancashire shore to Eastham Church on the Cheshire shore including the shores and waters of the River Weaver to Frodsham Bridge. And we do hereby appoint the following places within the said Port of Runcorn to be Legal Quays for the loading and unloading of Goods and do declare the bounds and extents of such Quays to be as follows that is to say:-

All that open place called the New Docks extending North East and South West on each side 180 feet bounded on the East by the River Mersey and on the West by the Town of Runcorn.

Also that open place called the Old Dock similarly bounded and situated extending on each side 400 feet.

Also that open place called Lower Basin similarly bounded and situated and extending on each side 490 feet.

Also that open place called Old Basin similarly bounded and situated extending on each side 970 feet.

Also that open place called Francis Dock similarly bounded and situated extending on each side 320 feet.

And also all that open place called Old Quay similarly bounded and situated extending on each side 1,011 feet.

Given under our Hands at the Treasury Chambers Whitehall this 31st day of March 1847.

JV Gibson Craig
O'Conor Don
H Rich

Imports into Runcorn during the year 1852

Warrington Guardian - 22nd October, 1853

Description:	Where from:	Tons:	
Potters Clay	Fowey	19,519	
	Poole	18,006	
	Teignmouth	3,699	
	Torquay	1,318	
	Various ports	2,074	
			44,616
Flints	Newhaven	6,292	
	Shoreham	2,627	
	Arundel	2,050	
	Rye	805	
	Various ports	3,255	
			15,029
China Clay and Stone	Fowey	10,174	
	Penzance	228	
			10,402
Slates	Caernarvon	19,685	
	Bangor	16,366	
	Dinorwic	3,785	
		1,753	
	Various ports	604	
			42,193
Pig Iron	Ardrossan	20,246	
	Glasgow	9,396	
	Whitehaven	3,159	
	Troon	2,848	
	Ayr	2,610	
	Irvine	1,260	
	Various ports	2,052	
			41,461
Pyrites	Wicklow	10,329	
	Arklow	7,481	
	Padstow	920	
	Conway	515	
	Various ports	506	
			19,751

Imports into Runcorn during the year 1852 (cont.)

Description	Where from:	Tons:	
Iron Ore	Barrow	12,793	
	Ulverston	1,755	
	Whitehaven	1,721	
	Ayr	90	
	Various ports	205	
			16,564
Copper Ore	Ulverston	1,481	
	Amlwch	605	
	Caernarvon	490	
	Swansea	281	
	Various ports	803	
			3,660
Oats and meal	Westport	1,019	
	Sligo	879	
	Ballena	772	
	Newry	682	
	Various ports	4,829	
			8,161
Timber (propwood)	Youghal	856	
	Conway	708	
	Wicklow	641	
	New Ross	543	
	Ulverston	431	
	Waterford	422	
	Various ports	2,233	
			5,834
Firebricks	Chester, etc.	3,578	
Railway iron	Newport, etc.	2,595	
Gypsum	Carlisle, etc.	1,311	
Manganese	Plymouth, etc.	813	
Blue stone	Amlwch, etc.	633	
Copper	Ulverston	453	
Lead	Chester, etc.	447	
Sand	Yarmouth	419	
Cromate iron	Lanark	380	
Barytes	Baltimore, etc.	308	
Oak bark	Ostend, etc.	237	
Bones	Dublin	210	
Yellow ochre	Amlwch	160	
Felspar	North Wales	138	
Flagstones	Thurso	126	

Imports into Runcorn during the year 1852 (cont.)

Description	Where from:	Tons:	
Tin plates	Newport	70	
Sundries (gun powder, hides, silk rollers, etc. - various)		353	11,928
			217,630

The Value of Foreign Exports at the Port of Runcorn 1859 to 1883[1]

	£
1859	7,259
1860	6,888
1861	9,376
1862	10,600
1863	16,758
1864	27,502
1865	20,509
1866	22,897
1867	27,342
1868	51,789
1869	28,480
1870	31,748
1871	44,553
1872	34,388
1873	46,403
1874	43,445
1875	32,545
1876	21,375
1877	22,325
1878	29,093
1879	25,453
1880	27,930
1881	25,453
1882	22,131
1883	22,122

1   Annual Statements of the Trade of the United Kingdom with Foreign Countries and British Possessions. Board of Trade. 1859 to 1860 p.37 1863 report; 1861 to 1865 p.37 1865 report; 1866 to 1870 p.29 1870 report; 1871 to 1874 p.28 1874 report; 1875 to 1877 p.28 1877 report; 1878 to 1881 p.28 1881 report; 1881 to 1883 p.29 1883 report.

The Value of Imports of Foreign and Colonial Merchandise at the Port of Runcorn from 1872 to 1883[1]

	£
1872	199,107
1873	129,001
1874	160,114
1875	117,178
1876	137,999
1877	141,685
1878	179,928
1879	101,000
1880	113,429
1881	74,962
1882	128,839
1883	118,027

1   Annual Statements of the Trade of the United Kingdom with Foreign
     Countries and British Possessions.
     1872 to 1874 p.16 1874 report;
     1875 to 1878 p.16 1878 report;
     1879 to 1883 p.16 1883 report.

Runcorn Population 1801 to 1901

1801	1,397
1811	2,060
1821	3,103
1831	5,035
1841	6,950
1851	8,688
1861	10,141
1871	12,444
1881	15,133
1891	20,050n
1901	16,491

N   The large increase in population which occurred between 1881 and 1891 and the subsequent decrease from 1891 to 1901 were due to the migration of the large workforce which was employed locally during the construction of the Manchester Ship Canal between 1887 and 1893.

The Runcorn District Council Badge

Bridgewater Navigation Company Limited

Statistics of Trade at Runcorn Docks (Including Old Quay) for 12 years ending 31st December 1884

	Vessels (arrived)		Vessels (departed)		Dockage Porterage Cranage	Landing Ware-housing Wharfage	Steam Towage	Earthenware Shipped	
	Foreign	Coast	Foreign	Coast	£	£	£	Tons	Packages
1873	178	2,318	142	2,295	7,427	63	1,693	17,514	43,785
1874	195	1,941	98	1,914	7,466	878	1,406	18,382	45,955
1875	186	1,742	53	1,851	5,805	1,333	1,246	20,409	51,022
1876	121	1,656	33	1,682	6,614	1,215	820	25,343	63,363
1877	168	1,662	87	1,743	7,449	820	853	33,244	83,110
1878	271	1,739	106	1,908	9,072	885	981	30,078	75,195
1879	178	1,835	87	1,836	8,932	1,536	1,092	33,181	82,952
1880	200	1,693	95	1,851	9,185	1,634	1,358	41,956	104,890
1881	167	1,625	87	1,670	9,104	2,070	1,369	39,422	98,555
1882	198	1,703	60	1,822	9,840	2,532	1,611	45,273	113,183
1883	133	1,742	66	1,771	9,969	2,303	1,702	48,129	140,323
1884	123	1,598	68	1,670	9,394	2,235	1,851	36,759	91,897
	2,118	21,254	982	22,013	100,257	17,504	15,892	389,690	994,230
Average for:									
10 years	186	1,991	84	1,857	8,089	1,296	1,242	30,480	76,201
12 years	176	1,771	82	1,834	8,354	1,459	1,332	32,474	82,850

Machinery:

11 hydraulic cranes
3 hydraulic hoists
7 steam cranes
4 steam hoists
3 hydraulic coal tips
9 hand cranes
6 jiggers

Labour:

Men employed at docks	438
Men employed at Runcorn boatbuilding etc.	204
Men employed on barges - Runcorn section	100
Men employed on canal tugs	75

Number of craft passed up and down the locks in 1883: 60,303
Number of craft passed up and down the locks in 1884: 55,961

Vessels:
Total In and Out 12 years 46,467
Averaging for 12 years   3,872

Minutes of evidence. Opposition by the Bridgewater Navigation Company and the Mersey and Irwell Navigation Company to the Manchester Ship Canal Bill in 1885. Bridgewater Dock Office, Runcorn.

Bibliography

Manuscript and Original Printed Sources

the location of material is given

Board of Trade, *Annual Statistics of the Navigation and Trade of the United Kingdom with Foreign Countries and British Possessions,* 1871-1893; Commerce Department, Central Libraries, Liverpool.

Board of Trade, *Annual Statements/Statistics of the Navigation and Shipping of the United Kingdom,* 1847-1893, Registrar General of Shipping and Seamen; Central Libraries, Liverpool.

Bridgewater Trustees, The Monthly Reports of the Superintendent of Lights and Buoys 1859-1872; Mr. W. Leathwood, Runcorn.

Bridgewater Trustees, Timetable of River Steamers 1839; The Manager, Bridgewater Department, Manchester Ship Canal, Runcorn.

Bridgewater Navigation Company, The Monthly Reports of the Superintendent of Lights and Buoys, 1872-1876; Mr. W. Leathwood, Runcorn.

Bridgewater Navigation Company, Statistics of Trade at Runcorn Docks 1873-1884. Evidence Submitted in Opposition to the Manchester Ship Canal Bill 1885; The Manager, Bridgewater Department, Manchester Ship Canal, Runcorn.

Bridgewater. Navigation Company, Notices and Regulations Relating to River Steamers, 1875.

Cholmondeley Collection, Runcorn Ferry, Gilbert Greenhall's Lease 1854, DCH E 92 VI County Record Office, Chester.

Cholmondeley Collection, Runcorn Ferry, Petition Against the Railway Bill, DCH 2 92X, BRA 984 1861 and 1864, The County Record Office, Chester.

Census, 1801, *Abstract of the Answers and Returns to the Population,* London, 1802.

Census, 1831, *Abstract of the Answers and Returns to the Population,* London, 1833.

Census Enumerator's books, 1841, 1851, 1861, and 1871; Local History Collection, Runcorn Library.

Lloyd's Registers of British Merchant Shipping; Commercial Department, Central Libraries, Liverpool.

Manchester Ship Canal Company, Engineer's Notebook 1902; The Manager, Bridgewater Department, Runcorn.

Manchester Ship Canal Company, Inventory, Canal Craft, Canal Tugs and River Steamers 1908; Bridgewater Department, Runcorn.

Manchester Ship Canal, Letter, J. Meadowcroft to J.H. Collier; Bridgewater Department, Runcorn.

Manchester Ship Canal Company, Letters to Importers and Shippers from J.H. Collier; Bridgewater Department, Runcorn.

Mersey and Irwell Navigation Company, Suggestions for the Improvement of the Rivers Mersey and Irwell for Sea Going Vessels to Manchester 1841; Central Libraries, Manchester.

Mersey Mission to Seamen, Runcorn Branch 1875-1921; The Local Collection, Runcorn Library.

Port of Runcorn, The Shipping Registers 1847-1850; H.M. Customs and Excise, Cunard House, Liverpool.

Port of Runcorn, The Shipping Registers 1862-1893; H.M. Customs and Excise, The Customs House, Runcorn.

Port of Runcorn, Crew Lists 1862-1914; County Record Office, Chester.

Port of Runcorn, The Limits of the Port and Legal Quays 1847 and 1862, The Annulment of the Port 1850 and 1893; H.M. Customs and Excise, Kings Beam House, London.

Port of Runcorn, The Registers of Canal Craft 1877-1946; The County Record Office, Chester.

Port of Liverpool, *Conservator's Report on the Navigation of the River Mersey,* 1858.

Port of Liverpool, The Shipping Registers 1786-1893; H.M. Customs and Excise, Cunard Building, Liverpool.

Port of Liverpool, The Customs Bills of Entry 1841-1880; The Local History Department, Central Libraries, Liverpool.

Port of Liverpool, *Annual Reports to the Conservancy Board,* 1857, 1877; Warrington Library.

Parish of Runcorn, The Constable's Accounts 1781-1834; The Local Collection, Runcorn Library.

Parish of Runcorn, The Baptismal Registers for 1816-20; The Parish Church, Runcorn.

Parish of Runcorn, The Annual Letters to the Parishoners and Parish of Runcorn, 1859-1883; Rev. J. Barclay, The Local Collection, Runcorn Library.

Upper Mersey Navigation Commission, Wrecks and Casualties; Mr. W. Snelson, Runcorn.

Upper Mersey Navigation Commission, Monthly Reports of the Superintendents of Lights and Buoys 1876-1902; Mr. W. Leathwood, Runcorn and Keeper of Shipping, Merseyside County Museums Liverpool.

Upper Mersey Navigation Commission, Upper Mersey Navigation Acts 1876 and 1879; Keeper of Shipping, Merseyside County Museums, Liverpool.

Upper Mersey Navigation Commission, Minute Books 1876-93; Keeper of Shipping, Merseyside County Museums, Liverpool.

Upper Mersey Navigation Commission, An Historical Account; Commander J. Rossiter of the Commission c.1930.

Upper Mersey Navigation Commission, An Inventory of Light vessels and Lighthouses 1870; Mr. W. Snelson, Runcorn.

Upper Mersey Navigation Commission, Charts of the Navigable Channels 1859-1902; The Keeper of Shipping, Merseyside County Museums.

Upper Mersey Navigation Commission, The Roll of Electors 1876; Mr. W. Snelson, Runcorn.

Registrar General of Shipping and Seamen, Transcripts of Ownership; Central Record Office, London BT 108/182.

Runcorn, *Detailed Returns of the Fully Licensed and Beer Houses, Clerk to the Peace,* Chester 1891; The County Record Office, Chester.

Runcorn, A Description of Runcorn About 1750, Manuscript by John Simpson, c. 1860; Local Collection, Runcorn Library.

Runcorn, A Letter Relative to a Bridge at Runcorn 1815; The Local Collection, Warrington Library.

Runcorn, Brooke of Norton Collection, Damage to Crops by Industrial Processes (1863) D 24B1, (1871) D 24B 7/15, (1873 D 25 A1; County Record Office, Chester.

Journals and Newspapers

The Chester Courant

The Liverpool Echo

The Liverpool Mercury

Lloyd's List

The Runcorn Guardian

The Runcorn Weekly News

The Warrington Guardian

The Warrington and Mid-Cheshire Examiner

The Widnes Weekly News

Scrapbooks of newspaper cuttings relating to the Upper Mersey Navigation Commission and to the construction of the Manchester Ship Canal 1876-1894 in the possession of Mr. W. Snelson, Runcorn.

Contemporary Accounts

Aikin, J., *A Description of the Country from Thirty to Forty Miles Around Manchester,* Stockdale, London, 1795.

Defoe, D., *A Tour Through the Whole Island of Great Britain, (ed.* P. Rogers), Penguin Books Ltd., Harmondsworth, 1971.

Fowler, G., *A Visitor's Guide to Runcorn and its Vicinity,* Walker, Runcorn, 1834.

Gresswell, J., *An Account of Runcorn and Its Environs,* Runcorn, 1811.

Holland, H., *A General View of the Agriculture of Chester,* Phillips, London, 1808.

Head, G., *A Home Tour Through the Manufacturing Districts of England in the Summer of 1835,* Murray, London, 1836.

Leland, J., *Leland's Itinerary in England and Wales, (ed.* Lucy Smith), Centaur Press, London, 1964.

Moss, W., *The Liverpool Guide,* Crane and Jones, London, 1795.

Priestley, J., *Historical Account of the Navigable Rivers, Canals and Railways Throughout Great Britain,* 1831; David and Charles reprint, Newton Abbot, 1969.

Directories

Bagshaw, S., *History, Gazatteer and Directory of the County Palatine of Chester,* 1850.

Gore, J., *Liverpool Directory, 1766, 1803, 1818.*

Kelly, *Post Office Directory of Cheshire,* 1857, 1865.

Morris and Company, *Commercial Directory and Gazatteer of Cheshire with Stalybridge,* 1874.

Pigot and Co., *Directory for the County of Lancashire,* 1834.

Pigot and Co., *The New Commercial Directory,* Manchester, 1822.

Pigot and Co., *Cheshire Directory,* 1828.

Slater, J., *Directory of Liverpool and Its Environs,* 1844.

Slater, J., *Directory of Manchester and Salford,* 1845.

Slater, J., *Directory of Cheshire,* 1855, 1890.

Universal British Directory, 1792.

Walker, W., Handbook and Directory of Runcorn, 1846.

White and Co., *History, Gazatteer and Directory of Cheshire,* 1860.

White and Co., *Runcorn Directory,* 1887.

Secondary Sources

Allison, J.E., *The Mersey Estuary,* Liverpool University Press, 1949.

Anderson, J., *Coastwise Sail,* Percival Marshall, London, 1948.

Anderson, R., *White Star,* Stephenson, Prescot, 1964.

Bagley, J.J., *A History of Lancashire,* Darwen Finlayson, Henley-on-Thames, 1956.

Barker, T.C. and Harris, J.R., *A Merseyside Town in the Industrial Revolution, St. Helens 1750-1900,* Cass, London, 1954.

Berry, R.J., "Ellen Weeton 1776-1850", *Transactions of the Lancashire and Cheshire Historic Society,* Vol. 106, 1954.

Boult, J., "A Littoral Survey of the Port of Liverpool", *Transactions of the Lancashire and Cheshire Historic Society,* Vol. 22, 1869.

Boscow, H., *Warrington. Its Heritage,* Teare, Warrington, 1947.

Campbell, W.A., *The Chemical Industry,* Longman, London, 1971.

Carter, C., *Cornish Shipwrecks,* David and Charles, Newton Abbot, 1976.

Carlson, R., *The Liverpool and Manchester Railway Project 1821-1831,* David and Charles, Newton Abbot, 1969.

Chandler, G., *Liverpool Shipping. A Short History,* Phoenix, London, 1960.

Chaloner, W.H., "William Furnival, H.E. Falk and the Salt Chamber of Commerce", *Transactions of the Lancashire and Cheshire Historic Society,* Vol. 112, 1961.

Chaloner, W.H., *The Birth of Modern Manchester and its Region,* Manchester University Press, 1962.

Cheshire Education Committee, *Runcorn River Crossings,* Archive Teaching Unit, Chester, 1978.

Craig, R. and Jarvis, R.C., *Liverpool Registry of Merchant Ships,* Chetham Society, Vol. XV (3rd Series), 1967.

Darbyshire, H., "Manchester Ship Canal Tugs Past and Present", *The Gog,* Vol. 4, No. 2., 1955.

Davies, J.E., "The Penmaenmawr and Trevor Quarries", *Caernarvon Record Office Bulletin,* No. 6, 1972.

Diggle, G.E., *A History of Widnes,* Widnes Corporation, Widnes, 1961.

Dore, R.N., *Cheshire,* Batsford, London, 1977.

Duckworth, C.L. and Langmuir, R., *West Coast Steamers,* Stephenson, Prescot, 1966.

Dunlop, G.A., "Early Warrington Fisheries", *Proceedings of the Warrington Literary and Philosophical Society,* 1929.

Eames, A., *Ships and Seamen of Anglesey,* Anglesey Antiquarian Society, 1973.

Edwards, M.M., *The Growth of the British Cotton Trade, 1780-1815,* Manchester University Press, 1967.

Farnie, D.A., *The Manchester Ship Canal and the Rise of the Port of Manchester,* Manchester University Press, 1980.

Greenhill, B., *The Merchant Schooners, David and Charles, Newton Abbot, 1968.*

Hadfield, C., *The Canal Age,* David and Charles, Newton Abbot, 1968.

Hadfield, C. and Biddle, G., *The Canals of North West England,* David and Charles, Newton Abbot, 1970.

Hardie, D., *A History of the Chemical Industry of Widnes,* I.C.I., 1950.

Hallam, W.B., *Manchester Ship Canal Tugs,* Swale Press. London. 1968.

Harris, J.R., "The Early Steam Engine on Merseyside", *Transactions of the Lancashire and Cheshire Historic Society,* Vol. 106, 1954.

Harris, J.R., "Michael Hughes of Sutton. The Influence of Welsh Copper on Lancashire Business 1780-1815", *Transactions of the Lancashire and Cheshire Historic Society,* Vol. 101, 1949.

Harris, J.R., (ed.), *Liverpool and Merseyside,* Cass, London, 1969.

Hayman, A., *Mersey and Irwell Navigation to Manchester Ship Canal 1720-1887,* Federation of Bridgewater Cruising Clubs, 1981.

Holden, G., *Historical Record. Liverpool Bay Lightships,* Mersey Docks and Harbour Company, Liverpool, 1973.

Hewitt, H., *Medieval Cheshire,* Manchester University Press, 1929.

Hyde, F.E., *Liverpool. The Development of the Port 1700-1970,* David and Charles, Newton Abbot, 1971.

Jarvis, R.C., "Liverpool Statutory Register of British Merchant Ships", *Transactions of the Lancashire and Cheshire Historic Society,* Vol. 105, 1953.

Jarvis, R.C., *A Customs Letter Book of the Port of Liverpool 1711-1813*, Chetham Society, 1954.

Lea, R., "Diary of Richard Lea. What was Runcorn Like in 1838?", *Holy Trinity Centenary Publication*, Runcorn, 1938.

Leathwood, W., "Workshop of the World", *Port of Manchester Review*, 1976.

Leech, B., *History of the Manchester Ship Canal*, Sherratt and Hughes, Manchester, 1907.

Lever Brothers, *The House of Hazlehurst 1816-1916*, Centenary Publication 1916.

Lindsay, J., *A History of the North Wales Slate Industry*, David and Charles, Newton Abbot, 1974.

Malet, H., *The Canal Duke*, David and Charles, Dawlish, 1961.

Mather, F.C., *After the Canal Duke*, Clarendon Press, Oxford, 1970.

McQueen, A., *Echoes of Old Clyde Paddle Wheels*, Cowans and Gray, Glasgow, 1924.

McRoberts, J., "The Mersey Lighthouses", *Sea Breezes*, Vol. 47 No. 336, 1973.

Mountfield, S., *Western Gateway. A History of the Mersey Docks and Harbour Board*, Liverpool University Press, 1965.

Musson, A.E., *Enterprise in Soap and Chemicals. Joseph Crosfield and Sons Ltd.*, Manchester University Press, 1965.

Neal, F., *Liverpool Shipping in the Early Nineteenth Century*, Cass, London, 1969.

Nickson, C., *A History of Runcorn*, Mackie Press, London, 1887.

Norton, P., *Waterways and Railways to Warrington*, Railway and Canal Historical Society, Hull, 1974.

Ogle, F.L., "Mainly About Flats", *Sea Breezes*, Vol. 45 No. 312, 1971.

Ormerod, G., *History of the County Palatine and City of Chester*, Helsby, London, 1882.

Paget-Tomlinson, E., *Mersey and Weaver Flats*, Wilson, Kettering, 1974.

Parkinson, C.N., *The Rise of the Port of Liverpool*, Liverpool University Press, 1952.

Poole, C., *A History of Widnes and its Neighbourhood*, Swale Press, Widnes, 1906.

Porteous, J.D., *Canal Ports. The Urban Achievement of the Canal Age*, Academic Press, London, 1977.

Rolt, T.L., *Navigable Waterways*, Longman., London, 1969.

Russell, R., *Lost Canals of England and Wales*, David and Charles, Newton Abbot, 1971.

Schofield, M.M., "Statutory Registers of British Merchant Ships for North Lancashire in 1786;" *Transactions of the Lancashire and Cheshire Historic Society*, Vol. 110, 1958.

Smith, W., (ed.), *A Scientific Survey of Merseyside*, Liverpool University Press, 1953.

Watkin, W.T., *Roman Cheshire*, E.P. Publications (reprint), Wakefield, 1972.

Ward, T., "Salt and its Export from the Mersey", *Proceedings of the Literary and Philosophical Society of Liverpool*, Vol. 30, 1875-1876.

Wheat, G., *On the Duke's Cut*, Transport Publishing Company, Glossop, 1977.

Willan, T.S., *The Navigation of the River Weaver in the Eighteenth Century*, Chetham Society (3rd Series), 1951.

Willan, T.S., *River Navigation in England 1600-1750*, Cass, London, 1964.

INDEX

Ice on canals	48, 75
Ice on River Mersey	48, 94, 99, 170
Iceland	83
Ince lighthouse	50, 93, 139, 155, 158, 179, 183
Ince marsh	17
Industrial pollution	37, 76, 135, 154
Iron barges	68
Iron ships	64-68, 128, 196, 198
Italy	6, 151
Isle of Wight	89
Janion, Kerfoot	27, 186
Johnson T and J.	36, 42, 54, 77, 194
Kelp	13
King, J.J. and Company	173
Kingstown	87
Knott Mill, Manchester	22
Labrador	6, 112, 124
Labour relations	145-147
Lagos	83
Leblanc process	62, 76
Le Havre	81, 82
Legal quays	58, 202
Leghorn	26
Leland, John	13, 14
Lightvessels	93, 97, 128, 129, 158, 159, 170, 171, 179, 180, 196
Limestone	9, 13, 101, 137, 183
Lisbon	83
Liverpool	5-8, 9-15, 18, 20, 21, 26, 29, 30-35, 38, 39, 42, 46, 48, 49, 53, 73, 80, 81, 88, 103, 116, 127, 128, 142, 143, 147, 148, 158, 162, 164, 167, 170, 172, 187, 189
Liverpool-Manchester Railway	46, 48, 49, 50, 52
Liverpool Town Dues	102-103
Liverpool Port Sanitary Authority	116
London and North West Railway Company	103, 107
Llandulas Stone Company	89
Lymm	21, 80
Manchester	9-15, 17, 19, 21, 28, 34, 35, 46-52, 73, 81,86, 88, 89, 90, 141, 158, 162-164, 167, 169, 173
Manchester, Port of	137, 147, 167
Manchester Ship Canal	46, 162-170, 173, 181, 182, 188, 190
Mariners' Mission Church	37, 78
Mason, Samuel	42, 58, 128, 193
Mason and Craggs	128
Marseilles	81
Mersey River Conservancy	53, 102-104

THETIS
"The Admiralty Regrets..."

The disaster in Liverpool Bay

C. Warren & J. Benson

Thetis - the Admiralty Regrets. The disaster in Liverpool Bay. A minute by minute account of the submarine disaster that cost the lives of 99 men...... Why didn't anyone cut open the submarine? Why was there no urgency in the Admiralty's rescue system? Did the Admiralty **really** regret? Contains previously unpublished photographs and documents.
By C. Warren & J. Benson. Foreword by Derek Arnold, a survivor's son, and postscript by maritime historian David Roberts.
ISBN 1 9521020 8 0. £9.50.

Lusitania - On the 7th May 1915 the Cunard vessel *Lusitania* was torpedoed by a German submarine off the Old Head of Kinsale on the south west coast of Ireland, resulting in the loss of the vessel itself and 1,201 men, women, and children. An act of brutal aggression? Or a cynical plot to bring the United States into the First World War?

More than eighty years on the story of the *Lusitania* continues to be shrouded in mystery and suspicion. What was her real cargo? Why wasn't she protected? Why did she sink so quickly?

Lord Mersey, the great grandson of the man who chaired the enquiry into the *Lusitania* disaster, (who he calls 'the Old Man'), has been extremely helpful and was kind enough to write a new foreword for this Special Edition.

Containing rare photographs from Germany and elsewhere, it is a truly intriguing and fascinating tale.

'A book that clamours to be read' - Observer.

'The truth at last' - The Sunday Times.

By Colin Simpson. ISBN 1 9521020 6 4. £9.50.

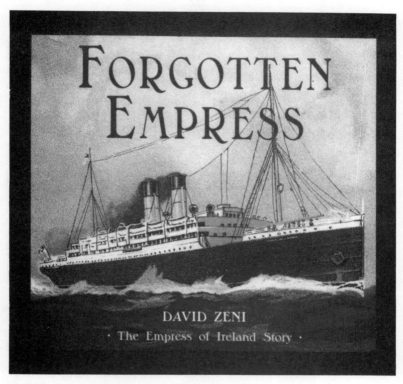

Forgotten Empress by David Zeni.
The fascinating story of the steamship *'Empress of Ireland'* which was lost at sea within two years of the sinking of the *'Titanic'*, and which was an even greater tragedy in terms of passenger fatalities.
Just one year later, the loss of the *'Lusitania'* completed a terrible triangle of maritime disaster.
Of the three, only the *'Empress of Ireland'* remains shrouded in the cloak of history, almost as impenetrable as the fog which caused her loss and the death of 1,012 souls on May 29, 1914.
Contains over 100 photographs. Hardback with full -colour dustjacket. ISBN 1 874448 80 9 £25.00

Life At Lairds - Memories of working shipyard men at Cammell Lairds world-famous shipyard in Birkenhead. *'The time may not be far off when young people will ask, what did they do, what were they like, those who worked there? This book answers the questions.'* - Sea Breezes.
'A book full of anecdotes and rich in humanity...a piece of social history.' - Liverpool Echo.
By David Roberts. ISBN 0 9521020 1 3 £6.99

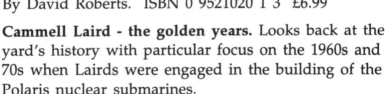

Cammell Laird - the golden years. Looks back at the yard's history with particular focus on the 1960s and 70s when Lairds were engaged in the building of the Polaris nuclear submarines.
'Captures life in the prosperous years of the historic Birkenhead shipyard' - Liverpool Echo.

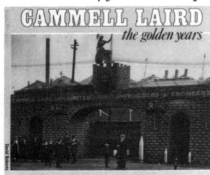

'Puts into perspective...the strikes...the Polaris contract...and those who worked at the yard' - Sea Breezes.
By David Roberts. Foreword by Frank Field MP.
ISBN 1 9521020 2 1. £5.99

David Roberts - Foreword by Frank Field M. P.

Life at Levers.
Memories of making
soaps at 'Billy' Lever's
Port Sunlight factory on
Merseyside. The
ordinary people who
worked there talk of
their lives and times
spent in the soapworks.
By David Roberts. ISBN
1 9521020 3 X. £6.99

**Faster Than The Wind - the Liverpool to Holyhead
Telegraph.** A guide to and history of this fascinating
maritime communications system from North Wales
to the busiest port in the world, Liverpool, in the
early 19th century. This book will take the reader on
two journeys. The first is a real journey, to places
with superb views along the North Wales and Wirral
coasts, including full
details of how to find the
substantial remains of the
Liverpool to Holyhead
Telegraph Stations. The
second is a journey into
the workings of such a
telegraph, and into the
experiences of the people

involved in creating and using the signalling system.
By Frank Large. ISBN 1 9521020 9 9. £8.95

THE CAMEO CONSPIRACY

The Real Story of the Cameo Murders

GEORGE SKELLY

The Cameo Conspiracy - the Real Story of the Cameo Cinema Murders.
Half a century ago one man was hanged and another served a long sentence for their part in this violent crime. Were they guilty, or were they the victims of a wicked conspiracy? A powerful and compelling investigation of this notorious Liverpool murder case in 1949.
By George Skelly. ISBN 1 9521020 9 6. £9.95

Off The Cuff - Ex-Merseyside Sergeant Swasie Turner tells the stories of real-life policing on the streets of the area. A book to raise your eyebrows - and sometimes your hair! Foreword by Alison Halford, former Asst. Chief Constable, Merseyside.
By Swasie Turner. ISBN 1 9521020 4 8. £8.99.

If The Cap Fits - The follow-up to the bestselling 'Off The Cuff' brings you more yarns from the sharp end of Merseyside police work. Foreword by Michael Chapman, Executive Producer of TVs 'The Bill'.
By Swasie Turner. ISBN 1 9521020 7 2.. £8.99.

Videos

Cammell Laird, Old Ships and Hardships - the history and true story of this world-famous shipyard - on video. Contains rare archive footage of famous vessels and comments from the men who built them. £12.99.

All In A Day's Work Vol. 1 - the story of a living, working river - the River Mersey - and the ordinary people that work upon it. Features : Mersey Pilots; Pilot Launch Crews; Shipbuilding and Shiprepairing workers; Dredger crews, and much more. £12.99

All In A Day's Work Vol 2 - More stories from the Mersey, on video. Features : Rock Boats; Mersey Ferries; Tugs and Tug management; the Bunker boats and crews; the Vessel Tracking System; New vessels on the river including cruise liners and car ferries, & much more. £12.99